THE LETTERS OF JOHN F. KENNEDY

THE LETTERS OF

★ ★ ★ ★ ★

John F. Kennedy

Edited by

MARTIN W. SANDLER

BLOOMSBURY

LONDON • NEW DELHI • NEW YORK • SYDNEY

First published in Great Britain 2013

Copyright © 2013 by Martin W. Sandler

The moral right of the author has been asserted

Bloomsbury Publishing plc
50 Bedford Square
London
WC1B 3DP

www.bloomsbury.com

Bloomsbury Publishing, London, New Delhi, New York and Sydney

A CIP catalogue record for this book is available from the British Library

ISBN 978 1 4088 3045 1

10 9 8 7 6 5 4 3 2 1

Designed by Rachel Reiss
Printed and bound in Great Britain by CPI Group (UK) Ltd, Croydon CR0 4YY

MIX
Paper from
responsible sources
FSC® C020471

Contents

★ ★ ★ ★ ★

Preface

★ ★ ★ ★ ★

FOR MANY OF US, it is almost impossible to believe that more than fifty years have passed since John F. Kennedy entered the White House, the youngest man ever elected president of the United States. It is perhaps even more startling to realize that an enormous percentage of our population has no personal recollection of the man who inspired Americans of all ages—young Americans especially—and captivated the imaginations of people around the world.

The man they called JFK was the most visible president the United States had ever had. Thanks to his movie-star good looks, his charisma, and the way in which he regarded photography not with the wariness displayed by almost all his predecessors, but as an ally, he became the most photographed person in the world. It was no accident that it was Kennedy who created the position of official White House photographer.

Even more than photography, however, it was television that endowed Kennedy with a visibility that no previous leader in world history had ever attained. John Kennedy was America's first television president, and from the beginning it was obvious that he and the medium were made for each other. Almost everything

that took place in his presidency—his speeches, his cold war battles, his motivation of the nation's young people—was molded by
his understanding of the ways in which television, unlike anything that had ever come before it, could both shape and sway
public opinion.

Before Kennedy, no American president had dared to conduct
televised press conferences live without delay or editing. Kennedy
not only did so but he elevated them to an art form. By the time his
presidency came to a tragic halt, he had held sixty-four news conferences, an average of one every sixteen days. The first of these
events, which took place less than a week after his inauguration,
was viewed by sixty-five million people. From the first, Kennedy's
press conferences revealed his quick intelligence and his understanding and command of the issues. And there was something
more—a wit and sense of humor rarely witnessed since Abraham
Lincoln graced the White House.

Yet for all John Kennedy's good looks and telegenic charm, at
his core he was a reader and a writer. Indeed, he was among the
best-read and most articulate presidents the United States has ever
had. Kennedy could read more than twelve hundred words a minute. Before he had entered the Navy, he had begun carrying a
loose-leaf notebook with him in which he wrote sentences he felt
were important to remember. While still a Harvard undergraduate he wrote a thesis that would become a bestselling book, and
his second book earned him a Pulitzer Prize. As biographers Robert Dallek and Terry Golway have reminded us, "He did not speak
in sound bites. The phrase had not yet been invented. He spoke in
literate paragraphs, and his speeches were filled with references to
history and literature that have all but disappeared from American political discourse." It is the premise of this book that one can
discover more about Kennedy the man, Kennedy the president,
and the extraordinary and harrowing times in which he lived by
reading his correspondence than through any number of the
scores of books that have been written about him.

President Kennedy's claim on history does not rest merely on charisma or eloquence, however. As historian Richard Reeves has written, "There was an astonishing density of events during the Kennedy years." If anything the remark is an understatement. The global contest between the United States and the Soviet Union that dominated every day of the Kennedy presidency could well have resulted in nuclear war, particularly over such issues as the divided city of Berlin or the placement of Soviet missiles in Cuba. At the same time, Kennedy was forced to grapple with protests, riots, and bloodshed that accompanied African Americans' unceasing struggle for rights and opportunities long denied. And, in a country called South Vietnam that few Americans had ever heard of, events were taking place that would present him with problems that promised only to get worse.

Despite the fact that from his earliest childhood until the day he died he was far more ill than the public would ever know, Kennedy met all these challenges with an energy that never failed to astound those around him. Reporting on one of the president's typical days, the *New York Times*'s James Reston wrote, "He did everything today except shinny up the Washington Monument." A United States senator stated, "When you see the President, you have to get in your car and drive like blazes back to the Capitol to beat his memo commenting on what you told him."

Kennedy regarded drive and energy, or vigor, as one of man's two most admirable qualities. The other was courage. "Everyone admires courage," he was fond of saying, "and the greenest garlands are for those who possess it." It was no coincidence that the title and theme of the book that propelled him into the national eye was *Profiles in Courage*.

All of those qualities were accompanied by another trait that would surprise those who had known him in his playboy prep school and Harvard days. In his inaugural address he inspired the world when he pledged that he and the nation would "pay any price, bear any burden, meet any hardship, support any friend, oppose any foe to assure the survival and success of liberty." In his June 26, 1963, speech at the Free University of Berlin, an address that may well have been his finest, he stated "Life is never easy. There's work to be done and obligations to be met—obligations to truth, to justice, and to liberty." It would be this unwavering sense of duty which would perhaps define him best of all.

That and something else. Commenting on how he felt history would judge Kennedy, his close aide Theodore Sorensen wrote, "History will surely record that his achievements exceeded his years. In an eloquent letter to President Kennedy on nuclear testing, Prime Minister Macmillan once wrote, 'It is not the things one did in one's life that one regrets, but rather the opportunities missed. It can be said of John Kennedy that he missed very few opportunities.'"

Macmillan's letter was but one of more than two million that flowed in and out of the White House during President John F. Kennedy's all-too-brief one thousand days in office. The vast majority of letters in this volume are housed in the John F. Kennedy Presidential Library and Museum, one of the world's richest and most accessible repositories of its kind. This massive collection encompasses papers from not just Kennedy's presidency but his whole life, as well as from other Kennedy family members and other members of his administration. Letters came to Kennedy from people from every walk of life and dealt with almost every subject imaginable, from the Vietnam War to physical fitness.

The Kennedy correspondence includes jocular letters to friends and family, formal missives to heads of state, and ringing declarations of principle, but all of it is revealing. No sequence of letters is more absorbing, or more important, than the long, ongoing secret correspondence between Kennedy and Soviet chairman Nikita Khrushchev. It provides insight into the personalities and leadership styles of two men miles apart in ideological beliefs, but trying desperately, together, to steer a path to safety along the lip of a nuclear volcano. It is not too much to say that this so-called pen pal correspondence became a critical factor in preventing the world from being literally blown apart.

Many of the other messages here are what former Archivist of the United States Allen Weinstein has termed "matters of conscience" letters, ones that challenged Kennedy to state his position on what their writers felt were crucial issues. It is in Kennedy's response to these letters that we often discover his earliest and clearest explanations of his positions and feelings on such matters as religion, civil rights, nuclear arms testing, and Vietnam.

Since the days of John Adams and Thomas Jefferson, American presidents have written to one another and as letters in this book reveal, the Kennedy years were no exception. What shines through in the correspondence between Kennedy and Herbert Hoover and Harry Truman and Dwight Eisenhower is a spirit of friendship and cooperation displayed by men who, whatever their views on policy, shared an understanding of the burden of the highest office in the land.

And there are the letters from children—hundreds of them in the Kennedy Archives, a sampling of them in this book. Not surprisingly they are among the most disarming of all the letters. Many are also among the most perceptive.

Collectively all the letters are, above all else, intensely human documents, testimony of a time when letter-writing was still an art, before e-mails and texting forever changed the nature of personal communication. All letters have been reproduced faithfully though minor corrections, if necessary for clarity, have been made in brackets. Journalist Hugh Sidey, who covered the White House for *Time*, wrote, "The special quality of John Kennedy that still defies those who would diminish him is that he touched something in the American spirit and it lives on." And in the letters that Kennedy wrote and received, we can still touch something in him.

CHAPTER 1

* * * * *

The Early Years

JOHN FITZGERALD KENNEDY was born in Brookline, Massachusetts, on May 29, 1917, into an extraordinary family defined, as the creators of the PBS documentary on his life have written, by "fantastic wealth, Roman Catholicism, Democratic politics, and patriarchal control." His father, Joseph, after working his way through Harvard, had become a multimillionaire, first by being elected, at the age of twenty-five, as the youngest bank president in America and then by establishing a number of thriving businesses ranging from investment and financial firms to a motion picture company. His mother, Rose, was the daughter of one of the most colorful and popular mayors the city of Boston had ever had.

Perhaps above all else, John Kennedy's childhood years were marked by his relationship with his older brother, Joe. Jr., and by his own fragile physical condition. His relationship with Joe Jr. was based on a rivalry, which, on more than one occasion, came to blows. As the *New York Times* noted, "All through childhood and early adolescence Joseph Jr. and John fought. The outcome was inevitable—John was smaller, slimmer and less developed than his brother. But still the boys fought. Their younger brother Robert remembered years later how he and his sisters had cowered in an upstairs room while the two boys fought below."

It was a rivalry that extended both to the schoolroom and the athletic fields, where John continually found himself in his older brother's shadow. Yet there was obviously something else, something deeper in their relationship. Years later, John Kennedy wrote, "I have always felt that Joe achieved his greatest success as the oldest brother. Very early in life he acquired a sense of responsibility towards his brothers and sisters. . . . I think that if the Kennedy children amount to anything now, or ever amount to anything, it will be due more to Joe's behavior and his constant example than to any other factor."

John Kennedy's childhood was also marked by one illness after another. Keeping track of her large brood was a formidable task, so Rose Kennedy resorted to recording each of her children's illnesses and medical treatments on file cards. The largest number of cards by far was devoted to young John. When he was not yet three, he almost died from scarlet fever. Then followed a succession of sicknesses, including chicken pox, whooping cough, measles, and even more serious ailments that went undiagnosed. He was ill so often that his younger brother Robert became fond of saying that if John were bitten by a mosquito, the insect would immediately perish from having tasted his brother's tainted blood. By the time John was in his teens, Robert had joked that if someone were to write a book about his brother its most appropriate title would be *John Kennedy: A Medical History.*

In 1931, fourteen-year-old John was sent off to Choate, a boarding school in Connecticut, where he became a leader of some of its most mischievous students. His academic accomplishments left much to be desired, and he excelled in only subjects that interested him, like history and English. Yet he was unquestionably the school's most popular student. And his classmates could not help but marvel that he had a daily subscription to the *New York Times*.

After graduating from Choate, Kennedy enrolled in Princeton where he immediately concentrated on what was to become a lifetime obsession—the conquest of beautiful women. But within weeks of entering the university, he fell ill with a sickness that had periodically afflicted him in the past and would continue to plague him for rest of his life. It was Addison's disease, an ailment that causes weight loss, weakness, and blood and gastrointestinal problems. He spent most of the school year recuperating and in 1936 returned to college, but not to Princeton; rather, to Harvard, his father's alma mater and where his brother Joe Jr. was attending.

He was still far from a serious student, and his freshman year at Harvard was characterized, for the most part, by a continued concentration on women. But then in the summer following his freshman year, he set off on a trip through Europe. He toured Hitler's Germany and Mussolini's Italy, and he spent time talking with men and women who had fled from the Spanish Civil War. Two years later, he again traveled abroad, visiting Germany, France, Poland, Latvia, Palestine, Turkey, and Russia. By this time, Joseph Kennedy Sr. had been appointed the U.S. ambassador to Great Britain, and the twenty-two-year-old Kennedy began sending long, detailed letters to his father, expressing his opinion on such subjects as the rising tensions throughout Europe, conditions in communist Russia, and the Zionist movement in Palestine.

Kennedy returned to Harvard for his senior year a changed young man. The world had changed as well. For his senior thesis, he decided to write about the conclusions he had drawn from his two European tours, particularly his feelings about why England's response to Adolf Hitler's rise and ambition for conquest had been so inadequate. With the considerable aid of his father, his completed thesis, which he had called "Appeasement at Munich," was published as a book titled *Why England Slept*. In the volume's introduction, Henry R. Luce, editor of *Time* magazine wrote, "If John Kennedy is characteristic of the younger generation—and I believe he is—many of us would be happy to have the destinies of the Republic handed over to his generation at once."

Why England Slept sold ninety thousand copies, vaulted onto the bestseller lists, and made its twenty-three-year-old author an instant celebrity. In the spring of 1941, with America's eventual entry into World War II becoming increasingly apparent, Kennedy volunteered for the U.S. Army but was rejected because of the back problems that had plagued him since his teens. Thanks once again to the influence of his father, however, he was accepted in the Navy. Given the rank of ensign, he was assigned to the naval office that compiled briefing information for the secretary of the navy. It was while he was carrying out these routine duties that the attack on Pearl Harbor took place, on December 7.

With the United States now at war, Kennedy wanted nothing more than to join the action. But there was a problem. He had entered into a romantic liaison with a beautiful *Washington Times-Herald* columnist named Inga Arvad. The Danish Arvad was not only married, but she was also known for having interviewed Adolf Hitler at least two times, for having written positive things about him, and for having been his companion at the 1936 Olympic Games in Germany. This led the FBI to place Arvad under surveillance as a possible German spy. When FBI director J. Edgar Hoover discovered that Arvad was carrying on an affair not only with a Navy ensign but the son of Joseph Kennedy Sr., whom he regarded as a Nazi appeaser, he hoped his men would uncover evidence proving that John Kennedy was sharing military information with his lover. Kennedy was suddenly transferred to a desk job in South Carolina, and within a short time his romance with Arvad came to an end.

In 1943, yet again with the help of his father, Kennedy was relieved of his desk duties, promoted to the rank of lieutenant, and sent to the South Pacific where he was given command of *PT-109*, a patrol torpedo boat. On August 1, 1943, as it was patrolling the waters of Blackett Strait off the Solomon Islands, *PT-109* was suddenly rammed and shattered apart by a Japanese destroyer. Two of Kennedy's men were killed instantly, and several others were badly injured. It was a disaster that could have placed the young boat commander in a very bad light, since it was highly unusual for such a fast, highly maneuverable vessel to be struck by so large a ship. But through his heroic actions, Kennedy more than redeemed himself.

Abandoning the sinking *PT-109*, Kennedy towed his most severely wounded crewman by clenching in his teeth the strap attached to the man's life jacket, and led the remainder of his crew first to one island and then to two others in search of help. Then, plunging back into the dangerous waters alone, he swam for more than an hour vainly seeking an Allied ship. Finally, the bedraggled crew was spotted by friendly natives who reported their whereabouts to naval units operating in the area. Six days after what has been termed "the most famous small-craft engagement in naval history," Kennedy and his men were rescued.

For the courage and leadership he displayed, Kennedy was awarded the U.S. Navy and Marine Corps Medal. But he had been sobered by the experience. Later asked how he had become a hero, he replied simply, "It was involuntary. They sank my boat."

★   ★   ★   ★   ★

As one of the first letters he ever wrote indicates, becoming a Boy Scout endowed twelve-year-old John Kennedy with a new sense of responsibility. Years later, still mystified by his inclusion of "Francis," which was not part of his name, in his signature, Rose Kennedy could only surmise that her son added the name of the kindly saint as a way of persuading his father to grant his wish.

A Plea for a raise
by Jack Kennedy

Dedicated to my
Mr. J.P. Kennedy

My recent allowance is 40¢. This I used for areoplanes and other playthings of childhood but now I am a scout and I put away my childish things. Before I would spend 20¢ of my $.40 allowance and In fixe [five] minutes I would have empty pockets and nothing to gain and 20¢ to lose. When I am a scout I have to buy canteens, haversacks, blankets searchlidgs [searchlights] poncho things that will last for years and I can always use it while I cant use a cholcolate marshmellow Sunday with vanilla ice cream and so I put in my plea for a raise of thirty cents for me to buy scout things and pay my own way more around.

Finis
John Fitzgerald Francis Kennedy

John Kennedy was in Connecticut attending Choate when the last of his eight siblings, Edward—soon to be known as "Teddy"—was born, an event that prompted him to make a very different kind of request, one that his parents granted him.

Feb 1932
The Choate School
Wallingford Connecticut

Young Jack Kennedy pleads with his parents for a raise in his allowance.

Dear Mother,

It is the night before exams so I will write you Wednesday.

Lots of Love.

P.S. Can I be Godfather to the baby

From the moment he entered Choate, Kennedy found himself, both academically and socially, in the shadow of his brother Joe, who was two years ahead of him. Except for in history and English, his grades were mediocre at best. And, as a letter from his housemaster to his parents indicates, he had other shortcomings as well.

THE CHOATE SCHOOL

REPORT OF: John F. Kennedy　　　　　IN: his House
FOR THE FOURTH QUARTER

I'd like to take the responsibility for Jack's constant lack of neatness about his room and person, since he lived with me for two years. But in the matter of neatness, despite a genuine effort on Jack's part, I must confess to failure.

Occasionally we did manage to effect a house cleaning, but it necessitated my "dumping" everything in the room into a pile in the middle of the floor. Jack's room has throughout the year been subject to instant and unannounced inspection—it was the only way to maintain a semblance of neatness, for Jack's room was a club for his friends.

I regard the matter of neatness or lack of it on Jack's

part as quite symbolic—aside from the value if [it] has in itself—for he is casual and disorderly in almost all of his organization projects. Jack studies at the last minute, keeps appointments late, has little sense of material value, and can seldom locate his possessions.

Despite all this, Jack has had a thoroughly genuine try at being neat according to his own standards and he has been almost religiously on time throughout the Quarter.

I believe Jack began to sense the fitness of things after his midwinter difficulties, and he has and is trying to be a more socially-minded person.

John J. Maker

When John Kennedy graduated from Choate in 1935, he stood 64th in a class of 112. But his classmates obviously saw something special in him and voted him "most likely to succeed." Two years after John's graduation, his father wrote a revealing letter to the dean of freshmen at Harvard. It was far from the last time that Joseph Kennedy Sr. used his influence to intercede on behalf of his second son.

JOSEPH P. KENNEDY
30 ROCKEFELLER PLAZA
NEW YORK, N.Y.

August 28, 1936

Delmar Leighton, Dean of Freshmen,
Harvard College,
9 University Hall,
Cambridge 38, Massachusetts

My dear Dean Leighton:

Thank you very much for your letter of August 14.

Jack was graduated year before last from Choate School, Wallingford, Connecticut, and I intended to enter him in the University of London as I did his older brother, Joe. I took him abroad last year but he had a recurrence of a blood condition and I brought him home to be near his doctors. He entered Princeton University where he stayed for about two months. His condition got no better and I sent him to the Peter Bent Brigham Hospital. After a period of two months there, I sent him South and then to Arizona. He seems to have recovered now and is in very good health.

Jack has a very brilliant mind for the things in which he is interested, but is careless and lacks application in those in which he is not interested. This is, of course, a bad fault. However, he is quite ambitious to try and do the work in three years. I know how the authorities feel about this and I have my own opinion, but it is a gesture that pleases me very much because it seems to be the beginning of an awakening ambition. If possible, I should like very much to have one of your assistants confer with Jack to decide whether or not this three-year idea is to be encouraged. He will be available at any time at Hyannisport, Massachusetts, and could come immediately to Boston if such a meeting can be arranged. I should like to have Jack do this before his adviser is appointed if possible.

I am leaving for Europe on business and shall be back in about a month, and at the beginning of the college term, I shall make it my business to go to Boston and talk with the teachers from whom Jack will receive instruction in his freshman year.

Assuring you of my willingness to help in any way possible, I am

Very truly yours,
Joseph P. Kennedy

Not surprisingly, no one was prouder of John Kennedy's accomplishment in producing Why England Slept *than Joseph Kennedy Sr. The ink was hardly dry on the first published copies when he began sending the book to some of the world's most important figures, including Prime Minister Winston Churchill.*

London, August 14, 1940

Dear Winston,

I am sending you herewith Jack's book which I have just finished reading and which I think is a remarkably good job, considering that it is the work of a boy of twenty-three. After all, it is a hopeful sign that youngsters in America are thinking this progressively. It is the first real story that's been published in America of this whole picture. Incidentally, it is already a best-seller in the non-fiction group.

Yours sincerely,
Joseph P. Kennedy

In September 1940, Joseph P. Kennedy Sr., still at his post in London during the German bombing raids, wrote a letter offering his son advice as to how he should proceed in the wake of the success of Why England

Slept. *Most notable were the ambassador's unequivocal statements regarding his feelings about the war.*

London, September 10,
1940.

Dear Jack:

It was nice to hear your voice ringing out on that record that you sent us and it made me plenty homesick. I couldn't be more pleased that you got away with such a marvelous start with the book and I think you are very wise in not attempting to write other articles until this book has had a long run, because, since the critics think this is all right, there is no sense in opening yourself up to attack on some other article you might write which might not go over so well. You will have plenty of time to do that. . . .

I am feeling very well. Haven't the slightest touch of nervousness. But I can see evidences of some people beginning to break down. Herschel Johnson was almost killed Sunday night when the house next door to him was blown right off the map. The Natural History Museum in Kensington was practically gutted by bombs and fire Sunday night, so all in all Jack, it is a great experience. The only thing I am afraid of is that I won't be able to live long enough to tell all that I see and feel about this crisis. When I hear these mental midgets talking about my desire for appeasement and being critical of it, my blood fairly boils. What is this war going to prove? And what is it going to do to civilization? The answer to the first question is nothing; and to the second I shudder even to think about it.

The second air raid warning is going off while I am dictating this to you at 4 o'clock in the afternoon, but until it gets really tough I am carrying on.

Good luck to you Boy, and I hope to see you soon.

Love
Dad

By the end of the first week of November 1940, Joseph Kennedy Sr., amid accusations of his being a Nazi sympathizer because of his stated conviction that the United States should stay out of the war in Europe, had resigned his ambassadorial post. He had been particularly stung by articles in the New York Herald Tribune *in which columnists Joseph Alsop and Robert Kintner had accused him of being both an appeaser and a defeatist. Determined to explain his position to the public, Kennedy Sr. decided to write an article of his own. John Kennedy was still only twenty-three years old, but it was to the young son who had gained such acclaim in writing* Why England Slept *that the father turned for advice on how the article should be written and what it should contain.*

December 5 1940

Ambassador Joseph P. Kennedy
North Ocean Blvd.
Palm Beach, Florida

Dear Dad:

. . . I am sending along to you a rough outline of some points that I feel it would be well for you to cover. It only shows an approach to the problem, it is not meant to be a finished form. Part of it is in article form; in other parts I have just mentioned points you might answer. I don't present it in the form of a finished article as I first of all don't know what your view point is on some questions, and secondly I think the article should be well padded with stories of your experiences in England in order to give it an authenticity and interest . . .

It must be remembered continually that you wish to shake off the word "appeaser". It seems to me that if this label is tied to you it may nullify your immediate effectiveness, even though in the long run you may be proved correct. . . . I don't mean that you should change your ideas or be all things to all men, but I do mean that you should express your views in such a way that it will be difficult to indict you as an appeaser unless they indict themselves as war mongers.

You might bring out in the point that you have always told the British frankly where you stood, that you have never given any Englishman the slightest hope that America would ever come into the war. You have done this for two reasons—because you believed it would be disastrous for America to come into the war and that Americans were firmly against it, and secondly because you felt that you would be doing the British just as great a disservice. It would have been much easier during the trying days of the summer to have held out some hope— but you thought it would have been a disservice to both the country to which you were accredited as well as the country from which you came. You might also make some mention that the diplomatic wires when released will bear you out. . . .

In reading Alsop and Kintner's latest remarks and their continual use of the word appeasement without amplifying its meaning, I received the impression that they, like so many other Americans, are guilty of throwing around the term when they never have stopped to think exactly what it meant. It might be a good idea to try to get a definition of what they mean. This is necessary because no one—be they isolationist, pacifist, etc.,—no one likes to be called an appeaser.... The word appeasement of course started at Munich; the background of it seems to be the idea of believing that you can attain a satisfactory solution of the points in dispute by making concessions to the dictators . . .

I would think that your best angle would be that of course you do not believe this, you with your background cannot stand the idea personally of dictatorships—you hate them—you have achieved the abundant life under a democratic capitalist system—you wish to preserve it. But you believe that you can only preserve it by keeping out of Europe's wars, etc. It's not that you hate dictatorship less—but that you love America more.

The point that I am trying to get at is that it is important that you stress how much you dislike the idea of dealing with dictatorships, how you wouldn't trust their word a minute—how you have no confidence in them—but that you feel that they can best be fought off, internally as well as externally, if we build ourselves up strong economically and defensively and we can only do that by following the procedure you advocate.

In that way you can prevent their fastening the word appeaser on you. You could take the word appeasement apart and question what it means. Does it mean fighting for the Dutch East Indies, etc. . . .

In talking about the gloom charge—it might be well

to mention that you don't enjoy being gloomy. It's much easier to talk about how pleasant things are. The only advantage of doing so is that you hope that it may prove of some value to the country. You believe that the optimists in England and France did their countries a profound disservice. It is not that you believe that come hell or high water—everything is going to be bad. I think you have to show some hope for the future—or otherwise people will say—"Oh well—no matter what we do—he says we are doomed." Rather you think that by preparing for the worst you may be able to meet it. You might bring it home by saying you have seen plenty of optimists cleaned out in the stock market before you went into the diplomatic service— and you have seen plenty of optimistic statesmen cleaned out since then.

It seems to me that you've got a wonderful point here, provided you make it appear that you are not gloomy for gloom's sake. You can bring out those French optimists who believed in the Maginot line, etc. You might bring out that it is necessary for politicians to stress the bright side of things—they are in politics and must get the people's vote—you don't care what people think—you are interested only in the long-run point of view of what is best for this country. . . .

Throughout their romantic relationship, Inga Arvad, whom Kennedy affectionately called Binga, sent him many letters, often lamenting both their continual partings and the fact that she was married. What is perhaps most notable in her correspondence is her assessment of her young lover's character and her belief in the fame she was certain he was destined to achieve. Arvad wrote the following letter after visiting Kennedy in Charleston, South Carolina.

TIMES HERALD

PUBLISHED DAILY AND SUNDAY

WASHINGTON, D.C.

Monday January 26,
1942

... Leaving [the station] I saw a figure on the platform. The further the train pulled away, the less visible was the young, handsome Boston Bean. ... There was the good old feeling of stinging eyes and a nasty pull at the heart-strings, which always show up when too great a distance is put between us. ...

And—about the man. He is full of enthusiasm and ex-pectations, eager to make his life a huge success. He wants the fame, the money—and what rarely goes with fame—happiness. He strives hard himself. More than any boy in the same cottonwool-position. He is a credit to the family and to his country. He is so big and strong, and when you talk to him or see him you always have the impression that his big white teeth are ready to bite off a huge hunk of life. There is determination in his green Irish eyes. He has two backbones: His own and his fathers. Some-how he has hit the bulls-eye in every respect. "He cant fail" I have said to myself very often. I love him more than anything else or anybody in the world.

It is funny. In reality, we are so well matched. Only because I have done some foolish things must I say to myself "NO". At last I realize that it is true "We pay for everything in life".

... Plan your life as you want it. Go up the steps of fame. But—pause now and then to make sure that you are accompanied by happiness. Stop and ask yourself

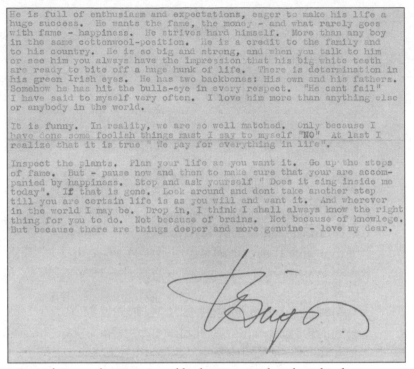

He is full of enthusiasm and expectations, eager to make his life a huge success. He wants the fame, the money - and what rarely goes with fame - happiness. He strives hard himself. More than any boy in the same cottonwool-position. He is a credit to the family and to his country. He is so big and strong, and when you talk to him or see him you always have the impression that his big white teeth are ready to bite off a huge hunk of life. There is determination in his green Irish eyes. He has two backbones: His own and his fathers. Somehow he has hit the bulls-eye in every respect. "He cant fail" I have said to myself very often. I love him more than anything else or anybody in the world.

It is funny. In reality, we are so well matched. Only because I have done some foolish things must I say to myself "NO" At last I realize that it is true " We pay for everything in life".

Inspect the plants. Plan your life as you want it. Go up the steps of fame. But - pause now and then to make sure that your are accompanied by happiness. Stop and ask yourself " Does it sing inside me today". If that is gone. Look around and dont take another step till you are certain life is as you will and want it. And wherever in the world I may be. Drop in, I think I shall always know the right thing for you to do. Not because of brains. Not because of knowlege. But because there are things deeper and more genuine - love my dear.

Danish Journalist Inga Arvad had an intense, but short-lived, romance with Jack. She signed this letter with his nickname for her, "Binga."

"Does it sing inside me today". If that is gone. Look around and don't take another step till you are certain life is as you will and want it. And wherever in the world I may be. Drop in, I think I shall always know the right thing for you to do. Not because of brains. Not because of knowledge. But because there are things deeper and more genuine—love my dear.

Binga

In October 1941, Kennedy was appointed an ensign in the U.S. Naval Reserve and assigned to the Office of Naval Intelligence (ONI). On

January 15, 1942, he was assigned to an ONI field office in Charleston, South Carolina. Throughout this time, he continued to exchange letters with his parents, often giving them his assessment of the direction in which America's participation in the war was headed.

25 February 1942

Dear Dad:

Thanks for Bill Hillman's letter—it was very interesting, and he really called Churchill's speech.

From what I've read and heard lately—the "Cliveden Set of Washington" article—the Daily News and the Times Herald editorials—Roosevelt's speech—these would all seem to indicate that the battle between isolationism and interventionism is just beginning its second major phase. If we get completely smothered in the Far East, Roosevelt is going to have his hands more than full achieving the necessary unity to begin the <u>fighting</u> phase of this war. Up to now this 40-hour week war with time and one-half for overtime and 2¼ for Sundays hasn't cost us anything but a small amount of sweat, a middling amount of toil, and a great amount of money. However, when the tears and blood phase begins and the Bells really start to Toll, then will come the great test. I imagine Roosevelt will swing it, he's got to swing it or he is presently and permanently down the drain. He will have to credit with and assist, however, the fact that even if the country is somewhat undetermined exactly why we want the Phillipines or exactly why we really need Java if we have all those synthetic rubber plants that are going up like—mushrooms I believe is the word that is being used—aside from this suspicion of doubt he'll be aided by the fact that no one wants to quit when the going gets particularly tough. The fight for the fight's sake will keep us in as will no amount of Four Freedoms or Atlantic Charters . . .

· It's a sad state of affairs in the world today when by looking at the worst it's always possible to be right. It's sad, but it's true.

Love,

At the time John Kennedy entered the U.S. Navy, Clare Boothe Luce was one of the most accomplished women in America. A Republican member of the House of Representatives from Connecticut, and wife of Time Inc. publisher Henry R. Luce, she was also an editor, a playwright, and a diplomat. Luce, a Kennedy family friend, sent the young naval officer a good luck coin that had belonged to her mother, a gesture that prompted a grateful response.

Sept. 29, 1942
Hyannisport
Massachusetts

Dear Mrs. Luce:

I came home yesterday and Dad gave me your letter with the gold coin. The coin is now fastened to my identification tag and will be there, I hope, for the duration.

I couldn't have been more pleased. Good luck is a commodity in rather large demand these days and I feel you have given me a particularly potent bit of it.

The fact that it had belonged to your mother—and then to you—and you were good enough and thought-

ful enough to pass it along to me—has made me especially happy to have it.

Just before coming home, I was considering getting
a St. Christopher medal to wear. Now, however, for me
St. Christophers are out—I'll string along with my
St. Clare.

Sincerely
Jack Kennedy

*Throughout the war, with her children scattered far and wide, Rose
Kennedy made a point of writing to them regularly in letters filled with
motherly advice.*

Hyannisport, Mass.
October 9, 1942

Dear Children:

I have been home all the week and it has been lovely
here. I have been working in my own little way, trying to
get all your clothes sorted out, etc. Dad came home from
New York on Wednesday as it was our twenty-eighth
anniversary.

We expected darling Teddy home over this weekend,
but it seems the little angel got into a water fight in the
lavoratory and "after he knew his way around he got full
of biscuits" and got himself into a little trouble, so he
was put on bounds for two weeks. It seems quite unfair
because I am sure the boys who were there before provoked him to mischief. Also, these are our last two weekends when he might come home as we now expect to

close the house about the 19th. I suppose he has learned
his lesson, but a little too late.

Bobby did not expect to get off for the holiday as
I can quite understand that they are steeping their brains
in study. He will have to keep on his toes to get used to
the new school and the new masters and the new requirements because everyone is going at a rapid clip in
order to get into college as soon as possible.

Joe wrote to us this morning and it seems his latest
concern is over a new mustache he is raising. He has
promised to have some photos taken later and so you will
see him all in his mustache glory. He is still busy with
his students and general flying business.

Jack, you know, is a Lieutenant, J.G. and of course he is
delighted. His whole attitude about the war has changed
and he is quite ready to die for the U.S.A. in order to
keep the Japanese and the Germans from becoming the
dominant people on their respective continents, believing that sooner or later they would encroach upon ours.
He also thinks it would be good for Joe's political career
if he died for the grand old flag, although I don't believe
he feels that is absolutely necessary. . . .

Kathleen wanted very much to get to Hot Springs
this weekend. It seems Zeke thought of going down, too.
She was trying to get Betty or Charlotte to go with her,
but they had other plans and I could not allow her to go
down there without a chaperone. We scanned the register for some mutual friend but could find no one and so I
do not know what her present plans are. She said everyone and his brother was to be at LaRue in New York this
weekend. Your father, by the way, said New York is a mad
house. You cannot get near the Capa Cabana [Copaca-
bana]. They are just standing on the street so the Maitre

d'hotel cannot see you even if you have an ambassadorial air. On some instances, even the beaming countenance of Ted O'Leary can not affect an entrance and so it is all too complicated. Jack is going over this weekend and your father has warned him and as usual has been making life easy for him by preparing the way at the various hot spots.

I do hope you will have a good time this weekend, Pat. I do not blame you for being bored and I wish you knew a few exciting swains in Cambridge or New Haven. It is really not your fault that you do not, as we really should make a few contacts for you and then you might follow them up. I am certainly going to do something about it pretty soon as there is no reason why you cannot be having your share of debutante excitement. By the way, I hear you are an excellent bridge player and I cannot understand how you accomplished that art.

I am sorry if you have to wear your old clothes, Jean, and I am quite ashamed that I have not been able to buy you any new ones, but I am going to New York in about another week. Your father and I are going to visit the Convent and I hope I shall have the pleasure of meeting Reverend Mother as I missed her last year. I also hope I shall hear words of praise for your application and industry. And please do not put on a lot of weight. It is so silly at school to eat that long bread roll, etc. . . .

Pat, do keep up your good work because as I said, there is always a record of your marks sent for every college year to whatever school or position you are taking. When I was applying for a secretary myself, I had complete records from Simmons College and Boston University of applicants who had studied there, their

May 14, 1945.

Dear Dad & Mother:-

Received your letter today and was glad to hear everyone was well. Things are still about the same here. We had a raid today but on the whole it's slacked up over the last weeks. I guess it will be more or less routine for another while. Going out every other night for patrol. On good nights it's beautiful - the water is amazingly phosphorescent - flying fishes which shine like lights are zooming around and you usually get two or three porpoises who lodge right under the bow and no matter how fast the boat goes keep just about six inches ahead of the boat. It's been good training. I have an entirely new crew and when the showdown comes I'd like to be confident they know the difference between firing a gun and winding their watch.

Have a lot of natives around and am getting hold of some grass skirts, war clubs, etc. We had one in today who told us about the last man he ate. "Him Jap him are good". All they seem to want is a pipe and will give you canes, pineapples, anything, including a wife. They're smartening up lately. When the British were here they had them working for 17 cents a day but we treat them a heck of a lot better. "English we no like" is their summating of the British Empire.

I was interested in what you said about MacArthur's popularity. Here he has none - is, in fact, very, very unpopular. His nick-name is "Dug-out-Doug" which seems to date back to the first invasion of Guadalcanal. The Army was supposed to come in and relieve the Marines after the beach-head has been established. In ninety-three days no Army. Rightly or wrongly (probably wrongly) MacArthur is blamed. He is said to have refused to send the Army in - "He sat down in his dug-out in Australia", (I am quoting all Navy and Marine personnel) and let the Marines take it.

What actually happened seems to have been that the Navy's hand was forced due to the speed with which the Japs were building Henderson Field so they just moved in ready or not. The Marines took a terrific beating but gave

Writing to his parents from the Pacific, Kennedy expressed skepticism about official war rhetoric.

courses and their marks during the four years, with rec-ommendations from their Professors or teachers as to their eligibility.

Much love to you all.

On April 23, 1943, Kennedy, after having been transferred to the Pacific, took command of PT-109. A month later, in a letter to his parents, he expressed his feelings on a range of subjects, including his opinion of General Douglas MacArthur's popularity, his prediction of how long the war would last, and the state of his health.

May 14, 1943

Dear Dad & Mother:

Received your letter today and was glad to hear everyone was well. Things are still about the same here. We had a raid today but on the whole it's slacked up over the last weeks. I guess it will be more or less routine for another while. Going out every other night for patrol. On good nights it's beautiful—the water is amazingly phosphorescent—flying fishes which shine like lights are zooming around and you usually get two or three porpoises who lodge right under the bow and no matter how fast the boat goes keep just about six inches ahead of the boat. It's been good training. I have an entirely new crew and when the showdown comes I'd like to be confident they know the difference between firing a gun and winding their watch.

Have a lot of natives around and am getting hold of

some grass skirts, war clubs, etc. We had one in today who told us about the last man he ate. "Him Jap his are good." All they seem to want is a pipe and will give you canes, pineapples, anything, including a wife. They're smartening up lately. When the British were here they had them working for 17 cents a day but we trust them a heck of a lot better. . . .

I was interested in what you said about MacArthur's popularity. Here he has none—is, in fact, very, very unpopular. His nick-name is "Dug-out-Doug" which seems to date back to the first invasion of Guadalcanal. The Army was supposed to come in and relieve the Marines after the beach-head had been established. In ninety-three days no Army. Rightly or wrongly (probably wrongly) MacArthur is blamed. He is said to have refused to send the Army in—"He sat down in his dug-out in Australia", (I am quoting all Navy and Marine personnel) and let the Marines take it.

What actually happened seems to have been that the Navy's hand was forced due to the speed with which the Japs were building Henderson Field so they just moved in ready or not. The Marines took a terrific beating but gave it back. At the end the Japs wouldn't ever surrender till they had found out whether the Americans were Marines or the Army, if Marines they didn't surrender as the Marines weren't taking prisoners. In regard to MacArthur, there is no doubt that as men start to come back that "Dug-Out-Doug" will spread—and I think would probably kill him off. No one out here has the slightest interest in politics—they just want to get home—morning, noon and night. They wouldn't give a damn whether they could vote or not and would probably vote for Roosevelt just because they knew his name.

As far as the length of the war, I don't see how it can

stop in less than three years, but I'm sure we can lick them eventually. Our stuff is better, our pilots and planes are—everything considered—way ahead of theirs and our resources inexhaustible though this island to island stuff isn't the answer. If they do that the motto out here "The Golden Gate by 48" won't even come true. A great hold-up seems to me to be the lackadaisical way they handle the unloading of ships. They sit in ports out here weeks at a time while they try to get enough Higgins boats to unload them. They ought to build their docks the first thing. They're losing ships, in effect, by what seems from the outside to be just inertia up high. Don't let any one sell the idea that everyone out here is bustling with the old American energy. They may be ready to give their blood but not their sweat, if they can help it, and usually they fix it so they can help it. They have brought back a lot of old Captains and Commanders from retirement and stuck them in as the heads of those ports and they give the impression of their brains being in their tails, as Honey Fitz would say. The ship I arrived on—no one in the port had the slightest idea it was coming. It had hundreds of men and it sat in the harbor for two weeks while signals were being exchanged. The one man, though, who has everyone's confidence is Halsey, he rates at the very top.

As far as Joe ranting to get out here, I know it is futile to say so, but if I were he I would take as much time about it as I could. He is coming out eventually and will be here for a sufficiency and he will want to be back the day after he arrives, if he runs true to the form of every one else.

As regards Bobby, he ought to do what he wants. You can't estimate risks, some cooks are in more danger out here than a lot of flyers.

Was very interested to know what your plans were and the situation at home. Let me know the latest dope whenever you can. Whatever happened to Timulty? Jerry O'Leary is out here to the South of where I am, but I hope he will get here soon one of these days. He has command of a 160 foot supply boat.

Feeling O.K. The back has really acted amazingly well and gives me scarcely no trouble and in general feel pretty good. Good bunch out here, so all in all it isn't too bad, but when I was speaking about the people who would just as soon be home I didn't mean to use "They"— I meant "WE."

I figure should be back within a year though, but brother from then on it's going to take an act of Congress to move me, but I guess that act has already been passed—if it hasn't it will be.

My love to every one.
(Signed) Jack.

P.S. Mother: Got to church Easter. They had it in a native hut and aside from having a condition read "Enemy aircraft in the vicinity" it went on as well as St. Pat's.

P.P.S. Airmail is better than V-Mail.

When Kennedy wrote to his parents on September 12, 1943, he had already become a war hero through his actions a month earlier during the sinking of PT-109. As his letter indicated, by this time Kennedy had learned through experience the difference between war talk and the reality of armed conflict.

_____

Sept. 12, 1943

Dear Mother & Dad:

Something has happened to Squadron Air Mail—
none has come in for the last two weeks. Some chowder-
head sent it to the wrong island. As a matter of fact, the
papers you have been sending out have kept me up to
date. For an old paper, the New York Daily News is by far
the most interesting. . . .

In regard to things here—they have been doing some
alterations on my boat and have been living on a repair
ship. Never before realized how badly we have been doing on our end although I always had my suspicions.
First time I've seen an egg since I left the states.

As I told you, Lennie Thom, who used to ride with
me, has now got a boat of his own and the fellow who
was going to ride with me has just come down with ul-
cers. (He's going to the States and will call you and give
you all the news. Al Hamm). We certainly would have
made a red-hot combination. Got most of my old crew
except for a couple who are being sent home, and am
extremely glad of that. On the bright side of an otherwise completely black time was the way that everyone
stood up to it. Previous to that I had become somewhat
cynical about the American as a fighting man. I had
seen too much bellyaching and laying off. But with the
chips down—that all faded away. I can now believe—
which I never would have before—the stories of Bataan
and Wake. For an American it's got to be awfully easy
or awfully tough. When it's in the middle, then there's
trouble. It was a terrible thing though, losing those two

men. One had ridden with me for as long as I had been out here. He had been somewhat shocked by a bomb that had landed near the boat about two weeks before. He never really got over it; he always seemed to have the feeling that something was going to happen to him. He never said anything about being put ashore—he didn't want to go—but the next time we came down the line I was going to let him work on the base force. When a fellow gets the feeling that he's in for it, the only thing to do is to let him get off the boat because strangely enough, they always seem to be the ones that do get it. I don't know whether it's just coincidence or what. He had a wife and three kids. The other fellow had just come abroad. He was only a kid himself.

It certainly brought home how real the war is—and when I read the papers from home and how superficial is most of the talking and thinking about it. When I read that we will fight the Japs for years if necessary and will sacrifice hundreds of thousands if we must—I always like to check from where he is talking—it's seldom out here. People get so used to talking about billions of dollars and millions of soldiers that thousands of dead sounds like drops in the bucket. But if those thousands want to live as much as the ten I saw—they should measure their words with great, great care. Perhaps all of that won't be necessary—and it can all be done by bombing.

Has Joe left yet—I hope he's still around when I get back. Saw Jake Pierrepont the other day who had received a letter from Marion Kingsland (of Palm Beach) who reported Joe in New York with two of "the most beautiful English girls she had ever seen." I hope, if Joe is planning to leave, he will leave a complete program with the names and numbers of the leading players. . . .

Love
Jack

P.S. Got camera and Reading glasses. Thanks. Summer beginning and it's getting hot as the devil hence letter blurred. If you should see Mrs. Luce would you tell her that her lucky piece came through for me. I understand she has five of them herself. At their present rate of luck production, there is no telling where it will all end.

One of the most candid letters Kennedy wrote while in the Pacific was to Inga Arvad, who obviously remained in his thoughts. It was a fatalistic letter as well, ending with a frank admission.

Dear Binga,

The war goes slowly here, slower than you can ever imagine from reading the papers at home. The only way you can get the proper perspective on its progress is put away the headlines for a month and watch us move on the map. It's deathly slow. The Japs have dug deep, and with the possible exception of a couple of Marine divisions are the greatest jungle fighters in the world. Their willingness to die for a place like Munda gives them a tremendous advantage over us. We, in aggregate, just don't have the willingness. Of course, at times, an individual will rise up to it, but in total, no. . . . Munda or any of those spots are just God damned hot stinking corners of small islands in a group of islands in a part of the ocean we all hope to never see again.

We are at a great disadvantage—the Russians could see their country invaded, the Chinese the same. The British were bombed, but we are fighting on some islands belonging to the Lever Company, a British concern making soap. I suppose if we were stockholders we would perhaps be doing much better, but to see that by dying at Munda you are helping to secure peace in our time takes a larger imagination than most possess. . . . The Japs have this advantage: because of their feeling about Hirohito, they merely wish to kill. An American's energies are divided: he wants to kill but he also is trying desperately to prevent himself from being killed.

The war is a dirty business. It's very easy to talk about the war and beating the Japs if it takes years and a million men, but anyone who talks like that should consider well his words. We get so used to talking about billions of dollars, and millions of soldiers, that thousands of casualties sound like drops in the bucket. But if those thousands want to live as much as the ten I saw, the people deciding the whys and wherefores had better make mighty sure that all this effort is headed for some definite goal, and that when we reach that goal we may say it was worth it, for if it isn't, the whole thing will turn to ashes, and we will face great trouble in the years to come after the war.

I received a letter today from the wife of my engineer, who was so badly burnt that his face and hands were just flesh, and he was that way for six days. He couldn't swim, and I was able to help him, and his wife thanked me, and in her letter she said, "I suppose to you it was just part of your job, but Mr. McMahon was part of my life and if he had died I don't think I would have wanted to go on living."

There are many McMahons that don't come through. There was a boy on my boat, only twenty-four, had three kids, one night, two bombs straddled our boat and two of the men were hit, one standing right next to me. He never got over it. He hardly ever spoke after that. He told me one night he thought he was going to be killed. I wanted to put him ashore to work. I wish I had. He was in the forward gun turret where the destroyer hit us.

I don't know what it all adds up to, nothing I guess, but you said that you figured I'd go to Texas and write my experiences. I wouldn't go near a book like that. This thing is so stupid, that while it has a sickening fascination for some of us, myself included, I want to leave it far behind when I go.

Inga Binga, I'll be glad to see you again. I'm tired now. We were riding every night, and the sleeping is tough in the daytime but I've been told they are sending some of us home to form a new squadron in a couple of months. I've had a great time here, everything considered, but I'll be just as glad to get away from it for a while. I used to have the feeling that no matter what happened I'd get through. It's a funny thing that as long as you have that feeling you seem to get through. I've lost that feeling lately but as a matter of fact I don't feel badly about it. If anything happens to me I have this knowledge that if I had lived to be a hundred I could only have improved the quantity of my life, not the quality. This sounds gloomy as hell. I'll cut it. You are the only person I'm saying it to. As a matter of fact knowing you has been the brightest point in an already bright twenty-six years. . . .

That Kennedy would indeed return home a hero was verified in a letter his father received from a naval officer.

MOTOR TORPEDO BOAT SQUADRON TWO

January 9, 1944

Dear Mr. Kennedy:

This is just a note to accompany the Purple Heart award for Jack. I am sending this to you as he's probably running around visiting and generally making up for his somewhat restricted existence out here. Hence, you can probably serve him with this, in fact, spring it on him in a family presentation.

Also, I want to tender a word of praise for Jack. We all regard ourselves fortunate indeed in knowing him as a friend, as he really is, in really the only words to express it—a swell guy. This regard is based entirely on his performance as we knew him. Jack never accepted any merits he did not actually earn. He performed all of his duties conscientiously and with admirable ease. He won the respect of officers and men alike by his disregard of himself and a quiet effective courage that manifested itself many times.

Jack has been recommended for a decoration for his work out here and I sincerely hope he will hear of it soon. He certainly deserves it.

I hope this doesn't sound like an official report, but I did want you and your family to know how very proud of your son you can be.

Give "Shafty" my regards and best wishes to you, sir.

He is a fine lad though he does seem to have Democratic inclinations.

> Republicanly yours,
> (Signed)A. P. Cluster
> Lt. U.S.N.

Joseph P. Kennedy Jr. skipped his final year at law school to begin officer and flight training in Florida. One of the letters he wrote to John while he was in Florida and John was home on leave in Hyannisport contained a brotherly warning, a reference to one of John's many girlfriends.

Tuesday

Dear Brother:

Just in case you are wondering what has happened to our silk. I gave it to Honey Fitz who promised that he would deliver it to Brooks Bros, and I then promised him a shirt out of it and Grandma a blouse. Will you please check on this, as he had Mrs. Posner on his brain, and that store will probably slice it to pieces. I also promised Timilty a shirt. Will you check up on this, and notify him, if the silk is there, and tell Brooks to send me the bill?

I understand that you and Bunny Waters are twosoming it, and the bets are that there will be a threesome before long, and it won't be in bundling clothes but it will have a long beak and a shotgun, and he will answer to the name of a Jolson, after he has given you a shot of lead up the ass.

You have ~~been~~ probably been giving the setting of your brothers station, through his enlightening letters to the Kennedy household, but Banana River speaks for itself, as does the town of Cocoa.

Keep me posted on your movements!

> Best from Brother
> *Joe*

Killfer left Miami yesterday, and ought to be around Boston ~~hor~~ ere long.

Among the letters Kennedy received after being awarded the Navy and Marine Corps medal was the following from his brother Joe. It would turn out to be perhaps the most poignant letter that John Kennedy would ever receive, given that it was written only two days before Joe Jr. was killed during a dangerous secret aerial mission.

> August 10, 1944
> England

My dear brother:

Your letters are always a great source of enjoyment to your noble frère, and my tardiness in writing is not attributable in any way to an attempt at discouragement of such a fine pen relationship, but rather to several pressing matters, which at this time have dwindled greatly. For the last ten days I have been stuck out in the country, far beyond striking distance of any town. Every day, I think will be my last one here, and still we go on. I am really fed up, but the work is quite interesting. The nature of it is secret, and you know how secret things are in the Navy. . . .

I read the piece in the *New Yorker* [John Hersey's account of *PT-109*], and thought it was excellent. The whole squadron got to read it and were much impressed by your intestinal fortitude. What I really want to know, is where the hell were you when the destroyer hove into sight, and exactly what were your moves, and where the hell was your radar. . . .

Tell the family not to get too excited about my staying over here. I am not repeat not contemplating marriage nor intending to risk my fine neck. . . . in any crazy venture.

I trust your back is OK at this point. Most of the letters from home are filled with bulletins about the progress of your back and stomach.

I should be home around the first of Sept, and should be good for about a month's leave. Perhaps you too will be available at that time, and will be able to fix your old brother up with something good.

I have already sent a notice home about my greying hair. I feel, I must make a pretty quick move, so get something that really wants a tired old aviator.

My congrats on the Medal. To get anything out of the Navy is deserving of a campaign medal in itself. It looks like I shall return home with the European campaign medal if I'm lucky.

Your devoted brother
Joe

In the years following the sinking of PT-109, *as John Kennedy's political star ascended, published accounts of the event increasingly appeared, many of them conflicting in nature. In November 1958, Kennedy received a letter from a key participant in the episode, a former Japanese naval officer anxious to set the record straight.*

Tokyo, November 15, 1958

Dear Senator Kennedy,

Please accept my hearty congratulations on your recent reelection to the U.S. Senate.

While I am maybe unknown to you, the fact is, I am ex-captain of the Japanese Navy that stood beside and commanded Mr. Kohei Hanami (then lieutenant-commander), skipper of the destroyer "Amagiri", as commanding officer of the 11th Destroyer Flotilla in the early dawn of that memorable 2nd August, 1943, when we chanced all of a sudden to collide into your *PT-109* boat.

As a matter of fact, it was by no means an intended ramming attack on our part. Finding the ship's course of my selection a bit too westerly, we had just changed course at high speed to North for our return voyage without in the least knowing your boat was there. Your boat however, suddenly bursting upon our view, "hard starboard" was hastily ordered to avoid collision but too late. We ran directly against your boat with the bow of our destroyer, which in her turn had her starboard propeller damaged by the hull of your boat. While my report by wireless to my C-in-C at the base stated the circumstances as they were, newspapers took up the incident, and probably in their attempts to pep up the morale of the nation headlined the news as "Enemy Torpedo Speed-boat Cut Right in Two", "Steering Right Across Enemy Torpedo Speed-boat, Feat Absolutely Unprecedented" and so on. . . .

While always with the memories of that night, I have kept from talking about me, because I was unknown to you. However, seeing your name illustriously headlined as reelected to the Senate in newspapers, I cannot but feel impelled to write you my hearty congratulations and best wishes for success in all your activities.

I had this my letter (in Japanese) translated into English (attached) by one of my classmates at former Etajima Naval Academy. He introduced me to the cover story of "Time" magazine of December 2, 1957. Thanks to his translation of the article, I have come to know about you much better. Among many things I have learned with delight and pride, it is my personal pain and grief that after many grave operations you are still suffering more or less in health. Let me only wish and pray that your toughness of character and your store of abilities will nonetheless carry you through successfully to any achievement you have justifiably in mind including the Presidency of the United States.

Yours Very Sincerely,
Katsumori Yamashiro

★ ★ ★ ★ ★

CHAPTER 2

Road to the White House

WHEN JOHN KENNEDY entered politics in 1946 as a candidate for Congress in Massachusetts's Eleventh Congressional District, several of those close to him were not convinced that, given his total lack of campaigning experience, he would be able to survive in the state's rough-and-tumble political arena. But he quickly proved them wrong. During one of his earliest campaign appearances, he was verbally accosted by a heckler who shouted, "Where do you live? New York? Palm Beach? Not Boston. You're a goddamned carpetbagger." Staring the heckler down, Kennedy replied, "Listen you bastard . . . nobody asked my address when I was on *PT-109.*" Facing another audience that had wildly cheered each of his rival candidates when they bragged about "coming up the hard way," he introduced himself by saying, "I'm the one who didn't come up the hard way." He won that crowd over as well.

After serving three terms in Congress, Kennedy was elected to the U.S. Senate in 1952. On September 12, 1953, he married Jacqueline Bouvier. Soon afterward the back problems that had long plagued him intensified and he was forced to undergo two serious operations. It was while he was recuperating that he wrote the highly acclaimed *Profiles in Courage.* By that time, the handsome young Kennedy's wit, charm, and magnetic speaking skills, combined with the way in which he and his attractive, elegant wife were increasingly becoming favorites of the media, had made him one of the Senate's most popular members. So popular, in fact, that as the 1956 Democratic National Convention convened in Chicago, there was serious talk that he would be selected as the vice presidential nominee. It was a prospect that Kennedy embraced and he actively began to pursue the nomination. Then, to the surprise of the convention, presidential nominee Adlai Stevenson threw his choice of running mate open to the "free vote" of the delegates. Kennedy came tantalizingly close, but after three ballots, he was beaten by Tennessee senator Estes Kefauver.

His narrow defeat was a blessing in disguise, given that he wasn't tainted by being part of the Democratic ticket that was soundly defeated that November. Yet his enormous television exposure at the convention propelled him, more than ever, into an attractive, promising national figure. And it gave him a thirst for an even higher goal. Told by a fellow senator that he would be a shoo-in for the next vice presidential nomination, Kennedy replied, "I'm not running for the vice-presidency anymore. I am running for the presidency."

He began his campaign for the Democratic Party's 1960 presidential nomination with a determination to do everything it took to gain what he now wanted most. But his party's leading luminaries, convinced that he was neither old enough nor experienced enough, were not encouraging about his prospects in 1960. "Senator," Harry Truman publicly asked, "are you certain that you are quite ready for the country, or that the country is ready for you in the role of President . . . ? [We need] a man with the greatest possible maturity and experience. . . . May I urge you to be patient?" Eleanor Roosevelt, the party's most influential woman, shared

Truman's concerns, often addressing Kennedy as "my dear boy." It was an issue that remained with Kennedy throughout the nomination campaign with the usually gracious Hubert Humphrey publicly admonishing him to "grow up and stop acting like a boy," and fellow hopeful Lyndon Johnson delighting in telling a joke about Kennedy's good fortune in having received a glowing medical report—from his pediatrician.

Rather than be discouraged by the assaults on his youth, Kennedy became, if anything, even more energized in his pursuit of the nomination. Night and day, with Jacqueline constantly at his side, he never stopped shaking hands, greeting workers, visiting every locale, large or small, that he could reach. "I am the only candidate since 1924, when a West Virginian ran for the presidency," he boasted, "who knows where Slab Fork is and has been there."

On July 13, 1960, Kennedy received the Democratic Party's nomination as its candidate for president. In his acceptance speech, he evoked the term "New Frontier" as a blueprint for the ways he intended to lead the nation aggressively into a new decade. The theme of the speech was one he repeated throughout his campaign, and one that was later echoed in a far more historic speech. "The New Frontier of which I speak," he told the delegates, "is not a set of promises—it is a set of challenges. It sums up not what I intend to offer the American people, but what I intend to ask of them."

Then he took to the road again, campaigning even more intensely than he had in his quest for the nomination. Ignoring the back that never stopped aching, constantly losing and regaining his voice, he traveled more than seventy-five thousand miles in his campaign plane, the *Caroline*. By this time he had become not only a seasoned campaigner but also an astute one. And his wit, charm, and grasp of the issues were resonating with millions of voters. But there was one issue that would not go away, one so serious that it threatened to derail his candidacy. Kennedy was a Roman Catholic, and throughout the nation there were many who believed that if he was elected president, his major decisions would be dictated by the head of the Catholic Church, the pope.

For Kennedy, it was not a new issue. He had been forced to confront it throughout his nomination campaign and had dealt with it effectively. Speaking to a largely Protestant crowd in Morgantown, West Virginia, he stated, "Nobody asked me if I was a Catholic when I joined the United States Navy." Then he asked, "Did forty million Americans lose their right to run for the presidency on the day they were baptized Catholics?" Gaining momentum he said of his brother Joe, "Nobody asked my brother if he was a Catholic or Protestant before he climbed into an American bomber plane to fly his last mission."

He won the crowd over that day, but at the midway point in his election campaign, his Catholicism was, according to many inside and outside the Democratic Party, the single most important issue in the election. Fuel was added to the fire when influential Philadelphia clergyman Dr. Daniel Poling charged that when Kennedy was a congressman, he had, on orders from the church, refused to attend a dinner honoring four chaplains who had gone down with their ship during World War II. The issue became even more intensified when one of the nation's best-known Protestant ministers, Dr. Norman Vincent Peale, publicly declared that he doubted whether any Catholic president could carry out his duties without being influenced by the Vatican.

Despite counsel to the contrary from some of his most influential advisers, an outraged Kennedy was convinced that he had to publicly respond. He got his chance when he was invited to address the religious issue by the Greater Houston Ministerial Association. On September 12, 1960, before three hundred ministers and more than a hundred spectators, he addressed the issue head-on. "I believe in an America," he said, "where the separation of church and state is absolute—where no Catholic prelate would tell the President (should he be Catholic) how to act, and no Protestant minister would tell his parishioners for whom to vote." He emphasized, "I am not the Catholic candidate for President. I am the Democratic Party's candidate for President who also happens to be Catholic. I do not speak for my church on public matters— and the church does not speak for me."

Following his speech, he was met with a barrage of questions, all of which he addressed effectively, including queries regarding Poling's accusation. What Poling had not made public, Kennedy explained, was that he had been invited to the dinner honoring the chaplains as "a spokesman for his Roman Catholic faith." This he could not do, Kennedy stated, since he had no credentials "to attend in the capacity in which I had been asked." Watching both the speech and Kennedy's response to the ministers' questions on television, Sam Rayburn, the legendary Democratic Speaker of the House, who had been a tepid Kennedy supporter at best, shouted out, "By God, look at him—and listen to him! He's eating 'em blood raw." A few days later Rayburn went out of his way to tell a Texas crowd that John Kennedy was "the greatest Northern Democrat since Franklin D. Roosevelt."

Kennedy's speech to the Houston ministers had come little more than a month before Election Day. Given the effect it had on its huge television audience, it was a prime example of the way American politics were being changed forever by the new medium. Just two weeks later, another television event had an even greater impact on the election. More than seventy million people watched the first-ever televised presidential debate. When it began, the vast majority were far more familiar with Richard Nixon than John Kennedy. When it ended, they had been exposed to a Kennedy who appeared healthier, wittier, and more poised than his opponent. Most important, as Richard Reeves observed, Kennedy "*looked* as presidential as the man who had been Vice President for the past eight years." Studies later found that of the four million people who made up their minds based on the first television debate, three million voted for Kennedy.

It was arguably the deciding factor in one of the closest elections in U.S. history. By a popular vote margin of one sixth of 1 percent of the nearly sixty-nine million votes cast, John Kennedy was chosen to lead the nation. Two months later, with eight inches of snow on the ground and the temperature well below freezing, he delivered an inaugural address that he had been revising since his election. "In the long history of the world," he stated, "only a few generations have been granted the role of defending freedom in its hour of maximum danger. I do not shrink from this responsibility—I welcome it." Calling upon the American people to enlist in "a struggle against the common enemies of man: tyranny, poverty, disease, and war itself," he reminded them of the sacrifices that would have to be made. "Ask not what your country can do for you—ask what you can do for your country."

It was a short speech—at 1,355 words, it was only about half as long as the average inaugural address. But as Kennedy biographers Robert Dallek and Terry Golway wrote, "When it was over and the day's commemorations of freedom were finished, those words lingered. They linger still."

★   ★   ★   ★   ★

As instrumental as Kennedy's PT-109 heroics were in setting the stage for his political career, it was, in the opinion of many political pundits, the national attention and acclaim he received from the publication of Profiles in Courage *that truly set him on the road to the White House. In January 1955, he sent a proposal for a "small book on 'Patterns of Political courage'" directly to Cass Canfield, the legendary president and chairman of Harper & Brothers. After Canfield indicated interest in the book and volunteered suggestions, Kennedy, who had considered profiling acts of courage by political leaders in various areas of government, responded by describing how he now believed it would be best to narrow his focus.*

January 28, 1955
Palm Beach, Florida

Mr. Cass Canfield:
Chairman of the Board
Harper & Brothers
49 East 33rd Street
New York, New York

Dear Mr. Canfield:

Many thanks for your very kind wire and letter concerning my proposal for a small book on "Patterns of Political Courage." I certainly appreciate your willing interest and helpful suggestions.

I agree with you wholeheartedly that each case history used should be considerably expanded, in order to establish more fully for the layman the historical contexts in which such events occurred and in order to heighten the dramatic interest by providing a fuller glimpse of the individuals involved, their background and their personalities. I am not certain, however, that I could expand each incident to a story of five to eight thousand words without losing in a mass of personal and historical detail the basic facts concerning the courageous deed which is the heart of the book. I believe that introductory and concluding chapters along the lines you mention can be worked out.

Meanwhile, I would submit this one additional thought—namely, to restrict the major examples to acts of political courage performed by United States Senators. It seems to me such a book might better hold together, and might present a more consistent theme—

particularly when it is to be written by a United States Senator. Consequently, I had considered dropping the example of John Adams defending the British soldiers at the British Massacre (not to be confused with his son, John Quincy Adams, who resigned from the Senate in the first example cited in the present draft); and adding to the manuscript three additional examples of political courage by Senators—involving William Giles of Virginia, Thomas Hart Benton of Missouri and Lucius Lamar of Mississippi. With these additions, I feel it would be more feasible to reach the length of forty to sixty thousand words that you suggest, without unduly burdening each story with detail. Unless you feel that restriction to Members of the Senate is too limited, I will proceed accordingly. In the concluding chapter, however, it is my intention to cite briefly many other examples of political courage—including those performed by non-Members of the Senate—including the John Adams story already mentioned, John Peter Altgeld, Sam Houston, Charles Evans Hughes, Robert Taft and others. I regret that the only example of recent times to be included is the brief mention of Taft (and his opposition to the Nuremberg trials); but I am unable to say whether we are too close in time to other examples for our political history to include them or whether this lack is due to a decline in the frequency of political courage in the Senate.

I intend to begin work on a complete book-length manuscript immediately, and I will be most appreciative of your further suggestions and assistance.

With every good wish, I am

Sincerely yours,
John F. Kennedy

From the moment Kennedy received a contract for the book and began to write it in earnest, the title of the volume became an issue of concern. Harper's was not thrilled with "Patterns of Political Courage." One of its top salesmen suggested "Patriots," but Kennedy was not enamored with that. As he would throughout his political career, he sought the advice of those close to him. Typical was a letter he sent to his sister Eunice.

July 26, 1955

Mrs. Eunice Shriver
220 East Walton Place
Chicago, Illinois

Dear Eunice:

Would you and Sarge and your friends mull over the following suggested titles for the book and let me know as soon as possible which you think is the best:

1. Men of Courage
2. Eight were Courageous
3. Call the Roll
4. Profiles of Courage.

Sincerely,

Published in 1956 with the finally agreed-upon title Profiles in Courage, *Kennedy's book immediately received widespread acclaim, and hundreds of laudatory letters poured into the senator's office. One of the earliest was from the distinguished American historian Arthur Schlesinger Sr., who had known Kennedy at Harvard. In typical profes-*

sorial manner, Schlesinger could not refrain from pointing out one of the errors in the book.

HARVARD UNIVERSITY

DEPARTMENT OF HISTORY

CAMBRIDGE, MASS.

HARVARD UNIVERSITY
DEPARTMENT OF HISTORY
CAMBRIDGE, MASS.

RECD JAN 19 1956

415 Widener Library
January 17, 1956

Dear Jack:

    I am not accustomed to writing "fan" letters to authors but Profiles in Courage obliges me to do so in your case. As a writer myself I admire the book's architecture, which I am sure was difficult to arrive at, and the text itself is thoughtful, stimulating and wise. You not only write fluently but convey a sense of holding back a great deal not directly relevant to your theme. Also you have the quality (which my son has so markedly) of making your characters come alive. In short, I am really enthusiastic about your book!

    No doubt you have caught the typographical error in the first line of chapter viii. Your later text makes clear that "1919" should be "1909."

    With cordial regards, I am

Sincerely yours,

Arthur M. Schlesinger

Senator John F. Kennedy
Washington, D. C.

Kennedy's second book, Profiles in Courage, *earned a fan letter from Harvard professor Arthur Schlesinger Sr.*

415 Widener Library
January 17, 1956

Dear Jack:

I am not accustomed to writing "fan" letters to au-
thors but *Profiles in Courage* obliges me to do so in your
case. As a writer myself I admire the book's architec-
ture, which I am sure was difficult to arrive at, and the
text itself is thoughtful, stimulating and wise. You not
only write fluently but convey a sense of holding back a
great deal not directly relevant to your theme. Also you
have the quality (which my son has so markedly) of
making your characters come alive. In short, I am really
enthusiastic about your book!

No doubt you have caught the typographical error in
the first line of chapter viii. Your later text makes clear
that "1919" should be "1909."

With cordial regards, I am

Sincerely yours,
Arthur M. Schlesinger

An enormous success, Profiles in Courage *remained on the bestseller list
for ninety-five weeks, a period in which Kennedy's daily mail included letters of praise from private citizens as well as well-known figures. In this
letter, a Louisiana man issued a special challenge to the book's author.*

1104 Second Street
New Orleans, La.
June 7, 1956

Honorable John F. Kennedy
United States Senate
Washington, D.C.

Dear Senator Kennedy:

I have read your book "Profiles in Courage" and have enjoyed it very much. Candidly I think that it should be required reading for all Senators and Congressmen and for any person who might aspire to be a Congressman or a Senator. But why stop at that? Make it required reading for all politicians.

There is so much that a man with the courage of his convictions can do now adays. If such a person happens to be a senator such as you are, he can do a great deal.

For example, you could help to stem the definite trend towards socialism that is going on in this country today. Or you could help to cut down all of the unnecessary spending that is going on in Washington. This would include the vast amount of waste by the federal government as well as the special requests that the federal government spend money locally on projects that rightfully belong to the states. (This last would include spending in your own district, Massachusetts.) There are a multitude of other ways that a man with the courage of his convictions could make himself felt.

All of this leads up to my question. Perhaps a hundred years from now someone else will write another "Profiles in Courage." Will the name of John F. Kennedy be included? Will you stand among the men you write about?

Very truly yours,
D.S. *Binnings*

Still highly popular today, Profiles in Courage *has had at least sixty-five printings in various editions with total sales of more than three million copies. To the day he died, John Kennedy continued to receive letters acknowledging the value of what he had written, none more gratifying than the one he received in May 1957.*

COLUMBIA UNIVERSITY

IN THE CITY OF NEW YORK

NEW YORK 27, N.Y.

ADVISORY BOARD ON PULITZER PRIZES

May 7, 1957

Senator John F. Kennedy
Senate Office Building
Washington, D.C.

Dear Senator Kennedy:

I take very great pleasure in confirming the fact that the Trustees of Columbia University, on the nomination of the Advisory Board on the Pulitzer Prizes, have awarded the Pulitzer Prize in Biography or Autobiography, established under the will of the first Joseph Pulitzer, to you for "Profiles in Courage" for the year 1956.

In accordance with that award, I enclose the University's check for $500 as tangible evidence to you of the selection of your work.

With renewed congratulations, I am

Sincerely yours,
John Hohenberg
Secretary

The combination of the acclaim that Kennedy received from both his PT-109 heroics and for Profiles in Courage *catapulted him into national prominence. As the 1956 Democratic Party's national convention approached, many in the party believed he would be an attractive vice presidential candidate. As the following letter to his father indicates, Kennedy had no doubts as to who the party's presidential candidate would be.*

June 29, 1956

Honorable Joseph P. Kennedy
Villa Les Fal Eze
Eze S/Mer, A.M.
France

Dear Dad:

As you know, the authorization for the Vatican bill passed the Senate unanimously yesterday. I think the appropriation bill will be all right too.

The office has probably sent you the article which appeared in the *New York Times* containing Governor Ribicoff's statement. I did not know he was going to say what he did, but when he keynoted the Democratic Convention at Worcester he had spoken to me about it. In the meantime he had John Bailey look into the matter further and I am enclosing a copy of John's letter.

Governor Roberts seconded Ribicoff's motion and Governor Hodges also indicated that it would be acceptable to him. The situation more or less rests there.

Arthur Schlesinger wrote to me yesterday and stated that he thought it should be done and that he was going to do everything that he possibly could. He is going to spend a month in Stevenson's headquarters.

I have done nothing about it and do not plan to although if it looks worthwhile I may have George Smathers talk to some of the southern Governors. While I think the prospects are rather limited, it does seem of some use to have all of this churning up. If I don't get it I can always tell them in the State that it was because of my vote on the farm bill.

We expect to get out of here in about three weeks and will then spend a couple weeks at the Cape before going to the Convention in Chicago. I expect to come to France with George Smathers right after the Convention.

Love,

P.S. Harriman was pretty well set back during the Governor's Conference and it looks sure that Stevenson will either be nominated on the 2nd or 3rd ballot.

Kennedy would lose the 1956 vice presidential nomination to Estes Kefauver. But his strong showing at the party's convention convinced him of the feasibility of a presidential run in the next election. When he began his bid for his party's presidential nomination, Eleanor Roosevelt was not only the most influential woman in the Democratic Party, but also one of the most powerful in the world. Kennedy was well aware that even though Roosevelt was a staunch supporter of Adlai Stevenson for the presidency, he could not afford to alienate her. On November 7, 1958, a genuine crisis erupted when, on the nationwide ABC television program College News Conference *the former First Lady made the serious accusation that Joseph Kennedy Sr. was attempting to "buy" the presidency for his son. Four days later, in what would be the beginning of a lengthy correspondence, Kennedy wrote to her, challenging her to prove her accusations.*

December 11, 1958
<u>PERSONAL</u>

Mrs. Franklin D. Roosevelt
211 East 62nd Street
New York, New York

Dear Mrs. Roosevelt:

I note from the press that on last Sunday afternoon, December 7, on the ABC television program "College News Conference" you stated, among other things, that Senator Kennedy's "father has been spending oodles of money all over the country and probably has a paid representative in every state by now."

Because I know of your long fight against the injudicious use of false statements, rumors or innuendo as a means of injuring the reputation of an individual, I am certain that you are the victim of misinformation; and I am equally certain that you would want to ask your informant if he would be willing to name me one such representative or one such example of any spending by my father around the country on my behalf.

I await your answer, and that of your source, with great interest. Whatever other differences we may have had, I'm certain that we both regret this kind of political practice.

Sincerely yours,
John F. Kennedy

December 11, 1958

PERSONAL

Mrs. Franklin D. Roosevelt
211 East 62nd Street
New York, New York

Dear Mrs. Roosevelt:

I note from the press that on last Sunday afternoon, December 7, on the ABC television program College News Conference, you stated, among other things, that Senator Kennedy's "father has been spending oodles of money all over the country and probably has a paid representative in every state by now."

Because I know of your long fight against the injudicious use of false statements, rumors or innuendo as a means of injuring the reputation of an individual, I am certain that you are the victim of misinformation; and I am equally certain that you would want to ask your informant if he would be willing to name me one such representative or one such example of any spending by my father around the country on my behalf.

I await your answer, and that of your source, with great interest. Whatever other differences we may have had, I'm certain that we both regret this kind of political practice.

Sincerely yours,

John F. Kennedy

JFK:gls

bcc: Mr. Philip L. Graham
Washington Post and Times Herald
1515 L Street, N. W.
Washington, D. C.

Kennedy responded swiftly—but carefully—to critical comments from liberal icon Eleanor Roosevelt.

Sixteen days later, Roosevelt replied, ending her letter by lecturing the senator.

MRS. FRANKLIN D. ROOSEVELT
202 FIFTY-SIXTH STREET WEST
NEW YORK 19, N.Y.

December 18, 1958

Dear Senator Kennedy:

If my comment is not true, I will gladly so state. I was told that your father said openly he would spend any money to make his son the first Catholic President of this country and many people as I travel about tell me of money spent by him in your behalf. This seems commonly accepted as a fact.

Building an organization is permissible but giving too lavishly may seem to indicate a desire to influence through money.

Very sincerely yours,
Eleanor Roosevelt

Kennedy, according to colleagues, was appalled by Roosevelt's reply. But he knew he had to tread softly with the person who led every public opinion poll in the United States as the most admired woman in the world. In a carefully worded letter that took him several days to construct and refine, he appealed to her "reputation for fairness" and asked her to "correct the record."

December 29, 1958

Mrs. Franklin D. Roosevelt
202 56th Street West
New York 19, New York

Dear Mrs. Roosevelt:

Thank you for your letter of December 18, 1958. I am disappointed that you now seem to accept the view that simply because a rumor or allegation is repeated it becomes "commonly accepted as a fact." It is particularly inexplicable to me inasmuch as, as I indicated in my last letter, my father has not spent any money around the country, and has *no* "paid representatives" for this purpose in *any* state of the union—nor has my father *ever* made the statement you attributed to him—and I am certain no *evidence* to the contrary has ever been presented to you.

I am aware, as you must be, that there are a good many people who fabricate rumors and engage in slander about any person in public life. But I have made it a point never to accept or repeat such statements unless I have some concrete evidence of their truth.

Since my letter to you, I assume you have requested your informants to furnish you with more than their gossip and speculation. If they have been unable to produce concrete evidence to support their charges or proof of the existence of at least one "paid representative" in one state of the union, I am confident you will, after your investigation, correct the record in a fair and gracious manner. This would be a greatly appreciated gesture on your part and it would be consistent with your reputation for fairness.

Sincerely yours,
John F. Kennedy

At the end of the first week of the new year, Roosevelt wrote back, telling Kennedy what she had done in response to his December 29 request.

MRS. FRANKLIN D. ROOSEVELT
202 FIFTY SIXTH STREET WEST
NEW YORK 19, N.Y.

January 6, 1959

Dear Senator Kennedy:

I am enclosing a copy of my column for tomorrow and as you will note I have given your statement as the fairest way to answer what are generally believed and stated beliefs in this country. People will, of course, never give names that would open them to liability.

I hope you will feel that I have handled the matter fairly.

Very sincerely yours,
Eleanor Roosevelt

Roosevelt's column did, in fact, contain Kennedy's denial of the allegations that the former First Lady and others had made about his father trying to buy the election. But Kennedy was still not satisfied. As far as he was concerned, it did not go far enough. Carefully including an apology for burdening her with "a too lengthy correspondence," he made his strongest statement in their exchange by asking her to state categorically that she had uncovered no evidence to indicate that Joseph Kennedy Sr. was attempting to buy the election.

January 10, 1959

Mrs. Franklin D. Roosevelt
202 56th Street West
New York 19, N.Y.

Dear Mrs. Roosevelt:

Thank you for sending me the copy of your column with the extract from my letter to you. Apparently there has been some misunderstanding of my reason for writing you.

While I appreciate your courtesy in printing my denial of the false rumors about my father and me, neither the article nor your letter to me deals with whether the rumors are true. In view of the seriousness of the charge, I had hoped that you would request your informants to give—not their own names—but the name of any "paid representative" of mine in any State of the Union. Or, if not the name, then mere evidence of his existence. I knew that your informants would not be able to provide such information because I have no paid representative.

Therefore, since the charges could not be substantiated to even a limited extent, it seemed to me that the fairest course of action would be for you to state that you had been unable to find evidence to justify the rumors.

You may feel that I am being overly sensitive about this issue. But when the record is as I have described it I feel that merely giving space to a denial that I have made leaves the original charge standing. The readers of your column and the listeners and viewers of the telecast of December 7 who do not have the benefit of our correspondence are forced to make their own judgments as to whether you or I am correct on the basis of your assertions and my denials.

I have continued what you may consider a too lengthy correspondence only because I am familiar with your long fight against the use of unsubstantiated charges and the notion that merely because they are repeated they attain a certain degree of credibility. If you feel that the matter was disposed of by your column, I certainly am prepared to let it rest on the basis of our correspondence.

Again I would like to express my appreciation for your courtesy in printing my denial of the charges.

> Sincerely yours,
> *John F. Kennedy*

Ten days later, in a letter notable for the former First Lady's acknowledgment that because her family, like the Kennedys, was wealthy, it too had been subjected to rumors, Roosevelt adopted the most conciliatory tone she had yet taken.

MRS. FRANKLIN D. ROOSEVELT
202 FIFTY-SIXTH STREET WEST
NEW YORK, NEW YORK

January 20, 1959

Dear Senator Kennedy:

In reply to your letter of the 10th, my informants were just casual people in casual conversation. It would be impossible to get their names because for the most part I don't even know them.

Maybe, like in the case of my family, you suffer from the mere fact that many people know your father and also know there is money in your family. We have always found somewhat similar things occur, and except for a few names I could not name the people in the case of my family.

I am quite willing to state what you decide but it does not seem to me as strong as your categorical denial. I have never said that my opposition to you was based on these rumors or that I believed them, but I could not deny what I knew nothing about. From now on I will say, when asked, that I have your assurance that the rumors are not true.

If you want another column, I will write it—just tell me.

Very sincerely yours,
Eleanor Roosevelt

Relieved that, at least for the immediate future, he had beaten back the onslaught from the woman he could not afford to have as an enemy,

Kennedy politely declined Roosevelt's offer of another column, seizing the opportunity to open the door to a closer relationship.

January 22, 1959

Mrs. Franklin D. Roosevelt
202 Fifty Sixth Street West
New York 19, New York

Dear Mrs. Roosevelt:

Many, many thanks for your very gracious letter of January 20. I appreciate your assurance that you do not believe in these rumors and you understand how such matters arise. I would not want to ask you to write another column on this and I believe we can let it stand for the present.

I do hope that we have a chance to get together sometime in the future to discuss other matters, as I have indicated before.

Again many thanks for your consideration and courtesy, and with every good wish, I remain

Sincerely yours,
John F. Kennedy

Their correspondence was still not quite over. True to her nature, Roosevelt was determined to have the final word. Nor, in a telegram, could she resist lecturing "my dear boy" one last time.

JANUARY 29 1959

HONORABLE JOHN F KENNEDY
SENATE OFFICE BUILDING
WASHINGTON DC

MY DEAR BOY I ONLY SAY THESE THINGS
FOR YOUR OWN GOOD I HAVE FOUND IN
LIFETIME OF ADVERSITY THAT WHEN
BLOWS ARE RAINED ON ONE, IT IS
ADVISABLE TO TURN THE OTHER
PROFILE.

MRS. ELEANOR ROOSEVELT

Later in their correspondence Mrs. Roosevelt gave the youthful
candidate some advice.

*In his run for the presidency, it would be Kennedy's good fortune to re-
ceive advice from such learned and important figures as economic and
foreign expert John Kenneth Galbraith, who regarded Kennedy, a personal friend, to be the best choice to lead the nation in troubled and dangerous times. The following letter, written in early 1958, would be the first
of what would become an ongoing correspondence between the two men.*

February 4, 1958

Mr. J. K. Galbraith
Littauer Center 207
Cambridge 38, Massachusetts

Dear Ken:

Many thanks for letting me have a preview of your
memorandum on "Democratic Foreign Policy and the
Voter." I have found this exercise in self-criticism conge-
nial with many thoughts which I myself have had over
the past months.

I quite agree with you that the emphasis of the Democratic Party, both in the broadsides issued by the Advisory Council and in Congressional speeches, has tended
to magnify the military challenge to the point where
equally legitimate economic and political progress have
been obscured. It is apparent, too, that there are members of the party who seem to feel that the world stood
still on January 20, 1953, and all we have to do is to pick
up some loose threads that were broken then. It is clear
also that, however tempting a target, the attacks on
Mr. Dulles have been taken too often as a sum total of
an alternative foreign policy—a new kind of devil theory
of failure.

With these narrow horizons, which take little account of economic aid or the United Nations, the political lessons you draw seem none too harsh. For my own part, I intend to give special attention this year to developing some new policy toward the underdeveloped areas, a field in which I know you also have special interest and far greater competence.

I have sent to you a copy of the Progressive article I wrote on India, which will be followed up with further speeches.

With kind regards and every good wish,

> Sincerely,
> John F. Kennedy

From his Harvard days, Kennedy, a voracious reader, had kept closely abreast of world affairs, a trait that was essential to him as a candidate for president. He was particularly taken with the writings of two-time Pulitzer Prize winner George Kennan who, along with having written seminal articles and books about U.S. policy regarding the Soviet Union, had served as an American diplomat in various countries from 1926 to 1953.

February 13, 1956

Honorable George F. Kennan
7 Norton Street
Oxford, England

Dear Mr. Kennan:

Having had an opportunity to read in full your Reith lectures, I should like to convey to you my respect for their brilliance and stimulation and to commend you for the service you have performed by delivering them.

I have studied the lectures with care and find that their contents have become twisted and misrepresented in many of the criticisms made of them. Needless to say, there is nothing in these lectures or in your career of public service which justifies the personal criticisms that have been made.

I myself take a differing attitude toward several of the matters which you raised in these lectures—especially as regards the underdeveloped world—but it is most satisfying that there is at least one member of the "opposition" who is not only performing his critical duty but also providing a carefully formulated, comprehensive and brilliantly written set of alternative proposals and perspectives. You have directed our attention to the right questions and in a manner that allows us to test rigorously our current assumptions.

I am very pleased to learn that these lectures will soon be published in book form, almost simultaneously with the appearance of the second volume of your magistral study of U.S.-Soviet relations after World War I.

With kind regards and every good wish for your stay in Oxford,

Sincerely yours,
John F. Kennedy

Among those in the Democratic Party who had embraced the Kennedy candidacy early on was influential Connecticut governor Abraham Ribicoff. In a letter acknowledging that Kennedy was entering a period in which "important and crucial decisions" about his nomination campaign approach needed to be made, Ribicoff offered the following advice.

ABRAHAM RIBICOFF
HARTFORD, CONNECTICUT
GOVERNOR'S RESIDENCE

December 16, 1959

Dear Jack:

Your vacation is well deserved. Being in the bosom
of your family and exposed to the southern sun should
give you the ease and relaxation you need. I know that
this is the period of making up your mind about important and crucial decisions.

I have tried to watch your activities with a dispassion-
ate eye even though I have been emotionally involved in
your campaign. You have been absolutely superb during
these past two years—busy, hectic, trying and provocative. You have gained in stature (opinion polls aside) and
people sense this. Your speeches, both in content and in
manner, have been of a nature to make a great impact on
those who have listened to you. In casting up the score,
you haven't made a strategic mistake. Provocation there
has been aplenty and you have had the constant patience
to give the soft word when the natural inclination would
have been to spit in someone's eye.

Your travels have been so wide and you have seen so
many people that as of now you, and only you, are the
best judge of future moves concerning individuals, their
word, and potential primaries. Jack, I don't think that
anyone can really advise you at this stage. You can tote
up the score until you are "blue in the face" but many of
these decisions cannot be resolved on an intellectual or

scientific basis. You have that rare quality that too few people possess and which is an absolute must if one is going to be a leader—the ability to make a split second decision from the heart and the viscera as well as the mind and without benefit of commissions, advisers or well-wishers. Use your own heart and "feel" in the month ahead and I am confident that the results will be all that one could expect.

All my best to you, Jackie, your father and the other members of the family during this holiday season. May the coming year bring good health and success at the end of the rugged and often lonely road.

Sincerely,
Abe

In the fall of 1943, author and journalist John Hersey met Kennedy while he was in the New England Baptist Hospital recuperating from malaria and back surgery. Based on interviews with Kennedy and his crew, Hersey wrote an article for the New Yorker *chronicling Kennedy's actions in the aftermath of the sinking of* PT-109. *The article drew national attention, particularly after an abridged version was published in* Reader's Digest. *In December 1959,* U.S. News & World Report *printed excerpts from Hersey's article in an assessment of Kennedy's presidential prospects. A month later, Hersey wrote what was obviously a good-natured protest letter to his friend Kennedy.*

JOHN HERSEY
HULL'S HIGHWAY,
SOUTHPORT, CONN.,
JANUARY 22, 1960.

The Honorable John F. Kennedy,
U.S. Senate,
Washington, D.C.

Dear Jack:

   A Hersey by-line over parts of the piece about your
adventures in the Solomons, in *U.S. News & World Report* of December 21, 1959, came as a surprise to me, as
David Lawrence, the editor, hadn't checked with either
me or *The New Yorker* for clearance before publication.
Upon our inquiry, Lawrence reported that he had been
given the piece by your office, and that it had carried
no copyright notice. As a lawmaker and a Pulitzer-prize-
winning author, Jack, you should be aware that that
kind of doings is agin the statutes. Please cease and
desist!
   As for the rest of life, best wishes to you in your current endeavors.

                                        Sincerely yours,
                                        John Hersey

*Kennedy's reply to Hersey was also good-natured, although it did end on
a serious note.*

                                        January 28, 1960

Mr. John Hersey
Hull's Highway
Southport, Connecticut

Dear John:

Thank you for your gentle letter of protest. In return for absconding with the copyright rights I hereby deed to you all reprint rights of *Why England Slept*, and all returns therefrom.

I hope the next time you come to Washington you will call me, because I would like to have lunch with you. If you are not going to be down this way, I would like you to give me your thoughts as to the conduct of this campaign whenever you feel moved to do so. I would very much appreciate your help.

With warmest regards,

Sincerely,
John F. Kennedy

As the 1960 presidential election approached, Thomas E. Murray, a former member of the Atomic Energy Commission, wrote a letter to all the aspiring candidates asking them to state their position on nuclear testing. Kennedy's reply gave him the opportunity to clearly articulate what his policies would be on one of the most hotly debated issues of the day.

Dear Mr. Murray:

Your thoughtful letter of September 6 is greatly appreciated.

I wholeheartedly concur in your opinion that the issue of nuclear weapon tests should not be exploited for partisan advantage. This subject, like all other public issues, is properly a matter for critical discussion and debate. But on this question—as on all other important issues—differences of opinion should be explored with responsible debate and with a full appreciation of the gravity of the question.

Your letter urges both presidential candidates to espouse the proposition that although the present ban on atmospheric tests should be retained, underground tests and tests in outer space should now be resumed, for the explicit purpose of developing nuclear weapons suitable for rational military purpose.

I do not agree that underground nuclear weapons tests should be resumed at this time. Should the American people choose me as their President, I would want to exhaust all reasonable opportunities to conclude an effective international agreement banning all tests—with effective international inspection and controls—before ordering a resumption of tests.

The Geneva Conference on Discontinuance of Nuclear Weapons Tests has been prolonged and generally discouraging. Even so, substantial progress has been made toward reaching agreement on some important phases of the problem.

The people of the United States, like millions of people all over the world, are anxiously hoping for an effective and realistic agreement outlawing nuclear tests—which means an agreement that is not dependent upon faith alone, but one enforceable through an effective system of international inspection controls.

I have always considered the conclusion of such an agreement of extreme importance not only to the people of the present nuclear powers, but for all mankind. This is true because new advances in technology have brought atomic weapons within reach of several additional nations.

For the United States to resume tests at this time might well result in a precipitate breakdown of the Geneva negotiations and a propaganda victory for the Soviets.

Under these circumstances I do not now recommend a resumption of testing. The question is not one of political courage. A man might courageously follow either course of action. The question is, which course of action is right.

It is possible that our negotiators, who have earnestly tried to negotiate a realistic and effective test ban, have exhausted every avenue of agreement, but since I have neither taken part in the negotiations nor had personal reports from the negotiators, who are not representatives chosen by me, I lack personal assurance of the futility of further discussions which alone would persuade me to urge the abandonment of so high an objective.

The Geneva Conference has been in progress, off and on, for almost 2 years. Despite the complexity of the subject, it should be possible within a reasonable period of time to find out whether the representatives of the Soviet Union are really prepared to enter into an effective test ban. If the Soviet Union still refused, after our earnest efforts, the world would then know where the responsibility lay.

Accordingly, it is my intention, if I am elected President, to pursue the following course of action

1. During my administration the United States will not be the first to begin nuclear tests in the world's atmosphere to contaminate the air that all must breathe and thus endanger the lives of future generations.

2. If the present nuclear weapons test conference is still in progress when I am elected, I will direct vigorous negotiation, in accordance with my personal instructions on policy, in the hope of concluding a realistic and effective agreement.

3. Should the current Geneva Conference have been terminated before January 20, 1961, I will immediately thereafter invite Great Britain, France, and the Soviet Union to participate in a new, and I would hope far more successful, conference on nuclear weapons test.

4. In either event, I intend to prescribe a reasonable but definite time limit within which to determine whether significant progress is being made.

    At the beginning of the period, I would direct the Atomic Energy Commission to proceed with preliminary preparations for underground tests of the type in which radioactive substances would be forever sealed within the explosive cavity. If, within the period, the Russians remain unwilling to accept a realistic and effective agreement, then the world will know who is to blame. The prompt resumption of underground tests to develop peaceful uses of atomic energy, research in the field of seismic technology and improvement of nuclear weapons should then be considered, as may appear appropriate in the situation then existing.

5. I would also invite leading nations having industrial capacity for production of nuclear weapons to a conference to seek and, if possible, to agree upon means of international control of both the production and use of weapons grade

fissionable material and also the production of
nuclear weapons.

6. I will earnestly seek an overall disarmament
   agreement of which limitations upon nuclear
   weapons tests, weapons grade fissionable material, biological and chemical warfare agents will
   be an essential and integral part.

John F. Kennedy

*On July 13, 1960, John Kennedy's handling of what Governor Ribicoff had
termed the "rugged and often lonely road" gained him the Democratic
presidential nomination. Among the scores of congratulatory letters and
telegrams he received was the following from one of the party's most
veteran and respected leaders, Senator Robert C. Byrd of Virginia.*

WESTERN UNION
TELEGRAM

1960 JUL 15 PM 12 48

THE HONORABLE JOHN F. KENNEDY
HOTEL BILTMORE LOSA:

HAVING LEFT LOS ANGELES THIS MORNING
AT 6 O'CLOCK, WHEN I WAS 135 MILES OUT OF
LOS ANGELES, I LEARNED OF YOUR GRACIOUS
INVITATION. I REGRET THAT INASMUCH AS I
HAVE ALREADY STARTED HOMEWARD BY
AUTOMOBILE AND MUST BE IN WASHINGTON
TO START EUROPEAN TRIP NEXT WEEK,
REGRETTABLY I WILL NOT BE ABLE TO BE

WITH YOU TONIGHT. I CONGRATULATE YOU
ON GREAT VICTORY AND I SHALL SUPPORT
YOUR CANDIDACY ENTHUSIASTICALLY. I
WANT EVEN NOW TO CONGRATULATE YOU
ON WINNING IN NOVEMBER. IT WILL BE A
PLEASURE TO WORK FOR AND SPEAK FOR THE
ELECTION OF THE 35TH PRESIDENT OF THE
UNITED STATES AND I SHALL DO ALL I CAN IN
YOUR BEHALF IN WEST VIRGINIA. I AM DE-
LIGHTED YOU WILL HAVE AS RUNNING MATE
OUR ABLE MAJORITY LEADER, SENATOR
LYNDON JOHNSON. I FEEL THIS ASSURES US
MORE THAN EVER OF AN UNBEATABLE
TICKET AND OF A SURE VICTORY THIS FALL.

ROBERT C BYRD USS.

*Legendary harpist and comedian Harpo Marx sent his own note of con-
gratulations on Kennedy's achievement on July 14, 1960.*

WESTERN UNION
TELEGRAM

SENATOR JOHN F KENNEDY
SPORTS ARENA LOSA

FIRST-CONGRATULATIONS. SECOND-DO
YOU NEED A HARP PLAYER IN YOUR CABI-
NET. THIRD-MY BEST TO YOUR MA AND PA-

HARPO MARX

———————————————

By July 1960, John Kenneth Galbraith had become one of Kennedy's most trusted advisers. The author of four dozen books and more than one thousand articles, Galbraith, during his lifetime, became the world's best-known economist. Kennedy particularly enjoyed his quick wit. Most important, he valued Galbraith's opinions on subjects that went well beyond economics. Days after Kennedy won the nomination, he received a letter from Galbraith offering advice on both his speaking style and the nature of his campaign speeches.

HARVARD UNIVERSITY

CAMBRIDGE, MASSACHUSETTS

July 16, 1960

Senator John F. Kennedy
Hyannis Port, Massachusetts

Dear Jack,

I hesitate to add to all the comment, liturgical and otherwise, you will have had on the acceptance speech. I listened to it here in Cambridge. But there are two matters which concern the future which I venture to bring up.

Let me say that I greatly approved the content. The New Frontier theme struck almost exactly the note that I had hoped for in my memorandum. So did the low key references to defense and Mr. K. [Khrushchev]. The reference to religion was good and indeed moving. By its nature much of the speech had to be an exercise in rhetoric, an art form in which I have never found it possible to practice, but it safely negotiated the delicate line that divides poetry from banality. I would hope that you would not need soon again to return to religion. You *could* succeed in making this an issue by speaking on it more frequently than is absolutely necessary. And your references to it are a license for others.

My suggestions concern construction of the speech itself—or rather those ahead. In the first place, your speech last night was essentially unfinished. It was badly in need of editing and polish. As a purely literary matter, the sentences could have been greatly smoothed. The images could have been much sharper and more vivid. Some superfluous words could have been drained out. The transitions could have been far smoother and more skillful. Your small transitions and changes of pace were insufficiently marked off from your major ones. This is partly a matter of speaking. But it is much more one of working into the text the warnings and signals (both to you and the audience) of the changes to come. Last night you were often well into the next sequence before the audience had realized that you had left the last. However, I do not wish to stress this point to the exclusion of others. The sharpening of images and allusions is also very important. All these matters not only make the speeches more effective. But they also make them much *much* easier to give. . . .

My next point concerns the nature of the speeches. It is evident that in straightforward exposition and argument you are superb. On the basis of your Los Angeles performance . . . I am prepared to argue that you have few masters in your time. When it comes to oratorical flights . . . you give a reasonable imitation of a bird with a broken wing. You do get off the ground but it's wearing on the audience to keep wondering if you are going to stay up.

The solution here is simple. You cannot avoid these

flights into space entirely—they are part of our political ritual. And maybe you could be less self-consciously awful in their performance although personally I would be sorry if you were. But the real answer is to keep this part of the speechmaking to the absolute minimum. My own guess is that people will welcome matter-of-fact and unpretentious discussion and anyhow that is what won you the primaries. In any case, I don't think you have a choice . . .

Do have a good rest—this would seem to me more important than anything else.

Sincerely,
J.K. Galbraith

To his credit, Kennedy, who had already gained a reputation as a masterful speaker, took Galbraith's constructive criticism most seriously. And soon he received a very different type of advice from political scientist Blair Clark.

Northeast Harbor, Maine
August 15, 1960

Dear Jack,

. . . As I told you in your office last week, Nixon's performance the night he was nominated, as he sat on a sofa in the Blackstone with his wife, daughters, mother and talked of humility, home, God, fate, the little gray home in the west, was enormously effective political soap opera. To me, it was almost thrillingly repulsive, a shameless exploitation of self. You would never do this, nor could you. But I think you might consider using some things in your own background which permit people to identify with you as a person, not you as a political figure. As one example of what I mean, you come from an impressive political background; I think most intelligent people now look on the Democratic city "bosses" as essential links between the immigrants and the cold and careless political establishment of those days. If there were crooks among them, there were at least as many among the bankers and business men (please, let's not talk about my great-great-grandpa Simon Cameron). What did your grandfather and his friends tell you, in the way of stories, when you were first getting into politics? My guess is that there is a rich vein to be mined here and that it would show your honorable ancestral origins and how they motivated you even as you rose above them to a more national role and to wider interests. I don't think this sort of personal story is undignified or to be avoided; on the contrary, it's the stuff of political parable and almost essential for the wide communication of ideas. Why leave all the corn to Nixon when your own hybrid brand could be so good? The above is just the beginning of a thought, but I think it's right.

Please let me know if I can do anything.

Yours, as ever,
Blair

From the time he announced his presidential aspirations, Kennedy knew that both his youth and his relative lack of experience would be major campaign issues. One month after his nomination, he received valued advice on these subjects from what might have been considered an unlikely source—his former rival Adlai Stevenson.

ADLAI E. STEVENSON
135 SO. LASALLE STREET
CHICAGO

August 29, 1960

Dear Jack:

I have been too long in following up on our conversation about "age and experience." This is probably a reflection of distaste for what is so obviously a phoney issue, at least on the merits.

The enclosed notes cover, I fear, only what is obvious. I have put them in as impersonal form as possible—in the unconscious desire, perhaps, to disassociate both of us from them:

Cordially yours,
Adlai

The "youth and inexperience" argument is an essentially false argument, significant only at the "image" level. This does not suggest that it can be disregarded. It means that it has to be dealt with as a "public impression" matter . . . it is reasonable to assume (i) that the "youth" element is much less significant than the "inexperience" element (particularly on a comparative basis); (ii) that the "inexperience" element has most of whatever significance it has in connection with the loose thinking about the business of "dealing with Khrushchev"; (iii) that this concern is felt more by women than by men.

Kennedy should not voluntarily take up this issue— as such—himself. Anything he says about it may appear defensive and accordingly contribute to the "image."

YOUTH

Kennedy should neither be defensive about his age nor try to appear older than he is. He should not argue that William Pitt or Napoleon or others were younger. All such tactics suggest that he is trying to vindicate himself of a charge. Leave that to others.

If the issue comes up under circumstances requiring comment on it by Kennedy he should treat it as being a "youth" (rather than "inexperience") issue. And youth is nothing to be ashamed of; in this campaign it is an asset. And the issue is irrelevant. The difference between 43 and 47 is inconsequential. If the Republicans are against young men, why did they nominate Nixon? Nixon was nominated for the Vice-Presidency at 39 and 43, and Dewey was nominated for the Presidency (in 1944) at 42. Bracketing Nixon in Kennedy's age group makes it harder for him to ride the maturity vs. youth issue. . . .

The point can also be made that America, founded by men in their thirties or forties and still a young country, has today a special need for leadership which can understand and be able to communicate effectively with the new generation of leadership coming to power all over the world.

EXPERIENCE

The "experience" element in the already developing Republican argument is more serious.

It is something new, by the way, for the Republicans to proclaim that the man most experienced in government is the man best qualified to be President. The record of the past 30 years shows that they have consistently chosen Presidential candidates who had less experience than the Democrats. Eisenhower had less than Stevenson. Dewey had less than Truman and less than Roosevelt. Willkie and Landon had less than Roosevelt. Hoover had less than Smith. . . .

Kennedy's own course of action should reflect his capacity for firm, thoughtful, courageous, decision-making. The public might be sensitive to any suggestion or petulance, argumentativeness, or either defensiveness or over-confidence. It will be important in the proposed television debates that obvious answers come tersely and directly but that the harder answers reflect full realization of the difficulties involved. . . .

To the extent that the "experience" issue relates less to actual past experience than to people's hunches as to how the two candidates will react to future demands and crises, the campaign may present opportunities for aggressive leadership. There will be a Nixon equivalent of "I shall go to Korea", if he can contrive one. This is not enough excuse for a Kennedy counterpart. But there is a basis even now for careful consideration whether the current crises (Congo, Cuba, disarmament, Russian rough stuff) warrant a dramatic *but responsible* proposal. If this can be done the "experience" issue will be won.

The importance of Kennedy's public identification with people who perhaps symbolize "experience" is too obvious to warrant more than mention. What is perhaps less obvious is the equal importance of this being done not as a matter of "endorsement," but rather as evidencing Kennedy's ability to command essential resources.

And, finally, there is opportunity for effective ridicule in the low state to which we have fallen in the past eight years of "age and experience"—at home and abroad.

Well before he received the presidential nomination, Kennedy's Senate office mailbags contained scores of letters from children. Among the most compelling of these was the one he received from a sixth grader informing him that in Walter Apley Jr., he had not only a supporter but an unsolicited campaign manager as well.

Salem Heights School
Salem, Oregon
February 29, 1960

Senator John Kennedy
c/o The Senate
Washington 6, D.C.

Dear Mr. Kennedy:

In view of the fact that the Presidential elections are being held this November, my sixth grade class decided to elect a President from the list of potential candidates.

The class first had a straw vote and the outcome was this:

Nixon	17
Stevenson	8
Kennedy	2
Humphrey	0
Johnson	0

RECEIVED ~~~~ 1 4 1960

Salem Heights School
Salem, Oregon
February 29, 1960

Senator John Kennedy
% The Senate
Washington 6, D.C.

Dear Mr. Kennedy:

In view of the that the Presidential elections are being held this November, my sixth grade class decided to elect a President from the list of potential candidates

The class first had a straw vote and the outcome was this:

Nixon	17
Stevenson	8
Kennedy	2
Humphrey	0
Johnson	0
Rockefeller	0
Symington	0

Our teacher, Mrs. Mendelson, asked for volunteers to head each candidate's campaign, and I volunteered to head yours. We all were allowed four posters.

Kennedy inspired young people as few American politicians ever had. As candidate and president he received thousands of letters from schoolchildren.

Rockefeller	0
Symington	0

Our teacher, Mrs. Mendelson, asked for volunteers to head each candidate's campaign, and I volunteered to head yours. We all were allowed four posters.

Two weeks later we had the arguments on who was the best man for President. After the arguments, we voted for a President.

Kennedy	12
Nixon	8
Stevenson	7
Humphrey	0
Johnson	0
Rockefeller	0
Symington	0

As you and Mr. Nixon were fairly close, we decided to vote again between you two.

Kennedy	15
Nixon	12

Good luck in the primaries.

Your Salem Heights
Campaign Manager,
Walter T. Apley, Jr.

One can only imagine the pride that Kennedy's response engendered in young Mr. Apley.

April 7, 1960

Mr. Walter T. Apley, Jr.
Salem Heights School
Salem, Oregon

Dear Walt:

I want to thank you for your letter. I was pleased to
see the results of your class's election, and I am grateful to you for your outstanding efforts in my behalf.
Certainly my victory in the second vote demonstrated
what an effective campaign manager you are, and I am
both proud and fortunate to have had you represent-
ing me.

I tentatively plan to be in Salem on Sunday, April 24,
for a Young Democrats reception. Should this materialize,
I hope that I will have an opportunity to thank you personally for your impressive work.

With every good wish, I am

Sincerely,
John F. Kennedy

*The letter Kennedy received from another young admirer contained a
candid observation.*

Box 352
Winton, N.C.

Dear Senator Kennedy,

I am an admirer of yours. My name is Lace Lewis. I am 14 years of age. I feel that you are the best possible candidate for the presidency.

My main reason for writing you is I would like more information on you and your family. Please, if you have "The Rules for Visiting the Kennedys" I would especially like to have that.

My sister Li Lu, age 6, is also one of your admirers but she thinks your brother, Robert, is better looking than you.

I wish you the best of luck in your campaign for president.

Yours sincerely,
Lace Lewis

In his reply to young Ms. Lewis, Kennedy assured her that he had informed his brother Robert that he had a brand-new admirer.

June 15, 1960

Miss Lace Lewis
Box 352
Winton, North Carolina

Dear Miss Lewis:

Thank you very much for your nice letter of recent date. I am glad to know that I can count on your support.

Regarding "The Rules for Visiting the Kennedys," this is a chapter in the book entitled *The Remarkable Kennedys* by Joe McCarthy. I am sure it is available in local bookstores.

My brother Robert will be happy to know that he has an admirer in your sister and I have passed your letter along to him.

Sincerely,
John F. Kennedy

Letters from young people continued to pour in after Kennedy secured his party's nomination. The most unique of all was in the form of a poem whose twelve-year-old creator demonstrated a surprising knowledge of events that had begun when she was only four.

July 17, 1960

Come on Kennedy, fight it out!
Let's give Nixon a reason to pout.
Lash out against the Republican party,
Scorn their candidate good and hardy.

You saw what happened these last eight years,
Many were the causes for sorrow and tears,
In Cuba, for instance, the terror is shocking,
'Tis not only Ike that Castro is mocking.
Where was our wonderful strength, and our
    spunk,
When our factories were stolen by that lousy
    Cuban skunk?

Perhaps Ike will say that the Communists bar us,
Well, things might have been a bit better, starting
　at Paris,
If he hadn't let that U2 plane loose,
Khrushchev's blunt rudeness would have no
　excuse.
He wouldn't have found it so easy to give Castro
　his way—
Now "U.S. Aggression" is all they need say,
The Cuban situation is going very badly,
The Republicans have handled our country quite
　sadly.

For instance, the taxes have never been higher
There's also a need for a good slum defier.
There's plenty of proof as you probably know,
To show that Republican's morales are low,
And so Kennedy, as you probably well see,
The odds are on Republicans, 1, 2, 3,

And in closing I just want to say,
Something which surely will brighten your
　day:
In our house, from basement, to front room, to
　attic,
Everyone is straight DEMOCRATIC

SLOGAN—NIX ON NIXON

By Doreen Sapir
3742 Silsly Rd.
Univ. Hts, 18, Ohio
12 years old

While young Cindy Baratz had not yet attained grammatical perfection, her letter to the candidate expressed clear reasons why Kennedy was her choice for president.

Thursday, October 23 1960

Dear Mr. Kennedy,

My Father was a Democratic and still is one for 10 years, but he never won.

I hope YOU are next President.

At school I not only say I vote you, but I tell all about the facts.

You want to build more school's, more college's, & Nixon says no, It's to much money & You want to help the poor Peapole.

I think that you think nicely.

I am seven years old.

Sincerly, Yours
Miss Cindy Baratz
145 Gable Rd.
Paoli, Pa.

Throughout his life, John Kennedy regarded courage as the greatest of virtues. When, during his campaign, he learned of a Pennsylvania schoolgirl's brave act on his behalf, he immediately wrote to her, expressing his gratitude:

———————————

October 29, 1960

Dear Judy:

I have learned of your persistence to remain in school despite the fact that the whole group was dismissed to hear Vice President Nixon speak.

I want to thank you for your devotion and spirit of independence at this time.

With every good wish, I am

Sincerely,
John F. Kennedy

Miss Judy Myers
743 South Front Street
Steelton, Pennsylvania

Kennedy could not help but be heartened by the expressions of support his candidacy received from the outset. But there was one issue that had also arisen from the moment he had announced his intention to run for the presidency, one so serious that it threatened his chances for election: Kennedy was Roman Catholic. Throughout the nation there were many who were convinced that a Catholic president would be bound to pledge greater allegiance to the Vatican and the church than to the United States Constitution. It was a concern clearly articulated in a letter sent to Kennedy by a Baptist minister.

16 January 1958

The Honorable John Kennedy
United States Senate
Washington D.C.

Dear Senator Kennedy:

   It is with an open mind that I am writing you, for it
does not seem Christian to actively oppose something
until one can be certain of the stand to be taken. As you
are constantly reminded many of the American people
are opposed to your running for the Presidency because
of your faith. It is not easy to forget that even today in
many parts of the world our Baptist missionaries are
being persecuted by the Roman Catholic Church.

   However, to me it is still an individual matter, and begins with the person not the church. You have my deepest sympathy in this situation. You cannot hope to please
everyone, and as a minister I am more than aware of that.

   Can you answer some questions for me? I am Mod-
erator of a group of Baptist Churches in this part of the
state, and I cannot actively support or oppose anything
either among the many churches or my own church
without knowing more than I do.

   The state of Texas is predominately Baptist, and the
Editor of the Baptist newspaper for the entire state and
I have discussed the possibility of your candidacy for the
Presidency in 1960. It would seem to be all but a "lead-
pipe cinch" that you will be the Democratic nominee.

   Unless we Baptists know EXACTLY where you stand
on major religious issues—we will be fighting your election down to the last inch.

If you would answer some questions that have been bothering me I would deeply appreciate it.

1. How do your beliefs coincide with the traditional stand of the country on separation of church and state?
2. Where do you stand on the appointment of an American ambassador to the Vatican?
3. In the event of pressure being applied where would your primary allegiance belong—to the Roman Catholic Church and the Vatican or to the United States and her people?
4. Would you advocate the use of public funds for Catholic or other sectarian schools? Would you <u>actively oppose</u> such usage of public funds?

Thank you very much for your gracious attention to this request, and I shall look forward to hearing from you at your earliest convenience.

Sincerely,
Mickey R. Johnston

Kennedy regarded Reverend Johnston's letter as a welcome opportunity to articulate where he stood on the religious issue.

February 5, 1958

Rev. Mickey R. Johnston
Grace Temple Baptist Church
Henrietta, Texas

Dear Reverend Johnston:

I am grateful to you for your letter of recent date and
I welcome the opportunity to try to illustrate my position on the questions you have raised; for, like you, I feel
that those of us who seek public office must be ready to
express opinions on issues as we see them.

In the first place, I believe that the position of the
Catholic Church with respect to the question of separation of church and state has been greatly distorted and
is very much misunderstood in this country. As a matter of fact, I am quite convinced that there is no traditional or uniformly held view on the subject. For my
own part, I thoroughly subscribe to the principles embodied in the Constitution on this point, particularly
those contained in the First Amendment. It is my belief
that the American Constitution wisely refrains from
involvement with any organized religion, considering
this most important but personal sphere not an area for
government intervention. To this view I subscribe without reservation.

I do not favor the establishment of diplomatic relations
with the Vatican, for I do not perceive any particular
advantage to the United States in sending an ambassador there—and it is my belief that this should be the
criterion in deciding on diplomatic relations.

I have no hesitancy in saying to you that in my public
life I act according to my own conscience and on the
basis of my own judgment, without reference to any
other authority. As a public official I have no obligation
to any private institution, religious or otherwise. My
obligation is to the good of all.

On the question of aid to private schools, my position
is also unequivocal. I support the Constitution without

reservation, and as I understand its principles it forbids aid to private institutions. In this respect you may be interested to see the attached copy of a bill which I have recently introduced to provide Federal aid for the construction of public schools.

I appreciate the good faith in which your letter was written and I hope that my reply will help to clarify my position.

With every good wish,

Sincerely yours,
John F. Kennedy

Despite Kennedy's continual explanations of his stance on religion, the issue would not go away. And, as the following letter and Kennedy's reply to it reveal, anti-Catholic sentiment took many forms.

La Grange
North Carolina
May 13, 1960

Senator John P. Kennedy
Congressional Halls
Washington, D. C.

Dear Senator:

Can you and will you tell me why the <u>Pre</u> dominant Catholic Countries are mostly illiterate, illegitimates and so poverty stricken?

Please differentiate between the two major parties, Democrat and Republican.

Though 85, born June 12, 1975 [1875], I want to be able to vote intelligently and conscientiously.

Thank you for an early reply.

Sincerely yours,
Mrs. M. S. Richardson

June 10, 1960

Mrs. M. S. Richardson
La Grange
North Carolina

Dear Mrs. Richardson:

I am sorry I haven't been able to reply to your letter before this. I believe that you will find that it is not possible to distinguish so-called Catholic countries on the basis of their wealth or social status. For instance, France is normally accepted as a Catholic country and I do not think that it has ever been charged that France is a nation of illiterates nor poverty stricken.

It is certainly true that in some countries where Catholics constitute a large portion of the population, stringent economic and social conditions do often exist but this can also be said of countries dominated by other Christian bodies or countries where the Christian church is in the distinct minority. It seems to me that poverty and illiteracy are related to other factors than the religion of the people.

There are many differences between the Republican

and Democratic Parties but I would say that the Democratic Party has been characterized in modern times by a pressing concern for the welfare of all the people, particularly those who are less fortunate and less able to care for themselves. It has been Democrats who have spearheaded some of our most important social legislation such as the Social Security Act and at the present time, a comprehensive health insurance program for our elderly citizens.

Again, I am sorry for the delay in replying to your letter. I trust that these few comments will answer the questions which are in your mind.

With every good wish, I am

Sincerely,
John F. Kennedy

As the 1960 election year began, Kennedy sent out a lengthy, detailed statement to his most influential supporters, outlining what he regarded as the major issues facing the nation and how he intended to address them in the campaign. Typical of the replies he received was one from Hulan Jack, in which New York City's powerful borough president could not refrain from reminding Kennedy of how important a role his religion was bound to play in the election.

PRESIDENT OF THE BOROUGH OF MANHATTAN
CITY OF NEW YORK
NEW YORK, N.Y.
HULAN E. JACK
PRESIDENT

January 11, 1960

Dear Jack:

I was delighted to receive your letter of December 28
with your enclosed statement of January 2, 1960, which
I accept as the preamble of the beginning of your historic campaign....

Your comprehensive statement clearly outlines the
momentous issues facing this nation of destiny. Your
courageous and forthright approach to the position of
responsibility is refreshing. In maintaining America's
leadership in human dignity, the security of the individual, the jealous guardianship of our democratic processes
and its expansion to give help, guidance, and leadership
to mankind to build a world of peace and plenty for all to
enjoy, we must aid in the economic development of the
emerging nations.

It is my profound hope that our Democratic Party will
recognize that the only sure road to winning in November is to have a fresh look in the person of our candidate
for the high office of President. I personally think that
our candidate must be young, with a dynamic as well as
a warm personality, a good family man, with a deep religious background, a great appeal to the women's vote, a
thorough familiarity with the issues facing this nation,
able to discuss them freely, willing to make decisions, a
man who truly demonstrates leadership.

I would strongly deplore the injection by any of our
citizens of the religious issue thereby denying all of the
people of our great democratic society the talents of a
noble and devoted public servant. I feel there is no room
in our land for this kind of bigotry. I think we have demonstrated a long time ago that the cornerstone of our

tradition is the principle of tolerance, understanding and equal trust. If these things are true then the right to worship as one pleases is inviolate, one's faith in God is paramount, his religion is his right of choice and will have nothing to do with his oath of trust and allegiance to serve all of our citizens alike, irrespective of race, creed, color or origin.

If religious mistrust sweeps this nation then the clock has been turned back much to the regret of us all. We will then be impeding the larger objective which God has destined for this nation, to lead our unhappy world to the heights of human dignity, peace and plenty. The emerging nations look to us, the enslaved nations plead with us wearily for their deliverance. The underdeveloped nations want our productive know how and guidance to develop their economy.

Will we accept the challenge? I am positive we will: Now is the hour to make the profound decision. We need the man with the mostest. Let us not rob ourselves and mankind because of the evil of bias.

May God give us the vision and unselfishness to get behind a good image.

With best wishes for success and kind regards.

> Sincerely yours,
> *Hulan E. Jack*
> President
> Borough of Manhattan

As the presidential campaign gained momentum, Arthur Schlesinger Jr. (the son and Harvard colleague of the historian whose letter appeared above) became an increasingly important Kennedy adviser. After discussing the candidate's approach to the religious issue with New York

Times columnist *James "Scotty" Reston and his wife, Schlesinger wrote to Kennedy with specific suggestions.*

HARVARD UNIVERSITY

CAMBRIDGE, MASSACHUSETTS

UNIVERSITY 4-9710

ARTHUR SCHLESINGER, JR.

April 26, 1960

Dear Jack:

I had a talk yesterday with Scotty and Sally Reston about the religious question, and it seems worthwhile to pass along one or two points which emerged.

I told Scotty that, while I thought the issues he raised against your ASNE [American Society of Newspaper Editors] speech were legitimate, the effect of his column was to give the Catholic-bloc issue an importance out of all proportion to its place in the speech and that, in doing this, he failed badly to do justice to what seemed to me in the main an exceptionally clear and courageous statement. We then talked about the general problem for a while. I think I now know what troubles the Restons, and others who, like them, are generally well disposed toward you but are still unsatisfied by your treatment of the religious problem. They are impressed by your own clear declaration of independence on the relevant issues; but they remain troubled, I think, by what they feel to be an implication in your discussion that bigotry is essentially a Protestant monopoly. They would respond to an attack by you on all bigots and on all those who vote their religion, whether Protestant or

Catholic. Their apprehension springs particularly, I believe, from the problems of small communities where
Catholic voting blocs have caused difficult problems for
the public schools.

In your ASNE speech you took steps to correct any
impression that you felt that an anti-Kennedy vote was
automatically an anti-Catholic vote. Of course you don't
believe that; and I think it is important to make this
abundantly clear time and time again. I think that it
would help to add to this a denunciation of religious bigotry in a way which would make it clear that you do not
regard intolerance as an exclusively Protestant failing,
that you recognize a tendency on the part of Catholics
too to vote as a bloc, and that you condemn all tendencies to vote *for* as well as *against* candidates on religious
grounds. ("I don't want a single Catholic to vote for me
for the reason that I am a Catholic any more than I want
a single Protestant to vote against me for that reason.")

You might also want to consider saying something
sometime about Nixon's astonishing statement before
the ASNE: "There is only one way that I can visualize
religion being a legitimate issue in an American political campaign. That would be if one of the candidates
for the Presidency had no religious belief." Apparently
Nixon wants to impose a religious test for office-holding
when none appears in the Constitution. The Constitution, was of course, designed to make America free for
irreligion as well as for religion. I think it would take
some wind out of the opposition's sails if you were the
first candidate to make this point.

Yours ever,
Arthur

*By August 1960, rumors and concerns regarding Kennedy's purported
"dangerous" ties to the Catholic Church and the pope continued to pro-
liferate. Among the most repeated was Daniel Poling's "four chaplains"
accusation, a charge that, as the following letter revealed, was having
serious political implications.*

104 Green Meadow Drive
Timonium, Maryland

August 9, 1960

Dear Senator Kennedy,

Both my husband and I, as Catholics, find ourselves
answering many questions concerning our religion since
your nomination. The questions of course, invariably
imply the possible conflict of religious beliefs with the
post of United States President.

We know you are extremely busy at this time, but we
hope for an answer from one of your secretaries or colleagues.

We are confronted with this problem. Two very fine
people connected with the Goucher College faculty,
and possessing a certain degree of influence, approached
us with this story: you accepted an invitation to speak
at a memorial service for the four heroic chaplains of
World War II. Then, so the story goes, the Bishop of your
diocese forbade you to speak at the service, and you ac-
quiesced to his wishes.

Our non-Catholic friends were disturbed and puzzled
by this action. All we could say was, "It doesn't sound
like the full story."

These two people, as a result of a half-told tale, have

decided not to vote in the coming presidential election! They are liberal-minded, educated and cultured,
yet, they are "frightened" by the implications of this
story.

We are anxious to do what we can to help you because
we believe in you and your ability. We will appreciate
greatly an answer, or possible reference material.

With best wishes for your success in the coming
election, we are

> Sincerely yours,
> *Mary Atherton*
> *George Atherton*

*Not all of the nation's non-Catholic religious leaders were as willing as
Norman Vincent Peale was to spread anti-Kennedy rumors. Arguably
the most respected of them all, the Reverend Billy Graham, refused to
circulate such stories, as he assured the candidate.*

> Billy Graham
> August 10, 1960

The Honorable Jack Kennedy
The United States Senate
Capitol Building
Washington, D.C.

Dear Senator:

I trust that you will treat this letter in strictest confidence. There is a rumor circulating in the Democratic
Party that I intend to raise the religious issue publicly

during the presidential campaign. This is not true. In fact, I would like to commend you for facing it squarely and courageously.

There was another matter concerning malicious gossip that I had overheard about you. I took it immediately to two of your closest friends and they clarified it. I promise you it has not gone beyond me. It is most unfortunate that political leaders are subject to these types of ugly rumors and gossip.

I shall probably vote for Vice President Nixon for several reasons, including a long standing personal friendship. I am sure you can understand my position. However, if you should be elected President, I will do all in my power to help unify the American people behind you. In the event of your election you will have my wholehearted loyalty and support.

With every good wish, I am

Cordially yours,
Billy Graham

On November 8, 1960, forty-two-year-old John F. Kennedy was elected president of the United States. Among the first congratulatory letters he received was one from family friend W. Averell Harriman. A former governor of New York and a candidate for the Democratic presidential nomination in 1952 and 1956, Harriman had also served as Franklin D. Roosevelt's special envoy to Europe and U.S. ambassador to the Soviet Union and to Great Britain. He would eventually carry out various diplomatic assignments in both the Kennedy and Lyndon B. Johnson administrations. Harriman's letter to the newly elected president was more than a congratulatory one. It was an assessment of what he envisioned might be the relationship between Kennedy and Soviet chairman Nikita Khrushchev, the man who would undoubtedly be the

new American president's main adversary in the explosive cold war
atmosphere that Kennedy had inherited.

November 12, 1960

Dear Jack:

Congratulations again. Yours was a great victory,
even though it was a bit close in some states. Nixon had
the fabulous advantage of having had eight years of
Madison Avenue build-up and the blind support of one
of the most popular men in our history. . . .

But congratulations are not the reason for this letter.

I had a most interesting talk yesterday with a Russian by the name of Alexander Korneichuk whom I had
known quite well in Moscow during the war. Among
other things he is a Russian playwright, a member of
the Communist Party Central Committee, high in the
Ukrainian government, and, I am told, quite close to
Khrushchev. He was over here with a group of Soviet
intellectuals for a conference at Dartmouth, at the invitation of Norman Cousins of the *Saturday Review*
and financed by the Ford Foundation, promoting
the exchange of ideas between a parallel group of
Americans.

We had a blunt and frank talk. He indicated that
Khrushchev wanted to make a fresh start, forgetting
the U-2 incident and all of the subsequent gyrations.
He expressed the opinion that arms limitation and
particularly nuclear control was a vital question. The
Russians don't want another devastating war—they
have too much at stake. They recognize the danger of

the present tensions, including the spread of nuclear weapons among other countries, unless an agreement is arrived at fairly soon.

He admitted the ideological conflict between us would continue on a world-wide basis, but he hoped that Khrushchev's statement, that the conflict could be carried on a competitive basis without war, would be accepted as sincere. I told him that I believed the single most important subject was to open up the Soviet Union still further and get away from their present closed society. He argued that much had been done in this direction, but I maintained that it was obviously not enough—and I got the impression that in his heart he agreed. However, the Soviet military and Khrushchev consider secrecy as a military advantage.

He asked me whether you would follow out FDR's policies. I said 'Yes' insofar as they concerned our 'good neighbor' relationships with the underdeveloped countries; that he could count on that, and Mr. Khrushchev would find much tougher competition in his attempts to communize them; but that there would be no appeasement on principle or on the positions our country had taken in our relations with the Soviet Union. I restated my personal opinion, which I had stated publicly fifteen months ago on my return from the Soviet Union, that I thought arms control should be the first subject of consideration between us. He didn't take issue with this. . . .

He asked me how I thought you and Mr. Khrushchev would get along if you met. I said Mr. Khrushchev would find you were not interested in scoring points in debate, and that you would be direct and clear in your discussion of the issues. I told him that if Mr. Khrushchev was sincere in trying to get back to where we left off before the May meeting, he would not mention the U-2 incident again. . . .

He said that he would report our conversation to Khrushchev. I naturally underlined that everything I had said was personal.

This conversation tends to confirm my interpretation of Khrushchev's message to you as being an indication that he wants to start afresh. . . .

I would like to have an opportunity to talk.

> Sincerely,
> *W. Averell Harriman*

Another congratulatory message he received was the following from Bernard M. Baruch, financier, statesman, and political and economic adviser to six presidents.

BERNARD M. BARUCH
597 MADISON AVENUE
NEW YORK 22, N.Y.

November 10, 1960

Dear Senator Kennedy:

Soon I must call your Mr. President.

My heartiest congratulations on your election. I know what satisfaction it must bring you and I know, too, what a burden you have assumed. No President has ever faced so many unsolved problems.

I join with every American in the hope that you will lead the country safely through these dangerous times.

If there is any way that I can help you in your tasks, you have but to call on me.

　　With all best wishes, I am

Sincerely yours,
Bernard M. Baruch

My best to your wonderful mother and father and my special favorite Pat.

On the day John Kennedy was elected president, eighty-seven-year-old Herbert Hoover was the nation's oldest living former chief executive. Despite his age, Hoover followed a time-honored tradition by congratulating his most recent successor and offering him what help he could provide.

THE WALDORF ASTORIA TOWERS
NEW YORK, NEW YORK

November 10, 1960

My dear Senator:

　　I use the above salutation as I do not know the precise moment when you should be addressed as President Elect.

　　In any event, this is just to express my good will and my desire to serve within my physical limitations.

Yours faithfully,
Herbert Hoover

———————————

One of those high on Kennedy's inaugural invitation list was Harry S. Truman. The former president replied in his usual direct manner.

January 3, 1961

Dear Mr. President:

I certainly appreciated your invitation to attend the Inaugural ceremonies and as you suggested to me I will have my high hat and my long tail coat.

As President of the United States you can tell me what you want me to do and I will be glad to do it.

Most Sincerely yours,
Harry Truman

Honorable John F. Kennedy
President of the United States
Senate Office Building
Washington, D.C.

One of the first letters Kennedy wrote as president was to his predecessor, Dwight D. Eisenhower. Although they were far apart on many key issues, Kennedy was most appreciative of Eisenhower's graciousness in making the transfer of power as smooth as possible.

————————————————

January 21, 1961

My dear Mr. President:

On my first day in office I want to send you a note of special thanks for your many acts of cordiality and assistance during the weeks since the election.

I am certain that your generous assistance has made this one of the most effective transitions in the history of our Republic. I have very much enjoyed personally the association we have had in this common effort.

With all good wishes to you and Mrs. Eisenhower in the days ahead, I am

Sincerely,
John F. Kennedy

Kennedy's inaugural address is widely regarded as one of the greatest speeches of its kind ever delivered. Of all the responses his words elicited, perhaps none was more warmly received by the new president than that from British prime minister Harold Macmillan, the man Kennedy was counting on to be his staunchest ally in the battle against the communist world. During his presidency, Kennedy met with Macmillan more than any other foreign leader and the two developed a relationship of mutual trust and a genuine friendship.

Admiralty House
Whitehall, SW 1
January 23, 1961

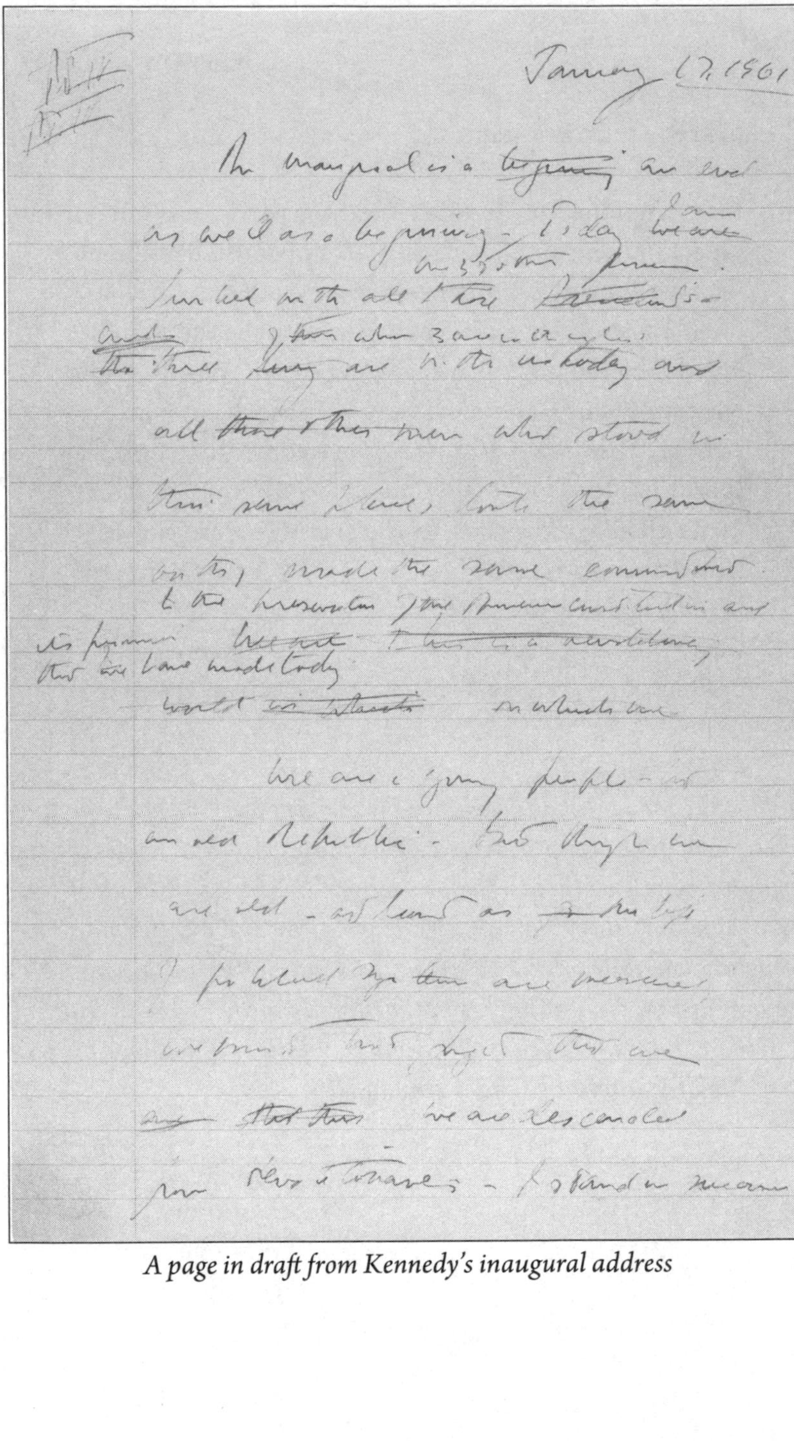

A page in draft from Kennedy's inaugural address

Dear Mr. President—

I have just seen my nephew, Andrew Devonshire, on his return from Washington. He has given me a most vivid account of all the ceremonies connected with your Inauguration. But in particular he has told me of the great kindness and hospitality which you and your family have shown to him and Debo. He tells me that not only did you invite him into your box for the parade, but also to the ball in the evening. All this has touched us very much.

May I add what a great impression your inaugural speech has made in this country. Everyone here is struck by its content as well as by its form. We were particularly struck by your phrase about considering what the United States and other countries can together do for the freedom of man. In that search, however long and perilous it may be, we are your enthusiastic allies.

Harold Macmillan

Kennedy's inaugural address elicited an overwhelmingly enthusiastic worldwide response. From far off Tanganyika, America's most popular actor interrupted his filmmaking to express his feelings.

ARUSHA 0900 FEB 3 1961

THE PRESIDENT
WHITEHOUSE

CONGRATULATIONS MR PRESIDENT IT WAS
THRILLING READING YOUR INAUGURAL

SPEECH HERE IN TANGANYIKA STOP IT
MADE US EVEN PROUDER THAT WE ARE
AMERICANS REGARDS

JOHN WAYNE

Not all of the hundreds of congratulatory letters, telegrams, and cables Kennedy received regarding both his election and his inaugural address were as warmly welcomed, particularly one sent by Walter Ulbricht, chairman of the communist-controlled section of the bitterly divided city of Berlin.

At a time of new beginnings and hope for a brighter world future, Ulbricht's cable was an inescapable reminder of the challenges that John Kennedy had inherited, as reflected by the State Department memorandum that stated, "Since the United States does not recognize the so called German Democratic Republic, which is a Soviet puppet regime imposed on the people of East Germany by the Soviet Union, no reply should be made to this cable."

THE WHITE HOUSE
WASHINGTON
WB077 INTL

S BERLIN 97 JAN 20 1539
ETATPRIORITE PRESIDENT JOHN F KENNEDY
WHITE HOUSE WASHINGTONDC

MR PRESIDENT: I SEND YOU MY BEST WISHES
ON YOUR TAKING OVER THE OFFICE OF
PRESIDENT OF THE UNITED STATES OF
AMERICA TODAY. I EXPRESS THE HOPE THAT

YOUR GOVERNMENT ACTIVITY WILL CON-
TRIBUTE TO THE RELAXATION OF INTER-
NATIONAL TENSION AND TO THE PEACEFUL
SETTLEMENT OF INTERNATIONAL QUES-
TIONS AT ISSUE. PERMIT ME IN THIS SENSE
TO WISH YOU SUCCESS IN FILLING YOUR
OFFICE TO THE BENEFIT OF THE PEOPLE OF
THE UNITED STATES OF AMERICA

WALTER ULBRICHT CHAIRMAN OF THE
STATE COUNCIL OF THE GERMAN DEMO-
CRATIC REPUBLIC.

*In 1952, thirty-five-year-old John Kennedy had confided to columnist
Joseph Alsop, "they tell me that the damn disease will get me in the
end. But they also tell me I'll last until 45, and that's a long way away."
Kennedy did not specify exactly what "damn disease" he was referring
to, but his family was constantly concerned about his health. This was
particularly true of his mother, who, as her son was beginning his run
for the presidency, wrote the following letter to his physician, Dr. Janet
Travell.*

Hyannis Port
Massachusetts

June 3, 1959

Dear Dr. Travell:

The other day when I talked with you on the telephone,
we discussed Jack's diet since the original list was rather

vague. As I recall, you said that he was allergic to the items marked with red and that he might have the unmarked items.

You also said that he might have root beer and V-8 juice, but could have no great quantity of milk. Does this apply to cream?

It was my understanding that you would send a revised list to his home in Washington and to me here in Hyannis Port. Undoubtedly, Jack has discussed all of this with [another of his physicians] Dr. de Garaj; but he is always so vague about his personal habits that it would help if I had an idea of just what he can eat.

Let me thank you for your attention in this.

Sincerely yours,
Rose Kennedy
(Mrs. Joseph P. Kennedy)

By the time he ran for the presidential nomination, there were serious rumors about Kennedy's health. India Edwards, a Southern Democratic Party leader and a strong supporter of Lyndon Johnson's campaign, told reporters that "Kennedy was so sick from Addison's disease that he looked like a spavined hunchback." Another Johnson campaign leader asserted that if Kennedy was elected, he "couldn't serve out the term" because "he was going to die." During both the race for his party's nomination and the presidential contest, Kennedy defused the charges by conducting extraordinarily vigorous campaigns. His physicians also sent him a letter "confirming" that he was in "superb physical condition."

From an early age John Kennedy was an avid reader and he became one of the most eloquent writers ever to serve in the presidency. His first book, *Why England Slept*, was originally written as his Harvard undergraduate thesis. It became a bestseller and gained Kennedy international attention. Here the young author poses at his typewriter, probably in 1940. (All photographs, unless otherwise indicated, are from the John F. Kennedy Presidential Library and Museum.)

The Kennedys were an extremely close-knit family. And from an early age, love of the sea was instilled in each of the children. The family gathered on the beach at Hyannis Port in 1931, with young Jack in white at left. Others (left to right) are Bobby, Eunice, Jean (in Joseph Sr.'s lap), Rose, Patricia, Kathleen, Joseph Jr., and Rosemary.

Even as a youngster, John Kennedy possessed a winning smile, something that would serve him well throughout his life. Here, he manages to flash a grin at a moment when his sisters were less cheerful.

A young John Kennedy (back row, second from left) poses with his parents and siblings in the Vatican before receiving an audience with Pope Pius XII in 1939. Kennedy's religion would play a major role in the 1960 presidential campaign.

Sailing was in John Kennedy's blood. It was a skill that he passed on to his younger brother Edward.

JOHN FITZGERALD KENNEDY

Born May 29, 1917, in Brookline, Massachusetts. Prepared at The Choate School. Home Address: 294 Pondfield Road, Bronxville, New York. Winthrop House. *Crimson* (2–4); Chairman Smoker Committee (1); St. Paul's Catholic Club (1–4). Football (1), Junior Varsity (2); Swimming (1), Squad (2). Golf (1). House Hockey (3, 4); House Swimming (2); House Softball (4). Hasty Pudding-Institute of 1770; Spee Club. Permanent Class Committee. Field of Concentration: Government. Intended Vocation: Law.

Kennedy's Harvard yearbook entry. Nothing in this early résumé indicates the greatness that lay ahead.

Before going to the Pacific, Kennedy had an intense romance with a beautiful Danish journalist, Inga Arvad, who was then working for the *Washington Times-Herald*.

Joseph P. Kennedy Jr. in his naval aviator's uniform. His father had groomed him from the time he was a young man to run for president, but Joe Jr. was killed on a dangerous mission in World War II.

The crew of *PT-109* poses with its commander, Lieutenant John Kennedy (far right). Kennedy showed courage and grit when his boat was sunk, rescuing injured men and swimming for hours to get help. When he was sworn in as president, several of his crew members took part in the inaugural festivities.

Although he would always remain modest about his actions following the sinking of *PT-109*, Kennedy would return home a war hero. Here he receives the Navy and Marine Corps Medal in June 1944.

The Kennedys in Hyannis Port, 1948. Jack is at far left, with (left to right) Jean, Rose, Joseph Sr., Patricia, Bobby, Eunice, and, in the foreground, Ted.

Despite his youth and political inexperience, Kennedy surprised the pundits with the effectiveness of his campaign for Congress in 1946. Here the candidate (at far left) marches in Boston's Bunker Hill Day Parade.

During his campaigns for Congress and the Senate, Kennedy was aided immeasurably by the support of his mother and sisters. Here the smiling candidate looks on as his mother extols his virtues.

Kennedy's ability to inspire young people was one of his greatest attributes. He signs copies of his second book, *Profiles in Courage*, for some youthful admirers.

The Kennedy brothers on vacation in Palm Beach, Florida, in April 1957. Both Robert and Edward would be vital contributors to John's presidential campaign and both would go on to important political careers of their own.

Kennedy had a delicate relationship with Eleanor Roosevelt, a living icon of New Deal liberalism who was initially critical of his candidacy for president. With assiduous effort—evident in a long exchange of letters—he earned her support. Here he visits her in early 1960. (United States Information Agency)

Those who opposed Kennedy's presidential candidacy because he was Catholic focused mainly on a single charge. If he was elected president, they proclaimed, his actions would be governed not by the U.S. Constitution but by the pope.

Kennedy's presidential campaign strategy included reaching out personally to as many voters as possible. Here he presses the flesh in a New Hampshire diner.

The torch is passed. President Dwight Eisenhower and president-elect Kennedy meet on the eve of the latter's inauguration, January 19, 1961.

Jacqueline Kennedy chats with Robert Frost at a White House dinner for Nobel laureates. Frost read at Kennedy's inauguration, and the two mutual admirers shared a warm correspondence.

John F. Kennedy was sworn in as president of the United States on January 20, 1961. More than fifty years later, his inaugural address is still regarded as among the greatest ever delivered.

Creating the Peace Corps was one of Kennedy's greatest triumphs. Here the president meets with Peace Corps trainees in the Rose Garden.

"We do not want our children to become a generation of spectators. Rather we want each of them to be a participant in the vigorous life," wrote Kennedy. Many schoolchildren wrote to the president with sharp comments about his physical education program.

Astronaut John Glenn shows Kennedy the inside of space capsule *Friendship* 7. Glenn's orbital flight moved the United States closer to achieving Kennedy's goal of landing a man on the moon and bringing him safely back.

Harry Truman entertains Kennedy and other guests at a White House dinner in Truman's honor. Although Truman would initially question Kennedy's presidential qualifications, he would become a great supporter and admirer.

Kennedy was a longstanding admirer of another gifted writer-statesman, Winston Churchill, shown here with his wife and daughter in 1963. The aging Churchill was touched when JFK led Congress to bestow honorary American citizenship on him. (Associated Press)

JANET G. TRAVELL, M.D.
9 WEST 16TH STREET
NEW YORK 11, N.Y.
WATKINS 9-2648

July 5, 1960

Senator John F. Kennedy
Senate Office Building
Washington, D.C.

Dear Senator Kennedy;

As your physicians for over five years, with knowledge of your medical record for over fifteen years, we wish to provide you with a straightforward brief medical statement concerning your health at the present time.

As stated in our recent letter to you of June 11th, we reiterate that you are in superb physical condition. Proof of this is your superior performance under a grueling and exhausting schedule of uninterrupted hard work and travel for the past two years. We emphasize again that performance is the final criterion of a person's physical fitness.

In the past you were treated for adrenal insufficiency which developed following extraordinary stress and malaria during the war period. You have not taken cortisone or hydrocortisone in several years, but on our advice have continued to take by mouth small doses of other corticosteroids even though the last ACTH stimulation test for adrenal function was normal. Adrenal insufficiency no longer presents any threat to a person who is fully rehabilitated on such simple oral therapy.

You see your doctors once or twice a year for a routine check-up which involves no elaborate or time-consuming examinations.

No limitations are placed on your arduous activities.

Very sincerely yours,
Janet Travell, M.D.
Eugene J. Cohen, M.D.

A letter detailing why Kennedy's health "should be a dead issue" was also sent to his campaign manager, his brother Robert.

JANET G. TRAVELL, M.D.
9 WEST 16TH STREET
NEW YORK 11, N.Y.
WATKINS, 9-2648

Mr. Robert F. Kennedy
Kennedy Headquarters
Hotel Biltmore
Los Angeles, California

Dear Mr. Kennedy;

The matter of Senator Kennedy's health should be a dead issue, but in case any further questions arise, you might wish to be guided by the following facts concerning his adrenal function.

1. Senator Kennedy does not have Addison's disease.

2. He was treated for adrenal insufficiency that developed following extraordinary stress and malaria during the war period.

3. In recent years, the function of his adrenal glands has shown excellent recovery and now approaches normal.

4. Old hospital records no longer apply to the present situation.

5. Prophylactically, Senator Kennedy takes a small dose of steroid by mouth, which his physicians expect eventually to discontinue.

6. No limitations of any kind are placed on his activities.

Sincerely yours,
Janet Travell, M.D.

After he was elected, Kennedy appointed Travell to the post of personal physician to the president. Although knowledge of his Addison's disease was kept from the public, Travell received scores of letters from citizens anxious to help the president solve his acknowledged back problems.

July 17, 1961

Dear Mr. Putich;

Your letter of June 26 addressed to President Kennedy was forwarded to me and is gratefully acknowledged. You were thoughtful to write about the remedy that helped your own back problem.

I wish to thank you for your interest in the President's

well-being, and was glad to know that you, yourself, no longer have any sign of a backache.

> Sincerely,
> *Janet Travell, M.D.*
> Personal Physician
> to the President

Mr. Joseph Putich
8660 Grayfield
Dearborn, Michigan

At least one of the letters, written directly to the president, must have given Kennedy a chuckle.

February 16, 1961

The President
White House
Washington, DC

Dear President Kennedy:

I would like you to solve a problem in my house between my husband and I.

We watched you on T.V. Wednesday, February 15th making a public speech. I remarked that you had false teeth. My husband says you don't. Do you?

Please solve the debate.

Thank you

Mrs. Eleanor Wiele
272 Saratoga Ave.
Brooklyn, NY

Kennedy's concerted efforts to present himself as a model of health and vigor did not go unnoticed. After receiving the following letter, Travell sent a memorandum to Kennedy's secretary Evelyn Lincoln stating, "Could you please ask the president to read this letter? There is much truth in what this doctor says. He is not the only one who writes about exposure to inclement weather."

Theodore H. Mendell, M.D.
2023 Spruce Street
Philadelphia
3

January 27, 1962

Hon. John F. Kennedy
President of the United States
The White House
Washington, D.C.

Dear Mr. President:

Forgive me for taking your time, so urgently needed on matters of state, to read this letter. Nevertheless, I could not withhold addressing you on what I believe to be vital to our country, more so in these crucial times; namely the health of our President.

The enclosed picture in the N.Y. Times on January 21st is one of several I have seen periodically in the newspapers during the past few months picturing you walking in snow or freezing weather without proper protection of an overcoat. I am sure you have heard this often, but I am also sure that I voice the concern of millions of our countrymen when I say: "Please, Mr. President, be more mindful of your health, you are taking unnecessary risks, we and the free world need John Kennedy too much to permit him to chance the slightest encounter with respiratory viruses or bacteria which thrive on such bodily exposure to the elements."

Last January, that important moment in history, when you delivered your inspiring Inaugural Address which I am sure will rate high with the greatest of American Documents—I was thrilled as the meaning and impact of your message touched mind and heart. And, I was proud that our country could present a new great president to the world. At the same time, as I viewed the inauguration on TV, I am sure I dropped a heart beat when I saw you strip your overcoat in that freezing weather.

Mr. President, there's a lot of work to be done if ever this sick world is to be bettered. And, the citizens of the United States know you can do it. With your leadership and our backing America will overcome every obstacle. We sense a return of greatness, long absent, in the White House. So please take better care of yourself. May God bless you always.

Very humbly yours,
Theodore H. Mendell, M.D.

★ ★ ★ ★ ★

CHAPTER 3

Man at the Center

As a U.S. senator, John Kennedy had responded to a reporter's question about his political ambitions by stating, "I suppose anybody in politics would like to be president. That is the center of the action, the mainspring, the wellspring, of the American system." Now he was the man at the center, the first president of the United States to have been born in the twentieth century. The cold war that he had inherited required him to deal constantly with explosive issues throughout the world, issues so vital to the very future of people everywhere that even most of his domestic policies and programs were motivated by the struggle between democracy and the spread of communism. Several of these programs had been germinating well before his election.

Kennedy had long been disturbed by research showing that potential American military recruits were being rejected at an alarming rate as physically unfit for duty. He was equally concerned that each year more than twice the number of American children failed physical fitness tests as did European youngsters and, particularly,

Russian young people. Shortly after his election, in an unprecedented move by a president-elect, he published an article in a national magazine describing a program he intended to introduce as soon as he entered the White House. Titled "The Soft American," the *Sports Illustrated* article stressed "the importance of physical fitness as a foundation for the vigor and vitality of the activities of the nation." Kennedy wrote, "Our struggle against aggressors throughout history has been won on the playgrounds and corner lots and fields of America."

At the heart of the article was Kennedy's belief that physical fitness was very much the business of the federal government. And with weeks of his taking office, the President's Council on Physical Fitness launched a massive awareness campaign that included thousands of posters, brochures, pamphlets, television and radio kits, and exercise books all designed to make physical fitness, especially for schoolchildren, a national agenda. The emphasis on physical fitness was embraced even by the nation's comic strip creators, seventeen of whom took up the subject, most notably Charles Schulz whose beloved character Snoopy encouraged youngsters to do their "daily dozen" exercises.

In an initial year in office that was marked by international setbacks and frustrations, the physical fitness program was one of Kennedy's genuine successes. In December 1961, 50 percent more American students passed a national physical fitness test than had passed a year earlier. Equally encouraging, schools around the country were placing greater emphasis on physical fitness programs.

Also successful was another program that had been incubating in Kennedy's mind well before his swearing-in. Just as he had been disturbed about how American youngsters lagged far behind their Russian counterparts in physical fitness, he was also concerned by the fact that while the Soviet Union "had hundreds of men and women, scientists, engineers, doctors, and nurses ... prepared to spend their lives abroad in the service of world communism," the United States had no such program. He had inspired the nation, particularly its young people, with his inaugural address. And he had entered the White House with plans for an ambitious project that would give life to his words "Ask what you can do for your country." Two weeks before his election, in a speech at San Francisco's Cow Palace, he had proposed "a peace corps of talented men and women" who would volunteer to devote themselves to the progress and peace of developing countries. Any doubt that Kennedy might have had of the appeal of such a program was removed when he received more than twenty-five thousand letters in response to his call. Under the direction of his brother-in-law R. Sargent Shriver, the Peace Corps, by providing thousands of American young people with the opportunity not only to aid millions in underdeveloped countries but also to serve as ambassadors of democracy and freedom, proved to be one of Kennedy's most enduring legacies.

John Kennedy arguably delivered more quotable and compelling speeches than any other American president, aside from Abraham Lincoln. None was more surprising or seemingly more implausible than the address he made to Congress on May 25, 1961. It was in this speech that Kennedy announced that he would be holding his first face-to-face meeting with Soviet premier Nikita Khrushchev later that spring. But the address will always be remembered for the astounding proposal he laid before the legislators. "I believe," he declared, "this nation should commit itself to achieving the goal, before this decade is out, of landing a man on the moon and returning him safely to the earth." Congress, as alarmed as Kennedy at the possible military ramifications of the Russians having sent cosmonaut Yuri Gagarin rocketing into space to make a complete orbit of Earth, reacted to the president's startling statement with thunderous applause. They even cheered when he told them that his "man on the moon" project would, over the next five years, require a budget of between $7 billion and $9 billion.

Despite congressional support, many were convinced that Kennedy's goal could not be met. Yet within a year both Alan Shepard and Virgil Grissom were launched into space. Then, on February 20,

1962, came John Glenn's historic 75,679-mile, three-orbital flight. In the weeks following Glenn's triumph, Kennedy stepped up his rhetoric in support of the space program, which had now captured the imagination of the nation. His most eloquent articulation of the importance he placed on conquering this new frontier came in a September 12, 1962, speech at Rice University, in Houston, Texas. "We set sail on this new sea," he stated, "because there is new knowledge to be gained, and new rights to be won, and they must be used for the progress of all people."

Few would question that there was "new knowledge to be gained." But it was another statement contained in the speech that best explained Kennedy's strongest motivation. "No nation," he declared, "which expects to be the leader of other nations can expect to stay behind in the race for space." He meant "behind the Soviet Union." Most revealing was the statement Kennedy made to NASA administrator James Webb. "Jim," he told the man whose main goal was to make the United States preeminent in acquiring scientific knowledge that was to be gained from space exploration, "you don't understand. I don't give a damn about scientific knowledge. I just want to beat the Russians."

Physical fitness, the Peace Corps, the space program—all in one way or another related to the communist threat. But Kennedy had also inherited an enormous challenge not related to issues abroad or in space. He had taken office at a time of tremendous racial turmoil at home. Throughout the South, African Americans and their supporters, committed to an unprecedented civil rights movement, were engaged in marches, sit-ins, demonstrations, boycotts, and other forms of protest in an effort to gain rights and opportunities long denied to them.

There was no question that Kennedy's personal sympathies lay with those whose rights had been denied. And he abhorred the violence with which their efforts were often being met. But a host of political realities—his narrow election victory, his small margin in Congress, his desire not to alienate white Southern Democrats who chaired key congressional committees, and not least, his hope for reelection—combined to make him cautious. Of the millions of letters Kennedy received while president, most of the angriest and most embittered would be from black leaders tired of waiting for justice to be served, weary of lip service and empty promises, and outraged at the bombings, beatings, and other atrocities they were forced to endure.

More than two and a half years into his presidency, Kennedy, having finally lost patience with the continued acts of defiance of federal law by Southern governors and local officials, was compelled to act as decisively as the black leaders had been urging for so long. On June 11, 1963, the same day that Governor George Wallace attempted to block African American students from enrolling at the University of Alabama, Kennedy delivered a televised address to the nation on civil rights. Defining the civil rights crisis as a moral issue, he reminded the nation that "one hundred years of delay have passed since President Lincoln freed the slaves, yet their heirs, their grandsons, are not fully free. They are not yet freed from social and economic oppression. And this Nation, for all its hopes and all its boasts, will not be fully free until all its citizens are free."

Kennedy then announced that he was submitting major civil rights legislation to Congress that would mandate African Americans receive "equal service in places . . . such as hotels, restaurants, and retail stores" and the right "to register to vote . . . without interference or fear of reprisal" and that would guarantee an end to segregation. The man who had been so reluctant to act at last put in motion the most far-reaching and effective civil rights legislation in the nation's history.

★   ★   ★   ★   ★

*Less than one month into his presidency, Kennedy received a most unex-
pected letter. It came from a Solomon Islander who had been instrumental in the rescue of the future American president and his PT-109 crew.
A grateful Kennedy sent off a warm reply.*

> From the Solomon
> Islands:
> February 6, 1961

Dear Sir,

In my reverence and sense of your greatness I write to
you. It is not fit that I should write to you but in my joy
I send this letter. One of our ministers, Reverend E. C.
Leadley, came and asked me, "Who rescued Mr. Kennedy?" And I replied, "I did."

This is my joy that you are now President of the United
States of America.

It was not in my strength that I and my friends were
able to rescue you in the time of war, but in the strength
of God we were able to help you.

The name of God be praised that I am well and in
my joy
I send this loving letter to you, my friend in Christ,
it is good and I say "Thank you" that your farewell words
to me
were those printed on the dime, "In God We Trust."

God is our Hiding Place and our Saviour in the time
of trouble and calm.

> I am, your friend,
> *Biuku Gaza*

───────────────

_____

March 11, 1961

Dear Biuku,

Reverend E. C. Leadley has recently sent me your very kind message, and I can't tell you how delighted I was to know that you are well and prospering in your home so many thousands of miles away from Washington.

Like you, I am eternally grateful for the act of Divine Providence which brought me and my companions together with you and your friends who so valorously effected our rescue during time of war. Needless to say, I am deeply moved by your expressions and I hope that the new responsibilities which are mine may be exercised for the benefit of my own countrymen and the welfare of all of our brothers in Christ.

You will always have a special place in my mind and my heart, and I wish you and your people continued prosperity and good health.

Sincerely,
John F. Kennedy

Binku Gaza
Madon
Wana Wana Lagood
British Solomon Island Protectorate

As Kennedy prepared for his inauguration, Stewart Udall, whom Kennedy would appoint secretary of the interior, suggested that America's great

poet Robert Frost be invited to read one of his poems at the ceremonies.
Kennedy, a longtime admirer of Frost and his work, readily agreed but
not before reminding Udall, "You know that Robert Frost always steals
any show he is part of." The day after Frost received Kennedy's tele-
gram inviting him to participate, he sent his own telegram of accep-
tance.

IF YOU CAN BEAR AT YOUR AGE THE HONOR
OF BEING MADE PRESIDENT OF THE
UNITED STATES, I OUGHT TO BE ABLE AT
MY AGE TO BEAR THE HONOR OF TAKING
SOME PART IN YOUR INAUGURATION. I MAY
NOT BE EQUAL TO IT BUT I CAN ACCEPT IT
FOR MY CAUSE—THE ARTS, POETRY, NOW
FOR THE FIRST TIME TAKEN INTO THE
AFFAIRS OF STATESMEN.

Having formed a bond with Frost, Kennedy, despite the demands of
his office, would stay apprised of the poet's activities.

March 8, 1961

Mr. Robert Frost
c/o American Friends of the Hebrew University
11 East 69th Street
New York 21, New York

   I am delighted to learn of your recent appointment
as the first Samuel Paley Lecturer in American Culture
and Civilization at Hebrew University in Jerusalem. I

know that your visit will provide the people of Israel with a rare cultural opportunity.

I wish you all success in your journey.

John F. Kennedy

One of the highlights of the Kennedy inauguration had been Frost's recitation of one of his poems. It marked the first time a poet had ever taken part in a presidential inauguration. Although he had written a new poem titled "Dedication" for the occasion, Frost had trouble reading the faintly typed poem. Instead, he recited his poem "The Gift Outright" from memory. In March 1961, Kennedy received a letter from Hyde Cox, an old friend and editor of the Selected Prose of Robert Frost. *In his letter, Cox thanked Kennedy both for his public recognition of Frost and for the unprecedented presidential attention to the arts.*

CROW ISLAND

MANCHESTER

MASSACHUSETTS

March 15, 1961

Dear Jack,

Robert Frost has been here recently to help me celebrate my birthday, and together we signed this little book he promised to send your daughter—the book of his for which I wrote the foreword.

Because of my long and close friendship with him,

and my friendly recollections of you, I feel that this is an appropriate moment for me to write the few personal words of congratulations that I have been tempted to send you before.

One of the things you are doing that touches me inevitably is your noticing the Arts—as they should be noticed; and I was especially touched by your recent, discerning recognition of Frost—so well expressed. He is a unique American asset.

But I do not mean to limit my praise of you to this friendship alone, or to the context of the Arts only. Believe me, you have—in more ways than these—the thoughtful best wishes and the admiration of an old acquaintance.

Very Sincerely,
Hyde Cox

Two months after receiving Cox's letter, Kennedy wrote to Robert Frost thanking the poet for sending him a very special gift.

May 8, 1961

Dear Mr. Frost:

It was most gracious of you to inscribe the four copies of the special printing of your dedicatory poem and my inaugural address. I only regret that Mrs. Kennedy and I could not join the enthusiastic throng which heard your reading at the State Department Auditorium last week. I know that both Caroline and John will treasure this book in years to come.

It was a pity that you were unable to join us this morning when Commander Shepard was received and honored at the White House. I hope that you have had a good stay here in Washington and will be back with us soon again.

With every best wish,

Sincerely,
John F. Kennedy

Mr. Robert Frost
35 Brewster Street
Cambridge, Massachusetts

The Kennedy/Frost relationship would develop into one of great warmth and mutual admiration. So much so that, despite the poet's age, in July 1962, Kennedy wrote to Frost asking him to undertake a special mission on behalf of the United States.

July 20, 1962

Dear Mr. Frost:

I have been informed by Secretary Rusk that the Soviet Union has expressed warm interest in the idea of an exchange of visits between two eminent American and Soviet poets, and your name has been mentioned as the logical American poet to initiate this exchange.

Ambassador Dobrynin has indicated that the Soviet Union would like to send the well-known Soviet poet, Alexander Tvardovsky, to our country as their part of this special exchange proposal.

Our great literary men are the ultimate custodians of the spirit and genius of a people, and it is my feeling that such an exchange of visits at this time would do much to enlarge the area of understanding between the people of the United States and the people of the Soviet Union.

I hope that you can represent the United States on this special mission. If you can accept this assignment please let me know, and I will have the State Department people contact you with regard to the plans and details.

Sincerely,
John Kennedy

Mr. Robert Frost
Ripton
Vermont

On the eve of his departure, Frost wrote to Kennedy expressing his feelings as only the already legendary Frost could do.

July 24, 1962

My dear Mr. President:

How grand for you to think of me this way and how like you to take the chance of sending anyone like me over there affinatizing with the Russians. You must know a lot about me besides my rank from my poems but think how the professors interpret the poems! I am almost as full of politics and history as you are. I like to tell the story of the mere sailor boy from upstate New York who by favor of his captain and the American consul at St. Petersburg got to see the Czar in St. Petersburg with the gift in his hand of an acorn that fell from a tree that stood by the house of George Washington. That was in the 1830's when proud young Americans were equal to anything. He said to the Czar, "Washington was a great ruler and you're a great ruler and I thought you might like to plant the acorn with me by your palace." And so he did. I have been having a lot of historical parallels lately: a big one between Caesar's imperial democracy that made so many millions equal under arbitrary power and the Russian democracy. Ours is a more Senatorial democracy like the Republic of Rome. I have thought I saw the Russians and the American democracies drawing together, theirs easing down from a kind of abstract severity to taking less and less care of the masses: ours creeping up to taking more and more care of the masses as they grew innumerable. I see us becoming the two great powers of the modern world in noble rivalry while a third power of United Germany, France, and Italy, the common market, looks on as an expanded polyglot Switzerland.

I shall be reading poems chiefly over there but I shall be talking some where I read and you may be sure I won't be talking just literature. I'm the kind of Democrat that <u>will</u> reason. You must know my admiration for your "Profiles". I am frightened by this big undertaking but I was more frightened at your Inauguration. I am glad Stewart will be along to take care of me. He has been a good influence in my life. And Fred Adams of the Morgan Library. I had a very good talk with Anatoly

3

HOMER NOBLE FARM
RIPTON : VERMONT

THE WHITE HOUSE
JUL 26 10 44 AM '62
RECEIVED

July 24,1962.

My dear Mr. President:

How grand for you to think of me this
way and how like you to take the chance of sending
anyone like me over there affinatizing with the Russians. You must know a lot about me besides my rank
from my poems but think how the professors interpret
the poems! I am almost as full of politics and history as you are. I like to tell the story of the
mere sailor boy from upstate New York who by favor
of his captain and the American consul at St.Peters-
burg got to see the Czar in St. Petersburg with the
gift in his hand of an acorn that fell from a tree
that stood by the house of George Washington. That
was in the 1830's when proud young Americans were
equal to anything. He said to the Czar, "Washington
was a great ruler and you're a great ruler and I
thought you might like to plant the acorn with me by
your palace." And so he did. I have been having a
lot of historical parallels lately: a big one between
Caesar's imperial democracy that made so many millions
equal under arbitrary power and the Russian democracy.
Ours is a more Senatorial democracy like the Republic
of Rome. I have thought I saw the Russian and the
American democracies drawing together, theirs easing
down from a kind of abstract severity to taking less
and less care of the masses: ours creeping up to
taking more and more care of the masses as they grew
innumerable. I see us becoming the two great powers
of the modern world in noble rivalry while a third
power of United Germany, France, and Italy, the common market, looks on as an expanded polyglot Switzerland.

I shall be reading poems chiefly over
there but I shall be talking some where I read and
you may be sure I won't be talking just literature.
I'm the kind of Democrat that will reason. You must

*Kennedy and poet Robert Frost, who read at his inauguration,
had a warm correspondence. Here Frost replies to an unusual invitation
from the president.*

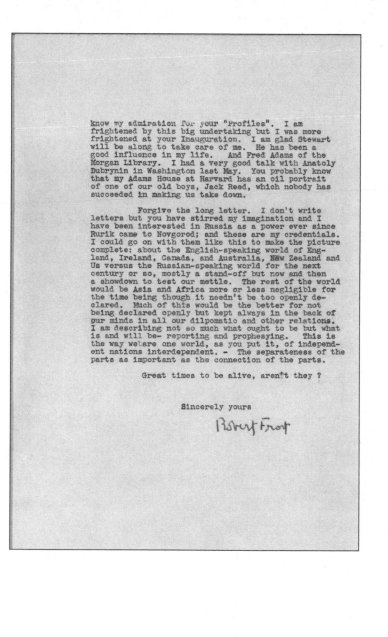

know my admiration for your "Profiles". I am
frightened by this big undertaking but I was more
frightened at your Inauguration. I am glad Stewart
will be along to take care of me. He has been a
good influence in my life. And Fred Adams of the
Morgan Library. I had a very good talk with Anatoly
Dubrynin in Washington last May. You probably know
that my Adams House at Harvard has an oil portrait
of one of our old boys, Jack Reed, which nobody has
succeeded in making us take down.

Forgive the long letter. I don't write
letters but you have stirred my imagination and I
have been interested in Russia as a power ever since
Rurik came to Novgorod; and these are my credentials.
I could go on with them like this to make the picture
complete: about the English-speaking world of England, Ireland, Canada, and Australia, New Zealand and
Us versus the Russian-speaking world for the next
century or so, mostly a stand-off but now and then
a showdown to test our mettle. The rest of the world
would be Asia and Africa more or less negligible for
the time being though it needn't be too openly declared. Much of this would be the better for not
being declared openly but kept always in the back of
our minds in all our dilpomatic and other relations.
I am describing not so much what ought to be but what
is and will be- reporting and prophesying. This is
the way we are one world, as you put it, of independent nations interdependent. - The separateness of the
parts as important as the connection of the parts.

Great times to be alive, aren't they ?

Sincerely yours

Robert Frost

Dubrynin in Washington last May. You probably know that my Adams House at Harvard has an oil portrait of one of our old boys, Jack Reed, which nobody has succeeded in making us take down.

Forgive the long letter. I don't write letters but you have stirred my imagination and I have been interested in Russia as a power ever since Rurik came to Novgorod; and these are my credentials. I could go on with them like this to make the picture complete: about the English-speaking world of England, Ireland, Canada, and Australia, New Zealand and Us versus the Russian-speaking world for the next century or so, mostly a stand-off but now and then a showdown to test our mettle. The rest of the world would be Asia and Africa more or less negligible for the time being though it needn't be too openly declared. Much of this would be the better for not being declared openly but kept always in the back of our minds in all our dilpomatic and other relations. I am describing not so much what ought to be but what is and will be—reporting and prophesying. This is the way we are one world, as you put it, of independent nations interdependent.—The separateness of the parts as important as the connection of the parts.

Great times to be alive, aren't they?

Sincerely yours
Robert Frost

The Kennedy presidency was little more than three months old when the Peace Corps was officially approved by Congress. Shortly afterward, Kennedy received a letter from one of the new organization's officials containing both welcome news and an important request.

———————————

The White House
Washington

May 16, 1961

Dear Mr. President:

You will be pleased to know that as of last night over 7,700 young men and women have answered your call as to what they can do for their country. Many of the letters and questionnaires from the applicants show that they have given a great deal of thought to their decision to join the Peace Corps since, as they say, it will change the whole pattern of their careers.

Mr. Wiggins asked me to speak to you about the attached letter which he would like to send out under your signature. The letter will be sent this week to the 7,700 Peace Corps candidates who have submitted questionnaires. The Peace Corps recruitment people are very encouraged by the large number of qualified applicants, but they fear that there may be some difficulty in making certain that they come to the examinations. Apparently a large number of students include college graduates and even postgraduate students. Most important of all there are many engineers, public health specialists and agricultural specialists etc.

Since Mr. Shriver has had good results on his recent trip, it is important that the Peace Corps have a large supply of applicants.

It is thought that a personal letter from you would certainly add to the enthusiasm of this group to sacrifice their time and efforts to the Peace Corps projects.

Also it would be a worthwhile means of stimulating public interest.

> Sincerely,
> *Deirdre Henderson*

Kennedy responded to Ms. Henderson's request the same day he received it, taking the opportunity to articulate to Peace Corps volunteers both the challenges they would face and the rewards they would receive.

THE WHITE HOUSE

WASHINGTON

May 22, 1961

Dear Peace Corps Volunteer:

I want to congratulate you for being among the first group to volunteer for service in the Peace Corps. As you know, you are now eligible to take the Peace Corps Entrance Examination on May 27 or June 5.

Nations in Latin America, Southeast Asia and Africa have already indicated their interest in having Peace Corps Volunteers serve with them. In the months ahead agreements with these nations will be concluded and Peace Corps projects announced. Once you qualify as a Volunteer you will be eligible for these undertakings.

As a Volunteer you will be called upon to exercise your skill or talent under difficult and unusual circumstances. The work will be hard and it may be hazardous. But, when your assignment is completed, you will have earned the respect and admiration of all Americans for having helped the free world in a time of need. You will have made a personal contribution to the cause of world peace and understanding.

I wish you the best of luck in your Peace Corps tests.

Sincerely
John Kennedy

Among the scores of letters that the White House received from Peace Corps volunteers in the field and their relatives, one of the most poignant was in response to a condolence letter Kennedy had written to a couple whose son had suffered a fatal illness while serving in Colombia.

West Plains, Mo.
June 2, 1962

Dear President Kennedy,

As humbly and sincerely as we know how we want to thank you for your letter concerning our David.

David hated war and had a driving passion for peace. In an early letter to us from Colombia he stated, "I had rather lose my life trying to help someone than to have to lose it looking down a gun barrel at them." David felt that the Peace Corps was the answer and there will never be a more loyal member.

Before David was born I prayed that my child would be a blessing to humanity. I believe God answered my prayer and I am grateful that through you and your program he had an opportunity to serve.

Be assured of our prayers, that you may look to God as you meet the great responsibilities that are yours

today. Also for your precious little Son that he may live
and love and serve as our David.

Sincerely yours,
Mr. and Mrs. R. L. Crozier

*From the beginning, Kennedy had envisioned Peace Corps volunteers
becoming American ambassadors of good will. By its third year of operations, the Peace Corps was meeting this goal.*

PEACE CORPS

WASHINGTON 25, D.C.

February 13, 1963

[President Kennedy:]

I thought you might be interested in seeing this statement by Monsignor J.J. Salcedo, member of the Board
of Directors of the Inter-American Literacy Foundation and Director General of the Accion Cultural Popular in Bogota, Colombia.

> The history of humanity will record the young
> people of the Peace Corps as heroes. Their
> admirable sacrifices, their conviction, the
> generosity they are showing, are the best
> thing you are doing today for the good name
> of the great American people. But the worth
> of their actions is not in the roads, houses or
> bridges they are building (their work is mainly
> manual), but in the heroic lesson they are

giving of true friendship. In the words of the
Gospel: "Greater love than this no man hath,
that a man lay down his life for his friends."
(St. John, XV, 13).

"These young people are conquering the
hearts of our people by means of their
example, their work, their true love for
the people."

Robert Sargent Shriver, Jr.

In his August 13, 1963, Progress Report by the President on Physical
Fitness, *Kennedy made special mention of the fact that, thanks to the
program that he and his administration had initiated, national awareness of the importance of staying fit was increasingly being reflected in
the White House mail, where, according to Kennedy, "fitness is one of the
main subjects of correspondence by young and old alike." Among the letters Kennedy cited was one from a Brooklyn schoolgirl who wrote, "I am
happy about your Physical Fitness Plan....I turn cartwheels every
chance I get. My parents are going out of their minds because I am always on my hands instead of my feet." A twelve-year-old Pennsylvania
boy, Kennedy reported, had written him stating, "I have took to mind
what you said about youth physical fitness. I not only take gym in
school, but I set aside an hour each day to have my own gym."*
    *Two letters in particular obviously amused the president. "Dear
President Kennedy," one youngster informed him, "I have walked 8
miles and I was thirsty." "Dear sir," wrote another, "would you please
send me a sample of your physical fitness." Of special note, Kennedy
stated, was a letter he had received from a student in a U.S. Army
school in Munich, Germany. "The purpose of my writing," the young
person explained, "is to congratulate you on your physical fitness program. All the students in my class take part in the program with great*

interest. *Through the program, we are developing an interest in fair play with each other. The responsibility through our training gives us great pride and an understanding of our responsibility as Americans."*

Not all the letters Kennedy received, however, unreservedly praised the program. Young Gladys McPherson not only pointed out what she regarded as a serious problem, but she also offered a solution.

1023 Berwick
Pontiac, Mich.
March 14, 1963

Dear Mr. Kennedy,

Your physical fitness program is in full swing and a very fine idea, except for one hitch. How can women and teenage girls be physically fit with deformed feet? It is impossible to find round toe, flat heel shoes to fit sub-teens in women's sizes, and difficult to find wedge or high heels with round toes. I'm sure you don't expect the army or marines to hike fifty miles in pointed toes, but even gym shoes and house slippers for women are pointed.

I have written letters to newspapers and shoe manu-facturers without success. But the solution is simple for you. Please convince Mrs. Kennedy to buy and wear in public round toe shoes, and every style conscious woman will demand the manufacturers make them.

Please, Mr. President, do this favor for the women of America to whom God gave rounded feet instead of pointed ones. We have suffered for a long time.

Respectfully yours,
Gladys D. McPherson

Another young woman, in sentiments well ahead of her time, described what she saw as another shortcoming of the physical fitness program.

It is a state law for all schools to have a Physical Fitness Program. We have a very fine gym but we girls are not about to use it for that purpose. The boys have many activities such as football, basketball, and etc. But we girls run around flabby! If we say anything to the Principal about the girls having a Program of any sort, he tells [us] to go home and do our own exercises. But Mr. President it is not fair to us girls because we want to do it as a group, not as individuals. The boys use the gym and we want to use it too.

In his letter, Richard Millington informed Kennedy of a problem that, in his opinion, threatened the success of the entire program.

Sacramento, Calif.
February 11, 1963

Dear President Kennedy,

I would like to know why, in this age of stress on physical fitness, there are still paunchy teachers around. These teachers are supposed to be good examples to us poor, disgusted kids. We kids do the exercise the teachers tell us, while the teachers stand around talking to other teachers. How are we supposed to believe exercises are worth it if the teachers don't seem to be interested?

I move that a new law be passed that requires teachers to keep themselves in the pink too. Thank you for your attention and please reply soon.

> Sincerely yours,
> *Richard Millington*

P.S. Even some of the Scoutmasters have midriff bulge.

Of all the letters that the physical fitness program elicited, it is difficult to imagine one that Kennedy welcomed more than following from nine-year-old Jack Chase.

Terrance, California
Mar. 3, 1963

Pennsylvania Ave.
The White House
Washington, D.C.

Dear President Kennedy:

I know you are a very busy man but I wanted to tell you what a wonderful President I think you are.

My teacher Mrs. Moneymaker, told us that you want all the children of America to be strong and healthy. You want us to do exercises every day to build up our bodies. Instead of riding a car to school you want us to walk. We should walk to the store, to the library and anyplace that is not too near and yet not too far.

I am going to do all these things because I know that

a strong boy makes a strong man and a strong man makes
a strong country.

Yours, truly,
Jack Chase
Age 9

The Soviet Union's achievement in launching a man beyond Earth's atmosphere signaled a race for space that became an integral part of the cold war. Although he received the news of cosmonaut Yuri Gagarin's accomplishment with far more concern than pleasure, Kennedy was quick to send Soviet chairman Nikita Khrushchev a congratulatory telegram.

WASHINGTON, APRIL 12, 1961, 1:24 P.M.

THE PEOPLE OF THE UNITED STATES SHARE
WITH THE PEOPLE OF THE SOVIET UNION
THEIR SATISFACTION FOR THE SAFE FLIGHT
OF THE ASTRONAUT IN MAN'S FIRST VEN-
TURE INTO SPACE. WE CONGRATULATE YOU
AND THE SOVIET SCIENTISTS AND ENGI-
NEERS WHO MADE THIS FEAT POSSIBLE. IT IS
MY SINCERE DESIRE THAT IN THE CON-
TINUING QUEST FOR KNOWLEDGE OF
OUTER SPACE OUR NATIONS CAN WORK
TOGETHER TO OBTAIN THE GREATEST
BENEFIT TO MANKIND.

JOHN F. KENNEDY

Kennedy's real feelings and his real goal as far as space exploration was concerned were clearly revealed in a communiqué he sent to Vice President Lyndon Johnson eight days after Gagarin's flight.

THE WHITE HOUSE

WASHINGTON

April 20, 1961

In accordance with our conversation I would like for you as Chairman of the Space Council to be in charge of making an overall survey of where we stand in space.

1. Do we have a chance of beating the Soviets by putting a laboratory in space, or by a trip around the moon, or by a rocket to land on the moon, or by a rocket to go to the moon and back with a man. Is there any other space program which promises dramatic results in which we could win?
2. How much additional would it cost?
3. Are we working 24 hours a day on existing programs. If not, why not? If not, will you make recommendations to me as to how work can be speeded up.
4. In building large boosters should we put out [our] emphasis on nuclear, chemical, or liquid fuel, or a combination of these three?
5. Are we making maximum effort? Are we achieving necessary results?

I have asked [science adviser] Jim Webb, Dr. [Jerome] Weisner, Secretary [of Defense Robert] McNamara and other responsible officials to cooperate with you fully. I would appreciate a report on this at the earliest possible moment.

After his orbital flight, John Glenn returned home to a hero's welcome not seen since Charles Lindbergh had crossed the Atlantic. From leaders of free nations throughout the world came letters and telegrams commenting on the particular importance of the fact that it was an American achievement.

AACS/FEB 22 1962 VIA MACKAYRADIO
SCHOENRIED 100 22 185P

THE HONOURABLE JOHN F. KENNEDY
PRESIDENT OF THE UNITED STATES OF
    AMERICA
THE WHITE HOUSE WASHINGTON DC

IT IS WITH GREAT PLEASURE AND IMMENSE
PRIDE WHICH I AM CERTAIN IS SHARED BY
THE ENTIRE FREE WORLD THAT I EXTEND
TO YOU AND TO THE PEOPLE OF THE
UNITED STATES CONGRATULATIONS ON
THE RESOUNDING SUCCESS OF THE OR-
BITAL SPACE FLIGHT OF COLONEL JOHN
GLENN STOP COLONEL GLENNS PERSONAL
COURAGE HAS WON UNIVERSAL ADMIRA-
TION AND THE SCIENTIFIC AND TECHNI-
CAL COMPETENCE OF THE UNITED STATES
THUS DEMONSTRATED GIVES ASSURANCE

OF THE PEACEFUL EXPLORATION OF SPACE
FOR THE BENEFIT OF MANKIND

RAINIER PRINCE OF MONACO

As the nation welcomed John Glenn into the ranks of its greatest heroes, many citizens wrote to Kennedy suggesting ways that the astronaut might be further utilized to give the United States a cold war advantage.

Hon. John F. Kennedy
President of the United States
White House
Washington, D.C.

My dear President:

May I humbly offer a suggestion to your Excellency?

Would it not be a splendid idea to appoint our famous Astronaut Col. John Glenn to be Ambassador of Good will to all Nations of the World that will want to know what is in outer space which Col. Glenn can explain so well?

This could inadvertently make the road for Khrushchev rockier.

Very truly yours,
Carl H. Peterson

As requests for personal appearances by John Glenn escalated, Kennedy had to decline one from the governor of Nebraska.

March 14, 1962

Dear Frank:

I am most grateful for your kind invitation to Astronaut John H. Glenn, Jr., to visit your State, and I can assure you that he, too, is grateful for this invitation. As you may be informed by now, the decision has been made not to send Colonel Glenn or the other astronauts on any extended tour in this country or abroad even though many people would be delighted to see him and to demonstrate their pride in the achievements made possible by him and the Project Mercury team.

The United States manned space flight program managed by the National Aeronautics and Space Administration will be pushed forward on the highest priority as it has been up to now, and each astronaut plays an important role as a result of his experience and training. Therefore, I feel this return to work is in the best interests of the program.

Sincerely,
John F. Kennedy

The Honorable Frank B. Morrison
The Governor of Nebraska
Lincoln, Nebraska

While the vast majority of letters that Kennedy received about the space program, particularly after Glenn's flight, were highly positive, there were some that expressed concern over placing so high a priority on such an expensive endeavor. Among the most compelling was that written by thirteen-year-old Mary Lou Reitler.

January 19, 1962
R.F.D. #1
Delton, Michigan

Dear President Kennedy,

I am thirteen years old and I'm in the eighth grade. Please don't throw my letter away until you've read what I have to say. Would you please answer me this one question? When God created the world, he sent man out to make a living with the tools he provided them with. They had to make their living on their own with what little they had. If he had wanted us to orbit the earth, reach the moon, or live on any of the planets, I believe he would have put us up there himself or he would have given us missiles etc. to get there. While our country is spending billions of dollars on things we can get along without, while many refugees and other people are starving or trying to make a decent living to support their families. I think it is all just a waste of time and money when many talents could be put to better use in many ways, such as making our world a better place to live in. We don't really need space vehicles. I think our country should try to look out more for the welfare of its people so that we can be proud of the world we live in. At school they tell us that we study science so that we can make our world a better place to live in. But I don't think we need outer space travel to prove or further the development of this idea. . . .

Sincerely,
Mary Lou Reitler

Despite the misgivings of those like young Ms. Reitler, John Glenn's
achievement provoked an overwhelming wave of support for the space
program. A number of letters that came into the White House actually
contained monetary donations to the effort. An Oregon state legislator
and his wife sent in a donation of a surprising amount.

March 19, 1962

Dear Mr. and Mrs. Howard:

The President has asked me to thank you for your
donation of $4.30 for the space program which you for-
warded in your letter of March 3, 1962. Your interest in
Colonel Glenn's successful flight is sincerely appreciated.
Your check will be forwarded to the National Aeronautics and Space Administration for their use in the space
programs under their jurisdiction.

Sincerely,
T.J. Reardon, Jr.
Special Assistant
to the President

The Honorable and Mrs. Norman R. Howard
Oregon House of Representatives
2504 S.E. 64th Street
Portland, Oregon

Kennedy had set the seemingly impossible goal of landing a man on the
moon by the end of the decade. But following Glenn's triumph and a
number of technical breakthroughs, he asked NASA administrator
James Webb to establish a 1967 target date for a lunar landing. Then, in

*the fall of 1963, after touring a number of NASA installations, he asked
Webb to prepare a report analyzing the possibility of a 1966 landing.*

*Webb responded with a letter outlining the ways in which all the
projects associated with a 1967 target date would have to be accelerated
and listing the considerable additional costs that would be required in
moving the target date up by a year. Webb concluded by stating that
despite these considerable challenges, NASA was "prepared to place the
manned lunar landing program on an all-out crash basis aimed at the
1966 target date if you should decide this is in the national interest."*

*Only days after receiving Webb's letter, Kennedy met with Webb and
other top NASA officials and made it clear that he was all for a 1966 lunar landing. As far as the funds needed for an accelerated program, he
told them that the money could be taken from certain NASA scientific
projects that he felt could be delayed. Webb, however, was far from thrilled
with that idea. Responding to Webb's arguments that many of the scientific projects were essential to the manned moon landing and that preemi-
nence in all of space was NASA's true goal, Kennedy asked the NASA
head to write him a "summary of our views on NASA's priorities."*

NATIONAL AERONAUTICS AND SPACE
ADMINISTRATION
WASHINGTON 25, D.C.
OFFICE OF THE ADMINISTRATOR

November 30, 1962

The President
The White House

Dear Mr. President:

At the close of our meeting on November 21, concerning possible acceleration of the manned lunar land-

ing program, you requested that I describe for you the priority of this program in our over-all civilian space effort. This letter has been prepared by Dr. Dryden, Dr. Seamans, and myself to express our views on this vital question.

The objective of our national space program is to become pre-eminent in all important aspects of this endeavor and to conduct the program in such a manner that our emerging scientific, technological, and operational competence in space is clearly evident.

To be pre-eminent in space, we must conduct scientific investigations on a broad front. We must concurrently investigate geophysical phenomena about the earth, analyze the sun's radiation and its effect on earth, explore the moon and the planets, make measurements in interplanetary space, and conduct astronomical measurements....

Although the manned lunar landing requires major scientific and technological effort, it does not encompass all space science and technology, nor does it provide funds to support direct applications in meteorological and communications systems. Also, university research and many of our international projects are not phased with the manned lunar program, although they are extremely important to our future competence and posture in the world community....

A broad-based space science program provides necessary support to the achievement of manned space flight leading to lunar landing. The successful launch and recovery of manned orbiting spacecraft in Project Mercury depended on knowledge of the pressure, temperature, density, and composition of the high atmosphere obtained from the nation's previous scientific rocket and satellite program. Considerably more space science data are required for the Gemini and Apollo projects. At higher altitudes than Mercury, the spacecraft will approach the radiation belt through which man will travel to reach the moon. Intense radiation in this belt is a major hazard to the crew. Information on the radiation belt will determine the shielding requirements and the parking orbit that must be used on the way to the moon.

Once outside the radiation belt, on a flight to the moon, a manned spacecraft will be exposed to bursts of high speed protons released from time to time from flares on the sun. These bursts do not penetrate below the radiation belt because they are deflected by the earth's magnetic field, but they are highly dangerous to man in interplanetary space.

The approach and safe landing of manned spacecraft on the moon will depend on more precise information on lunar gravity and topography. In addition, knowledge of the bearing strength and roughness of the landing site is of crucial importance, lest the landing module topple or sink into the lunar surface. . . .

In summarizing the views which are held by Dr. Dryden, Dr. Seamans, and myself, and which have guided our joint efforts to develop the National Space Program, I would emphasize that the manned lunar landing program, although of the highest national priority, will not by itself create the pre-eminent position we seek. The present interest of the United States in terms of our scientific posture and increasing prestige, and our future interest in terms of having an adequate scientific and technological base for space activities beyond the manned lunar landing, demand that we pursue an adequate, well-balanced space program in all areas, including those not directly related to the manned lunar landing. We strongly believe that the United States will gain tangible benefits from such a total accumulation of basic scientific and technological data as well as from the greatly increased strength of our educational institutions. For these reasons, we believe it would not be in the nation's long-range interest to cancel or drastically curtail on-going space science and technology development programs in order to increase the funding of the manned lunar landing program in fiscal year 1963....

With much respect, believe me

Sincerely yours,
James E. Webb
Administrator

Webb's letter proved persuasive. Finding himself in agreement with all of Webb's arguments, Kennedy abandoned his push for an earlier lunar landing. In the all-too-brief remaining months of his presidency, he publicly proclaimed that America's goal was to become preeminent in every area of the nation's space program. Kennedy would not live to see an American land on the moon.

Although it seems contradictory to Kennedy's passion for winning the battle with the Soviet Union for the conquest of space, Kennedy also expressed a determination to work with the Russians on joint space endeavors.

In 2011, thanks to the Freedom of Information Act requests, two communiqués written by Kennedy just days before he was killed were made available. In one, Kennedy ordered NASA administrator James Webb to develop a program of cooperation with the Soviet Union for both space exploration and lunar landings.

November 12, 1963

I would like you to assume personally the initiative and central responsibility within the Government for the development of a program of substantive cooperation with the Soviet Union in the field of outer space, including the development of specific technical proposals. I assume that you will work closely with the Department of State and other agencies as appropriate.

These proposals should be developed with a view to their possible discussion with the Soviet Union as a direct outcome of my September 20 proposal for broader cooperation between the United States and the USSR in outer space, including *cooperation in lunar* landing programs. All proposals or suggestions originating within the Government relating to this general subject will be referred to you for your consideration and evaluation.

In addition to developing substantive proposals, I suggest that you will assist the Secretary of State in exploring problems of procedure and timing connected with holding discussions with the Soviet Union and in proposing for my consideration the channels which would be most desirable from our point of view. In this connection the channel of contact developed by Dr. Dryden between NASA and the Soviet Academy of Science has been quite effective, and I believe that we should continue to utilize it as appropriate as a means of continuing the dialogue between the scientists of both countries.

I would like an interim report on the progress of our planning by December 15.

John F. Kennedy

In other correspondence, written the same day, Kennedy ordered the director of the CIA to release to him secret documents held within the agency concerning UFOs. "One of his concerns," author William Lester, who succeeded in obtaining the communiqués, has stated, "was that a lot of these UFOs were being [reported] over the Soviet Union and he was very concerned that the Soviets might misinterpret these UFOs as U.S. aggression, believing that it was some of our technology."

November 12, 1963

Director, Central Intelligence Agency

As I had discussed with you previously, I have initiated and have instructed James Webb to develop a program with the Soviet Union in joint space and lunar exploration. It would be very helpful if you would have the high threat cases reviewed with the purpose of identification of bona fide as opposed to classified CIA and USAF sources. It is important that we make a clear distinction between the knowns and unknowns in the event the Soviets try to mistake our extended cooperation as a cover for intelligence gathering of their defense and space program.

When this data has been sorted out, I would like you to arrange a program of data sharing with NASA where unknowns are a factor. This will help NASA mission directors in their defensive responsibilities.

I would like an interim report on this data review no later than February 1, 1964.

John F. Kennedy

———————————————————————

It was not surprising that a president as popular as John Kennedy—who was forced to deal with issues more critical than those any American chief executive had ever before faced, and who, thanks to television, was seen by more people at one time than any other previous world leader—would receive a staggering number of letters on every conceivable subject from individuals from every walk of life.

Many of the letters that Kennedy would write as president would deal with some of the most thorny and dangerous issues with which any American president had ever had to contend. Others, like the one he sent to John Galbraith's son on his birthday, would be characterized by the Kennedy wit.

January 26, 1961

Dear Jamie:

I understand that you were born in the last year of the last Democratic Administration and are now celebrating your ninth birthday in these first two weeks of mine. I hope that the long Republican years have not hurt you too much, that you will grow up to be at least as good a Democrat as your father but possibly of a more convenient size.

My best wishes for a happy birthday.

Sincerely,
John F. Kennedy

Master James Kenneth Galbraith
30 Francis Avenue
Cambridge 38, Massachusetts

Nelson Rockefeller was the governor of New York and one of the Republican Party's leading candidates to oppose Kennedy when he ran for reelection in 1964. In November 1961, Rockefeller's youngest son, Michael, disappeared while studying the Asmat tribe and its unique art in southern New Guinea. Despite an intense and prolonged search, the twenty-three-year-old Rockefeller was never found. Two weeks into the search, the grateful and still-hopeful governor wrote to Kennedy to thank him for his concern and assistance.

STATE OF NEW YORK

EXECUTIVE CHAMBER

ALBANY

NELSON A. ROCKEFELLER

GOVERNOR

December 1, 1961

Dear Mr. President:

The deep human understanding which motivated your wire last week, at the time of Michael's disappearance, with your offer of all possible assistance, is something I shall never forget, and is something for which I shall be eternally grateful to you.

Thanks importantly to your personal concern, no possible means of search was overlooked. The Department of State and Defense as well as CIA gave every assistance. The Department of Defense enlisted the full support of the Netherlands air and naval units to supplement the all-out effort of their civilian personnel, and also an Australian air and army helicopter unit which did a superb job. In addition, the Seventh Fleet, as well as the Air Force in Hawaii offered to send task forces. However, these latter two offers were declined with the deepest appreciation in view of the fact that every possible avenue of approach was being covered.

I would like to add that both the Dutch Catholic and American Protestant missionaries were uniquely kind and generous in their help.

While as yet no trace of Mike has been found, over 1,500 square miles of sea, 150 miles of coastline have been searched and all of the villages in the area have been visited. The search will continue in a jungle area of approximately 1,000 square miles, conducted by native Papuans, and I'm confident that if he was able to make the shore, he will be found.

> With best wishes,
> Sincerely,
> *Nelson*

Kennedy's presidency would be marked by an almost continuous exchange of letters with his chief cold war adversary, Soviet chairman Nikita Khrushchev. It would, in fact, be this unprecedented exchange that would seriously affect the course of history. Not all of the correspondence between the two men would be antagonistic, as evidenced by this letter from Kennedy thanking Khrushchev for having sent Caroline the puppy Pushinka, whose mother had flown in space.

Washington, June 21, 1961

Dear Mr. Chairman:

I want to express to you my very great appreciation for your thoughtfulness in sending to me the model of an American whaler, which we discussed while in Vienna. It now rests in my office here at the White House.

Mrs. Kennedy and I were particularly pleased to receive "Pushinka." Her flight from the Soviet Union to the United States was not as dramatic as the flight of her mother, nevertheless, it was a long voyage and she stood it well. We both appreciate your remembering these matters in your busy life.

We send to you, your wife and your family our very best wishes.

Sincerely yours,
John F. Kennedy

John and Jacqueline Kennedy's unprecedented opening of the White House to the world's most accomplished artists and performers did more than turn the executive mansion into a cultural showcase. It gave some of these artists such as cellist and conductor Pablo Casals the opportunity to express the confidence they had in the young president.

Pablo Casals
Isla Verde K 2 - H 3
Santurce, Puerto Rico

October 16, 1961

The President
The White House
Washington, D.C.

Dear Mr. President:

Your kind invitation to the White House has honored me and given me great pleasure.

Over a year ago I addressed an open letter to the *New York Times* as I felt that a Democratic victory was essential for the universal reestablishment of faith and trust in the great American nation.

Never before has humanity faced such crucial moments and the desire for universal peace is a prayer of all. Everyone must join in doing their utmost to achieve this goal.

I know that your aim is to work for peace based on justice, understanding and freedom for all mankind. These ideals have always been my ideals and have determined the most important decisions—and the most painful renunciations—of my life.

Your generous foreign aid program and your many welfare plans all prove your practical idealism and have already given hope to those who yearn for liberty.

Therefore I look forward to the opportunity of meeting you personally. May the music that I will play for you and for your friends symbolize my deep feelings for the American people and the faith and confidence we all have in you as leader of the Free World.

Please accept, Mr. President, my respects and my highest esteem.

Sincerely,
Pablo Casals

As evidenced by the following letter to author and poet Carl Sandburg, Kennedy found that sometimes there were unplanned benefits from his being in contact with many of the creative individuals he so admired.

———————————————

May 19, 1961

Dear Mr. Sandburg:

You were most kind to send me the article you wrote for the Chicago TIMES in 1941. The President enjoyed it—he particularly liked the phrase "Rest is not a word of free peoples—rest is a monarchial word."

He may steal it from you some day.

Again many thanks.

Sincerely,
Pierre Salinger
Press Secretary to the
President

In January 1962, Kennedy received a letter from Arthur Schlesinger Sr. in which the historian asked him if, despite his "crushing duties," he would take the time to join some seventy "students of American history" in filling out a ballot ranking who they thought had been the nation's greatest presidents. Kennedy's reply showed the introspection he had gained after a full year in office. It also provided an early indication of one of the projects he might take on after he left the White House.

January 22, 1962

Dear Professor Schlesinger:

Thank you for your letter in regard to our past Presidents.

A year ago I would have responded with confidence

to a request to rate their performance in office, but now I am not so sure. After being in the office for a year I feel that a good deal more study is required to make my judgment sufficiently informed. There is a tendency to mark the obvious names. I would like to subject those not so well known to a long scrutiny after I have left this office. Therefore, I hope you will forgive me for not taking part in what I regard as a most interesting and informative poll. . . .

>   With kind regards,
>   Sincerely,

In early June 1962, the American Booksellers Association held its annual convention in the nation's capital. Kennedy used the occasion to send a telegram to the president of the organization containing both a heartfelt statement and a mock complaint.

JUNE 4, 1962

AS AN AUTHOR, LOYAL TO THE TRADITIONS OF HIS CRAFT, I AM DEEPLY SORRY NOT TO BE ABLE TO JOIN YOU IN PERSON IN ORDER TO DISCUSS THE INADEQUACY OF THE SALES OF A BOOK CALLED "WHY ENGLAND SLEPT". HOWEVER, MY BROTHER [ROBERT], WHOSE BOOK SOLD EVEN LESS WELL THAN MINE, WILL COME AMONG YOU TONIGHT, AND I ADVISE NO ONE TO APPEAR WITHOUT COPIES OF [HIS] "THE ENEMY WITHIN". I TRUST THAT THE ATTORNEY GENERAL'S APPEARANCE WILL INSPIRE YOU ALL TO SELL MORE

BOOKS TO MORE PEOPLE THAN EVER BEFORE
IN THE NEXT TWELVE MONTHS. NOW THAT
READING IS BECOMING INCREASINGLY
RESPECTABLE IN AMERICA, I WANT, BOTH AS
AN AUTHOR AND AS A READER, TO EXPRESS
MY GRATITUDE TO THE MEN AND WOMEN
WHO HAVE LIVED WITH BOOKS, LOVED
THEM, SOLD THEM, AND KEPT THEM AN
INDISPENSABLE PART OF LIFE.

The mock complaint in Kennedy's telegram was obviously taken seriously by some who read it, including Pike Johnson Jr., editor in chief of Anchor Books, publisher of the paperback version of Why England Slept.

June 6, 1962

The Honorable John F. Kennedy
The White House
Washington, D. C.

Dear Mr. President:

I read in yesterday's *New York Times* your telegram to the American Booksellers Association in which you spoke of "the inadequacy of the sales of a book called "WHY ENGLAND SLEPT".

Recognizing the spirit in which this telegram was sent, and recognizing also that no author is ever satisfied with the sales of his book, I am, nevertheless, pleased to inform you that the Dolphin edition of "WHY ENGLAND SLEPT", which has been out approximately two weeks, has already sold 17,000 copies, which is about three times as good as any of our other paperback books have done in many years.

We shall, however, continue to put adequate pressure upon the booksellers of the country to increase this number.

Sincerely,
Pyke Johnson, Jr.
Editor-in-Chief

By Kennedy's second year in office, he and Eleanor Roosevelt had developed a warm, supportive relationship. So much so that Kennedy had sought to have one of the world's highest honors bestowed upon her.

February 1, 1962

Dear Mr. President:

I have learned through Mr. Lee White and Mr. Abba Schwartz that you have sent a letter nominating me for the Nobel Peace Prize in 1962. I am overcome by such an idea and I must frankly tell you that I cannot see the faintest reason why I should be considered. Of course, I am grateful for your kindness but I shall not be surprised in the least if nothing comes of it but my gratitude to you for having thought of this gesture will be just as great.

With my warm good wishes,

Very cordially yours,
Eleanor Roosevelt

One letter Kennedy received was quintessentially Harry Truman.

> Harry S. Truman
> Independence, Missouri
>
> June 28, 1962
>
> Dear Mr. President:
>
> It looks as if the Republerats haven't changed a bit since 1936. President Roosevelt had his troubles with them—so did I.
>
> Mr. President, in my opinion you are on the right track. Don't let 'em tell you what to do. You tell them, as you have! Your suggestions for the public welfare, in my opinion, are correct.
>
> This is a personal and confidential statement for what it may be worth. You know my program with these counterfeits was "Give 'em Hell" and if they don't like it, give them more of the same. I admire your spunk as we say in Wisconsin.
>
> Sincerely
> *Harry S. Truman*
>
> This is a pretentious note but I had to write it.
> Do as you please with it. Perhaps it ought to go into the "round file."

By the middle of Kennedy's second year in office, Kennedy and Truman had engaged in regular correspondence. And Kennedy, knowing that he would get a well-considered reply, had seriously begun asking the

HARRY S. TRUMAN   June 28, 1962
INDEPENDENCE, MISSOURI

Dear Mr. President:—

It looks as if the Republicans
have n't changed a bit since 1936.
President Roosevelt had his troubles
with them — so did I.

Mr. President, in my opinion you
are on the right track. Don't let 'em
tell you what to do. You tell them, as
you have! Your suggestions for the public
welfare, in my opinion, are correct.

This is a personal and confidential
statement for what it may be worth.

You know my program with these
counterfeits was "Give 'em Hell" and if

*A typically plainspoken letter from former president
Harry Truman to Kennedy*

former president for advice on a number of important matters, includ-ing his Trade Program.

January 25, 1962

Dear Mr. President:

I am anxious that you have directly from me a copy of the special message which I am sending to Congress on the Trade Program.

The wonderful reaction to your address at the dinner Saturday evening has been most gratifying. It certainly pleased me to have you speak out as you did. I know that as we enter the debate phase no help will be more important than yours.

With warmest regards,

Sincerely,
John F. Kennedy

February 6, 1962

Dear Mr. President:

I certainly did appreciate your letter of January 25th, enclosing a copy of your "Message on Trade" to the Congress on January 24th.

Your letter came while I was back East and I have just now had an opportunity to read it carefully. It is a great message and I think hits the nail on the head right where it ought to be hit.

I sincerely hope for the successful passage of the

legislation, which you requested, as it ought to solve a great many of our problems.

Again, I want to tell you that I appreciate your thoughtfulness, in sending me a copy of the message with your own personal letter attached, more than I can tell you.

Sincerely yours,
Harry S. Truman

Among the hundreds of letters Kennedy received from college students was a specific request from a Yale undergraduate. Neither the sender nor the president could have predicted that this particular student would, some forty-five years later, come within thirty-five electoral votes of gaining the presidency himself, or that he would eventually serve as the nation's secretary of state.

1078 Yale Station
September 24, 1962

To whom it may concern:

Dear Sir:

I am at the moment involved in the preparation for a debate on the resolved; "That the Kennedy administration's Domestic Program has failed to meet the challenge(s) of the future."

I would greatly appreciate an administration statement on this issue as soon as possible—if available. I already intend to speak against the resolved but I would naturally be interested in a first hand idea of what the administration feels on this issue and how it would approach its naturally negative answer.

In all hopes that I am not taking your time nor trying your patience.

Sincerely,
John Forbes Kerry

As both a student of history and a statesman, Kennedy was an ardent admirer of Winston Churchill. So much so that early in his presidency he began to advocate for the bestowal of American citizenship on the legendary British leader whose alliance with the United States had been forged in World War II. On August 14, 1961, the twentieth anniversary of the signing of the historic Atlantic Charter, Kennedy sent Churchill a telegram commenting on both the importance and the enduring legacy of the Charter.

AUGUST 14, 1961

TODAY MARKS THE 20TH ANNIVERSARY OF THE ATLANTIC CHARTER. TIME HAS NOT CHANGED AND EVENTS HAVE NOT DIMMED THE HISTORIC PRINCIPLES YOU THERE EXPRESSED WITH PRESIDENT FRANKLIN ROOSEVELT. OUR TWO NATIONS ARE STILL UNITED ON THE COMMON GOALS YOU TWO SO ELOQUENTLY CHARTED AT SEA. WE STILL BELIEVE THAT ALL NATIONS MUST COME TO THE ABANDONMENT OF THE USE OF FORCE. WE STILL SEEK A PEACE IN WHICH ALL THE MEN IN ALL THE LANDS MAY LIVE OUT THEIR LIVES IN FREEDOM FROM FEAR AND

WANT. AND WE ARE STILL DETERMINED TO
PROTECT THE RIGHT OF ALL PEOPLES TO
CHOOSE THE FORM OF GOVERNMENT UN-
DER WHICH THEY WILL LIVE—AND TO OP-
POSE ALL TERRITORIAL CHANGES THAT DO
NOT ACCORD WITH THE FREELY EXPRESSED
WISHES OF THE PEOPLE CONCERNED.

YOUR OWN NAME WILL ENDURE AS LONG AS
FREE MEN SURVIVE TO RECALL THESE
WORDS.

(S) JOHN F. KENNEDY

THE RIGHT HONORABLE
SIR WINSTON CHURCHILL
LONDON, ENGLAND

*A day after receiving Kennedy's telegram, Churchill replied, reaffirming
the Atlantic Charter's principles and reminding Kennedy of the vital role
he now played in world affairs.*

1961 AUG 15 PM 1 05

VWN2 88 VIA RCA
WESTERHAM ENGLAND 1512 AUGUST 15 1961
THE PRESIDENT
THE WHITE HOUSE WASHINGTON

MR PRESIDENT I AM INDEED GRATEFUL TO
YOU FOR YOUR MESSAGE STOP THE TERMS OF
THE ATLANTIC CHARTER OF TWENTY YEARS

AGO EMPHASIZED THE PRINCIPLES WHICH
THEN AND NOW GUIDE THE POLICIES OF OUR
GREAT DEMOCRACIES STOP LET US NEVER
DEPART FROM THEM NOR DESIST FROM OUR
EARNEST ENDEAVOUR TO ESTABLISH THEM
THROUGOUT THE WORLD STOP I SEND YOU
MY HEARTFELT GOOD WISHES FOR THE
MOMENTOUS AND PREEMINENT PART YOU
PLAY IN THE SHAPING OF OUR DESTINIES

WINSTON S CHURCHILL

*One of the strongest supporters of Kennedy's desire to bestow American
citizenship on Winston Churchill was a remarkable woman named Kay
Murphy Halle. A glamorous Cleveland department store heiress, Halle
became best known for the ways in which she formed close personal
friendships with many of the leading figures of her day, including
Churchill and Franklin D. Roosevelt. On August 19, 1961, Halle wrote to
Kennedy stressing the urgency of granting citizenship to Churchill, a letter also notable for its unique glimpse into the aging Churchill, his
thoughts, and his surroundings.*

August 19, 1961

President John F. Kennedy
The White House
Washington, D. C.

Dear President Kennedy:

I thought it would please you to know that Randolph
and I spent the day with Sir Winston and his family at

Chartwell. We found him seated on the terrace overlooking his water gardens girdled by the crenelated raw-
liver-red brick walls he had built with his own hands
which make Chartwell seem not unlike a castle close. A
light-beige-colored South African campaign hat shaded
his eyes as he watched the gambols of a gray pony that
had escaped from a nearby gypsy camp and leapt the
walls into a Chartwell pasture where his Belted Galloway cattle were grazing. Not a combination of its gypsy
owners, a Scotland Yard detective, a London Bobby and
Vincent, the head gardener was able to corral the
freedom-loving pony. Sir Winston could not help cheer-
ing the pony's determination to avoid capture.

When lunch was announced, we were lifted to the din-
ing room in an elevator—a present from his friend, Lord
Beaverbrook—and my host bade me sit next to him at
the table. Several times he turned to speak to me of "That
splendid leader, your President." When the fish course
arrived, he waved away any assistance from his red-haired
nurse as he rose from the anesthesia of his great age and
lifted his glass of hock. Then, turning to me, he proposed
a toast, "To your great President Kennedy and . . . and . . .
ours." I told him I had seen you on the eve of my departure and that you had sent him warmest greetings.
He smiled a jack-o'-lantern grin and I could see he was
pleased. He asked me, "Is there a picture of me now at the
White House?" Lady Churchill's eyes signaled "No." He
muttered that perhaps I could take one to you.

I had brought with me a clipping from the Paris edition of the *New York Herald Tribune* of the full exchange
of messages between ~~Churchill~~ you and ~~President Ken-
nedy~~ Sir Winston on the twentieth anniversary of the
signing of the Atlantic Charter. He read it through,
then promptly invited me to his bed-study to see the

original draft copy of the August 14, 1941 Joint Declaration of the Atlantic Charter, with some suggested changes for Point III written in his own hand to President Roosevelt. Thereupon he presented me with a copy, taking particular care to point out the significance of Point III—"That's mine!"—which was to become Point III of the United Nations Charter: "They respect the right of <u>all</u> people to choose the form of government under which they will live."

It was only one of many of the historic mementoes that ringed his room. Most dramatic were the three flags hanging from oaken beams in the high ceiling of his study. One of these was the Cinque Ports, a medieval league of coastal cities of which Churchill was warden which Churchill enjoyed hanging from his manor house in Chartwell and on his car by special decree of the Queen. The other two were the Flag of the Knight of the Garter and—most dramatic of all—a tattered Union Jack sent him by General Montgomery, the first flag to fly over Rome after the Allied entry.

On awakening each morning, his eyes would first rest on a wall opposite his bed on which were hung an engraving of Lord Nelson, a new painting of Bernard Baruch, and a fine drawing of John, Duke of Marlborough. I was amused to note a Bible lying on the shelf of his bedside table.

On top of The Holy Book, he had placed an autographed photograph of Stalin face downwards, perhaps in the hope that the Communist leader might absorb its contents!

Discussions concerning *The Daily Express*' "monstrous position on Berlin" and the eddies of British politics all swirled around his head. It mattered not to him. All he seems to brood upon is Anglo-American amity. I

leaned close to him all through lunch to catch his frag-
mentary words. Some reminded me so much of his sentences in a speech he gave July July 4, 1950 in London.
"The British and the Americans do not war with races
and governments as such. Tyranny external or internal
is our foe whatever trappings or disguise it wears, whatever language it speaks or perverts." "Undying fraternal
association" was much on his lips.

The best way to describe the appearance of the
Great Man at this moment, with his beautifully ordered house, loving staff and family around him, is in
the words he used in his profile on the aging Admiral
Lord "Jackie" Fisher. 'As in a great castle which has
long contended with time, the mighty central mass of
the donjon towered up intact and seemingly everlast-
ing. But the outworks and the battlements had fallen
away, and its imperious ruler dwelt only in the special
apartments and corridors with which he had a life
long familiarity.'

I fear, Mr. President, that if the Honorary American
Citizenship we discussed is not bestowed on Sir Winston soon, even his 'mighty central mass' will have
crumbled. Though his cheek was warm when I kissed
him farewell, both hands were cold. I left him, glasses
on the end of his nose, reading Thomas Hardy's TESS
OF THE D'URBERVILLES.

Faithfully
Kay Murphy Halle

*Granting U.S. citizenship to even as giant a figure as Winston Churchill
required the approval of the United States Congress, a process that, for
Kennedy, would take an agonizingly long two years. In the meantime,*

the Kennedy/Churchill correspondence would continue, as evidenced
by this exchange of telegrams occasioned by a serious illness Churchill
had suffered.

JULY 6, 1962

THE HONORABLE WINSTON CHURCHILL

DEAR SIR WINSTON, WE HAVE BEEN ENCOUR-
AGED BY THE REPORTS OF THE PROGRESS
YOU HAVE MADE AND HEARTENED AGAIN BY
YOUR DISPLY [DISPLAY] OF INDOMITABLE
COURAGE IN THE FACE OF ADVERSITY. THE
WISHES OF ALL OUR PEOPLE, AS WELL AS
THOSE OF MRS. KENNEDY AND I, GO TO YOU.

PRESIDENT JOHN. F. KENNEDY

WA360 40 PD
ZL LONDON (via WU cables) JULY 7, 1962 551P EDT

THE PRESIDENT
THE WHITE HOUSE

I AM MOST GRATEFUL TO YOU MR. PRESI-
DENT AND TO MRS. KENNEDY FOR YOUR
MESSAGE AND SYMPATHY WHICH I
RECEIVED WITH THE GREATEST PLEASURE
ALL GOOD WISHES.

WINSTON CHURCHILL.

*Finally, in the beginning of April 1963, it became clear that the U.S.
Congress was about to enact Public Law 88-6 declaring "that the Pres-
ident of the United States is hereby authorized and directed to declare
that Sir Winston Churchill shall be an honorary citizen of the United
States of America." Informed of the impending act, the ever-eloquent
Churchill wrote to Kennedy.*

28, Hyde Park Gate
London, S.W.7

6 April, 1963

Mr. President,

I have been informed by Mr. David Bruce that it is
your intention to sign a Bill conferring upon me Honorary Citizenship of the United States.

I have received many kindnesses from the United
States of America, but the honour which you now accord me is without parallel. I accept it with deep gratitude and affection.

I am also most sensible of the warm-hearted action
of the individual states who accorded me the great com-
pliment of their own honorary citizenships as a prelude
to this Act of Congress.

It is a remarkable comment on our affairs that
the former Prime Minster of a great sovereign state
should thus be received as an honorary citizen of another. I say "great sovereign state" with design and
emphasis, for I reject the view that Britain and the
Commonwealth should now be relegated to a tame
and minor role in the world. Our past is the key to our

future, which I firmly trust and believe will be no less fertile and glorious. Let no man underrate our energies, our potentialities and our abiding power for good.

I am, as you know, half American by blood, and the story of my association with that mighty and benevolent nation goes back nearly ninety years to the day of my Father's marriage. In this century of storm and tragedy I contemplate with high satisfaction the constant factor of the interwoven and upward progress of our peoples. Our comradeship and our brotherhood in war were unexampled. We stood together, and because of that fact the free world now stands.

Nor has our partnership any exclusive nature: the Atlantic community is a dream that can well be fulfilled to the detriment of none and to the enduring benefit and honour of the great democracies.

Mr. President, your action illuminates the theme of unity of the English-speaking peoples, to which I have devoted a large part of my life. I would ask you to accept yourself, and to convey to both Houses of Congress, and through them to the American people, my solemn and heartfelt thanks for this unique distinction, which will always be proudly remembered by my descendants.

Winston S. Churchill

On April 9, 1963, Public Law 88-6 was officially enacted and was signed by Kennedy in a ceremony attended by dignitaries from both the United States and Great Britain. Four days later, Sir Winston wrote once again to the president.

13 April, 1963

Private

My dear Mr. President,

When Mr. David Bruce called on me to bring me the Act of Congress by which I was made a Citizen of the United States, he also handed me your gift of the signatures of those present at the ceremony and the pen with which you signed the Act of Congress.

I have already expressed to you, Mr. President, and to the people of America the strong sentiments that your action aroused in me. I would now like to add my very warm thanks to you personally, both for the part you played in bestowing this signal honour on me, and for these most agreeable gifts with which you accompanied it. They will be cherished in my archives for my family, and they will be a constant reminder to me of your goodwill and that of the American people.

With all good wishes,

I remain, Yours very
sincerely,
Winston S. Churchill

As chief executives before Kennedy had learned, even the presidency did not offer protection from the solicitations of entrepreneurial citizens eager to hawk their wares.

W.N. HYDER
Real Estate and Insurance
Insurance in Cash
43 Devereux Building
Utica, New York
October 9, 1962

President John F. Kennedy
White House
Washington, D.C.

Dear Mr. President:

We have just been retained to sell an estate on Dark
Island in the St. Lawrence River, usually referred to as
"Stone Castle", owned by the LaSalle Military Academy.

The property consists of a Main Building of 28
rooms, with 9 master bedrooms each with bath, is of
stone construction, on 7 acres of land, on an island, that
is not accessible except by boat or plane.

It is in the main channel of the St. Lawrence River,
high above the water, a Scottish Castle with beautiful
trees in abundance, nice lawns, has its own electric
plant, with two Boat Houses, and a Squash Court Building 25' × 54'.

Although this could be used for a Hotel, Show Place,
or Tourist attraction, or International Yacht Club, the
writer remembers visiting the Secretary of State Dulles
on Duck Island, not too far away, where the Republican
leaders talked over strategy and other matters of national interest.

MY THINKING, KNOWING A LITTLE OF
WHAT YOU WILL BE FACING SOON, TELLS ME

THAT THIS IS JUST THE PLACE FOR A PRESI-
DENTIAL HIDEAWAY, where you can have peace of
mind, secretly consult with whoever requires attention
from you, (without) interference or observance.

Replacement Cost	$1,000,000.00
Sale Price	225,000.00

Sincerely Yours
W.N. Hyder, Broker

*The Kennedy wit and sense of humor which became trademarks of his
presidency were evident in the following exchange of letters between
him and his friend Leonard Lyons, the popular* New York Post *columnist. In late August 1961, Lyons passed by the window of an autograph
shop that contained a display of presidential autographs along with the
price each signature was fetching. In his initial letter to Kennedy, Lyons
issued a lighthearted warning.*

Leonard Lyons

October 2, 1961

Dear Mr. President:

In the event you might be anxious about how you
rate in history, I think you should know about this market: a manuscript and autograph framing shop on 53rd
Street and Madison Avenue has a window display of
framed presidential autographs. In each is either a tinted
photo or a medallion of a President.

George Washington's sells for $175, U.S. Grant's sells

for $55, Franklin D. Roosevelt's for $75, Teddy Roosevelt's for $67.50, John F. Kennedy's for $75.

Please don't bother to acknowledge this, for two reasons:

(1) You're too busy; and
(2) If you sign your name too often, that would depress the autograph market on E. 53rd Street.

Sylvia joins me, of course, in sending you fondest regards.

Sincerely,
Leonard

A tongue-in-cheek Kennedy responded by demonstrating that he was heeding Lyon's warning.

THE WHITE HOUSE
WASHINGTON

October 11, 1961

Dear Leonard:

I appreciate your letter about the market on Kennedy signatures. It is hard to believe that the going price is so high now. In order not to depress the market any further I will not sign this letter.

Best regards,

Delighted by Kennedy's response, Lyons wrote back, asking the president's permission to share it with his readers.

> New York Post
> Leonard Lyons
>
> October 16, 1961

Dear Mr. President:

Sylvia and I laughed and laughed at your unsigned response regarding depressing the market for presidential autographs.

Naturally such a communication is privileged; but since it's so amusing, I am writing for permission to print it and share the amusing aspects with my readers.

I assume that your reply, one way or another, will be signed. Now that you know about the market, I hope you don't think I am seeking unjust enrichment. As a swap, therefore, I'm enclosing two Republican autographs—Tom Dewey's and Richard Nixon's. Not that one of your autographs isn't worth two of theirs: it's just that yours will be signed "Jack" and theirs are signed in full.

> With best regards,
> Sincerely,
> *Leonard*

By using his press secretary Pierre Salinger to grant Lyons permission to print the letter, Kennedy made sure he delivered the last word in the playful exchange.

———————————————

Dear Leonard:

With regard to your letter of October 16th, you have permission to print the President's response.

By having me write this letter, the President again avoided signing the letter.

> Best regards,
> *Pierre Salinger*
> *Press Secretary to the*
> *President*

And always there were the letters from children, some of which elicited a personal response from the president.

October 28, 1961

Dear Michelle:

I was glad to get your letter about trying to stop the Russians from bombing the North Pole and risking the life of Santa Claus.

I share your concern about the atmospheric testing of the Soviet Union, not only for the North Pole but for countries throughout the world; not only for Santa Claus but for people throughout the world.

However, you must not worry about Santa Claus. I talked with him yesterday and he is fine. He will be making his rounds again this Christmas.

> Sincerely,
> *John Kennedy*

Miss Michelle Rochon
Marine City, Michigan

Many of the more than two million letters that poured into or out of the Kennedy White House, like the following he wrote to his chief of protocol for the State Department, Angier Biddle Duke, dealt with issues that are still paramount today.

March 13, 1961

Dear Angie:

Please extend my best wishes to Chairman Edward Ennis, Chairman of the Board, and to the Directors of the American Immigration and Citizenship Conference on the occasion of its annual conference on March twenty-fourth. The A.I.C.C. performs a valuable function in assembling information, in developing sound and humane immigration policies, and in keeping the American people fully informed.

I am pleased to note the theme of your conference: "Immigration and Refugees – The Task Ahead." We can be proud of the total record made by our nation over the years. In the post-war period alone, we have welcomed millions of men, women and children to our shores, but the problems we face today are the problems of the future.

The tasks we face in revision of our immigration policy must be keyed to the tasks we face in connection with every aspect of our rapidly changing world. The emergence of new nations in Asia and Africa, the assumption of power by any totalitarian tyranny, the cries for assistance when disaster strikes, all call for the best in our American traditions. Our immigration programs must be free from any taint of racism or discrimination.

We must never forget that we are a nation of immigrants, and that our land has always been—and must continue to be—a haven for the persecuted and oppressed who seek the air of freedom.

Sincerely,
John Kennedy

Honorable Angier Biddle Duke
President
American Immigration and
Citizenship Conference
509 Madison Avenue
New York 22, New York

One of the first to openly question the depth of John Kennedy's commitment to the goals of the civil rights movement was sports legend Jackie Robinson, the man who courageously broke the color barrier in major league baseball. Early in Kennedy's presidential campaign, Robinson, who was then an executive at a restaurant company, wrote to the candidate, criticizing him for meeting with the governor and other officials of the deeply segregated state of Alabama. Kennedy's reply to the letter included one of his earliest articulations of his position on civil rights while also indicating the political tightrope he felt he needed to walk both as candidate and president.

UNITED STATES SENATE
WASHINGTON, D.C.

July 1, 1960

Mr. Jackie Robinson
c/o Chock Full O'Nuts Company
425 Lexington Avenue
New York, New York

Dear Jackie:

It was good to see you at [foreign policy adviser] Chet Bowles' the other evening. I have long admired your contribution to the world of baseball and good American sportsmanship. Hearing your great personal concern about the denial of civil rights to American citizens by reason of their race or color and your dedication to the achievement of first-class citizenship for all Americans, I believe I understand and appreciate your role in the continuing struggle to fulfill the American promise of equal opportunity for all. I trust that you now understand better my own concern about this problem and my dedication to these same ideals. It is time for us to fulfill the promise of the Declaration of Independence—to make good the guarantees of the Constitution—to make equal opportunity a living reality in all parts of our public life.

I have said this on many occasions in the past and will of course continue to say it. I have called for an end to all discrimination—in voting, in education, in housing, in employment, in the administration of justice, and in public facilities including lunch counters. I have also spoken in favor of the right of peaceful protest, saying that the recent demonstrations have been in the American tradition of people standing up for their rights, even if the new way of standing up for one's rights is to sit down. You may be interested in the enclosed interview in *The Pittsburgh Courier* of June 25, 1960, which goes into detail on some of these points.

But saying these things is not enough. What is required now above all is effective, creative, persuasive Executive leadership. This is not just a matter of law and order. For great moral issues are involved.

You have questioned my talk over sixteen months ago with the Governor of Alabama and some members of his state cabinet. As I told you, any responsible person in my position must be ready to talk with the governor or leading public officials of every state. I suppose I have talked with most of the governors of our states in the last few years. That does not imply my agreement with them or their agreement with me on particular issues. In my one brief meeting with Governor Patterson civil rights was not discussed, but I am sure that he knows that we do not have similar views on this matter.

                                        Sincerely,
                                        John Kennedy

Four months into the Kennedy presidency, Harris Wofford, Kennedy's special assistant for civil rights, received a letter from Roy Wilkins, executive director of the National Association for the Advancement of Colored People (NAACP), critiquing the administration's civil rights record thus far. Regarded by his fellow activists as "the acknowledged champion of civil rights in America," Wilkins remained a moderate but insistent voice for action throughout the civil rights movement. In this letter, however, he left little doubt about how he felt about Kennedy's civil rights approach.

April 5, 1961

Mr. Harris Wofford

For as long as I can remember, the NAACP (commonly thought of as the opposers, the protesters) has been seeking something far beyond mere opposition. It was a pioneer in trying to be "in better gear with the Government." Its trademark, almost, has been "the use of the law and of government to fulfill the promise of the Constitution."

The Kennedy Administration has done with Negro citizens what it has done with a vast number of Americans: it has charmed them. It has intrigued them. Every seventy-two hours it has delighted them. On the Negro question it has smoothed Unguentine on a stinging burn even though for a moment (or for perhaps a year) it cannot do anything about a broken pelvis. It has patted a head even though it could not bind up a joint.

All this is good, not only because people like to have their immediate hurts noticed and attended to, but because the attention to them helps to create a useful moral (and political) climate.

Experienced observers know that snags have developed, that changes have had to be ordered, that some obeisance to pressures has had to be made. This is politics.

The point is not so much whether we have come out thus far with all we were due (we have not), but whether the lines have been set in such a way that we cannot later recover our proper share.

It is plain why the civil rights legislative line was

abandoned, but nothing was accomplished by the ma-
neuver. It did not save the minimum wage bill from
gutting and it will not save other legislation. The Southerners and their Northern satellites, Halleck, Mundt,
Bonnett, Saltonstall and Company, function whether a
civil rights bill is proposed or withheld.

An administration gets as much by whacking them as
by wooing them. JFK might as well have had a civil rights
bill in the hopper; he might as well have won the Senate
rules fight (he could have) so he would have a procedure
open when he *does* decide to get behind a civil rights bill.

I don't suppose we have a quarrel. We do have a difference with the Kennedy Administration and perhaps
that difference is rooted in the purpose of the NAACP
as contrasted with the purpose of the government of all
the people in a time of world crisis. We are concerned
(as much as our financial and personnel resources will
permit) with Big Integration, but we must, because of
the very nature of the domestic scene and of our *raison
d'être*, be concerned with Little Integration. . . .

Sincerely,
Roy Wilkins
Executive Secretary

*Another important civil rights leader, James Farmer was national di-
rector and cofounder of the Congress of Racial Equality (CORE), an organization with a clearly stated approach to pursuing its goals. CORE's
approach, Farmer said, meant "advising your adversaries or the people in
power just what you are going to do, when you are going to do it, and how
you were going to do it, so that everything would be open and above
board." Highest on the list of those in power that Farmer wished to inform
was the president of the United States.*

April 26, 1961

The President
The White House
1600 Pennsylvania Avenue, N.W.
Washington D.C.

My dear Mr. President:

We expect you will be interested in our Freedom Ride, 1961. It is designed to forward the completion of integrated bus service and accommodations in the Deep South.

About fifteen CORE members will travel as inter-state passengers on Greyhound and Trailways routes. We leave Washington early in May and, traveling through Virginia, North and South Carolina, Georgia, Alabama and Mississippi, plan to arrive in New Orleans on Wednesday, May 17th.

The group is interracial. Two-thirds are Southerners. Three are women. We propose to challenge, en route, every form of segregation met by the bus passenger. We are experienced in, and dedicated to, the Gandhian principles of non-violence.

Our plans are entirely open. Further information is available to all.

Freedom Ride is an appeal to the best in all Americans. We travel peaceably to persuade them that Jim Crow betrays democracy. It degrades democracy at home. It debases democracy abroad. We feel that there is no way to overstate the danger that denial of democratic and constitutional rights brings to our beloved country.

And so we feel it our duty to affirm our principles by asserting our rights. With the survival of democracy at stake, there is an imperative, immediate need for acts of self-determination. "Abandon your animosities and make your sons Americans," said Robert E. Lee. Freedom Ride would make that, "*All* your sons—NOW!"

Sincerely yours,
James Farmer

In Dr. Martin Luther King Jr., the civil rights movement found its most eloquent spokesman and its iconic figure. Espousing the nonviolent methods embodied in the teachings of Mahatma Gandhi, King, as president of the Southern Christian Leadership Conference (SCLC), relentlessly pursued his goal of a color-blind society, establishing himself in the process as one of the greatest orators in the nation's history. In this telegram, one of the earliest of the many communications King sent to Kennedy, King reminded the president of the nation's vital obligations at home as well as beyond its shores.

1961 DEC 10

THE PRESIDENT
THE WHITE HOUSE

WE URGE YOU ISSUE AT ONCE BY EXECUTIVE ORDER A SECOND EMANCIPATION PROCLAMATION TO FREE ALL NEGROES FROM SECOND CLASS CITIZENSHIP. FOR UNTIL THE GOVERNMENT OF THIS NATION STANDS AS FORTHRIGHTLY IN DEFENSE OF DEMOCRATIC PRINCIPLES AND PRACTICES HERE AT HOME AND PRESSES AS UNCEASINGLY FOR EQUAL RIGHTS OF ALL AMERICANS AS

IT DOES IN AIDING FOREIGN NATIONS WITH
ARMS, AMMUNITION AND THE MATERIALS
OF WAR FOR ESTABLISHMENT DEFENSE OF
HUMAN RIGHTS BEYOND OUR SHORES,
THEN AND ONLY THEN, CAN WE JUSTIFY
THE CLAIM TO WORLD LEADERSHIP IN THE
FIGHT AGAINST COMMUNISM AND TYR-
ANNY. WE URGE YOU FURTHER TO USE
EVERY MEANS AVAILABLE TO RELEASE AT
ONCE THE HUNDREDS OF PERSONS NOW IN
JAIL IN ALBANY GEORGIA FOR SIMPLY SEEK-
ING TO EXERCISE CONSTITUTIONAL RIGHTS
AND TO STAND UP FOR FREEDOM.

DR. MARTIN LUTHER KING JR PRES SCLC DR
V G ANDERSON PRES ALBANY NON-VIOLENT
MOVEMENT RALPH D. ABERNATHY SEC OF
TEXAS SCLC

*Throughout his ongoing letters and telegrams to Kennedy, King con-
tinually pleaded with the president to pursue every avenue "to make
the negro a full participant in every phase of American life."*

JOHN F KENNEDY
THE PRESIDENT
THE WHITE HOUSE

URGENTLY REQUEST YOUR SERIOUS CONSID-
ERATION OF JUDGE WILLIAM H HASTIE AND
JUDGE THURGOOD MARSHALL FOR APPOINT-
MENT TO THE SUPREME COURT BENCH.
BOTH MEN ARE EMINENTLY QUALIFIED TO

FILL VACANCY. THIS IS SUPERB OPPORTU-
NITY FOR THE ADMINISTRATION TO REVEAL
TO WORLD ITS SERIOUS DETERMINATION TO
MAKE THE NEGRO A FULL PARTICIPANT IN
EVERY PHASE OF AMERICAN LIFE, IN THIS
CRUCIAL PERIOD OF HISTORY SUCH AN
APPOINTMENT WOULD BE ONE OF THE FIN-
EST WAYS TO DEMONSTRATE THE NATIONS
COMMITMENT TO THE IDEAL OF EQUALITY
OF OPPORTUNITY YOURS VERY TRULY

MARTIN LUTHER KING JR

PRESIDENT SOUTHERN
CHRISTIAN LEADERSHIP
CONFERENCE.

In September 1962, black air force veteran James Meredith was, for the fifth time, denied admission to the fully segregated University of Mississippi. Determined to overcome this defiance of federal law, President Kennedy and Attorney General Robert Kennedy exchanged telephone conversations with Mississippi governor Ross Barnett. When these phone calls failed to convince Barnett to comply with federal law, Kennedy wrote to the governor leaving no doubt as to how he viewed Barnett's determination to prevent Meredith from attending the university.

SEPTEMBER 29, 1962

HON. ROSS BARNETT
GOVERNOR
STATE OF MISSISSIPPI
JACKSON, MISSISSIPPI

SEPTEMBER 29, 1962

HON. ROSS BARNETT
GOVERNOR
STATE OF MISSISSIPPI
JACKSON, MISSISSIPPI

TO PRESERVE OUR CONSTITUTIONAL SYSTEM THE FEDERAL
GOVERNMENT HAS AN OVERRIDING RESPONSIBILITY TO ENFORCE
THE ORDERS OF THE FEDERAL COURTS. THOSE COURTS HAVE
ORDERED THAT JAMES MEREDITH BE ADMITTED NOW AS A STUDENT
AT THE UNIVERSITY OF MISSISSIPPI. THREE EFFORTS BY FEDERAL
LAW ENFORCEMENT OFFICIALS TO GIVE EFFECT TO THE ORDER
HAVE BEEN UNAVAILING BECAUSE OF YOUR PERSONAL PHYSICAL
INTERVENTION AND THAT OF THE LIEUTENANT GOVERNOR
SUPPORTED BY STATE LAW ENFORCEMENT OFFICERS. A FOURTH
WAS CALLED OFF AT THE LAST MINUTE BY THE ATTORNEY GENERAL
ON ADVICE FROM YOU THAT EXTREME VIOLENCE AND BLOODSHED
WOULD OTHERWISE RESULT. BY VIEW OF THIS BREAKDOWN OF
LAW AND ORDER IN MISSISSIPPI AND IN ACCORDANCE WITH OUR
TWO TELEPHONE CONVERSATIONS TODAY, I WOULD LIKE TO BE
ADVISED AT ONCE OF YOUR RESPONSE TO THE FOLLOWING QUESTIONS:

*During the crisis over integrating the University of Mississippi, Kennedy
sent a pointed telegram to Mississippi's Governor Ross Barnett—
increasing the pressure by releasing it to the press.*

FIRST, WILL YOU TAKE ACTION TO SEE THAT THE COURT
ORDER IS ENFORCED AND PERSONALLY FOLLOW THE COURT'S
DIRECTION TO YOU?

SECOND, IF NOT, WILL YOU CONTINUE TO ACTIVELY INTERFERE
WITH ENFORCEMENT OF THE ORDERS OF THE COURT THROUGH
YOUR OWN ACTIONS OR THROUGH THE USE OF STATE LAW ENFORCEMENT
OFFICIALS OR IN ANY OTHER WAY?

THIRD, WILL STATE LAW ENFORCEMENT OFFICIALS COOPERATE
IN MAINTAINING LAW AND ORDER AND PREVENTING VIOLENCE IN
CONNECTION WITH FEDERAL ENFORCEMENT OF THE COURT ORDERS?
IN THIS CONNECTION, WILL YOU AT ONCE TAKE STEPS TO PROHIBIT
MOBS FROM COLLECTING IN THE OXFORD AREA DURING THIS
DIFFICULT PERIOD, AND WILL YOU CALL ON THE UNIVERSITY OFFICIALS
TO ISSUE REGULATIONS TO PREVENT STUDENTS FROM PARTICIPATING
IN DEMONSTRATIONS OR MOB ACTIVITY? AS GOVERNOR OF THE
STATE OF MISSISSIPPI, WILL YOU TAKE THE RESPONSIBILITY FOR
MAINTAINING LAW AND ORDER IN THAT STATE WHEN THE COURT
ORDERS ARE PUT INTO EFFECT?

I WOULD LIKE TO HEAR FROM YOU THIS EVENING BY WIRE.

I HOPE FOR YOUR COMPLETE COOPERATION AND ASSISTANCE
IN MEETING OUR RESPONSIBILITIES.

JOHN F. KENNEDY
PRESIDENT OF THE UNITED STATES

TO PRESERVE OUR CONSTITUTIONAL
SYSTEM THE FEDERAL GOVERNMENT HAS
AN OVERRIDING RESPONSIBILITY TO EN-
FORCE THE ORDERS OF THE FEDERAL
COURTS. THOSE COURTS HAVE ORDERED
THAT JAMES MEREDITH BE ADMITTED
NOW AS A STUDENT AT THE UNIVERSITY
OF MISSISSIPPI. THREE EFFORTS BY FED-
ERAL LAW ENFORCEMENT OFFICIALS TO
GIVE EFFECT TO THE ORDER HAVE BEEN
UNAVAILING BECAUSE OF YOUR PERSONAL
PHYSICAL INTERVENTION AND THAT OF
THE LIEUTENANT GOVERNOR SUPPORTED
BY STATE LAW ENFORCEMENT OFFICERS.
A FOURTH WAS CALLED OFF AT THE LAST
MINUTE BY THE ATTORNEY GENERAL
ON ADVICE FROM YOU THAT EXTREME
VIOLENCE AND BLOODSHED WOULD OTH-
ERWISE RESULT. BY VIEW OF THIS BREAK-
DOWN OF LAW AND ORDER IN MISSISSIPPI
AND IN ACCORDANCE WITH OUR TWO
TELEPHONE CONVERSATIONS TODAY, I
WOULD LIKE TO BE ADVISED AT ONCE OF
YOUR RESPONSE TO THE FOLLOWING
QUESTIONS:
    FIRST, WILL YOU TAKE ACTION TO SEE
THAT THE COURT ORDER IS ENFORCED AND
PERSONALLY FOLLOW THE COURT'S DIREC-
TION TO YOU?
    SECOND, IF NOT, WILL YOU CONTINUE TO
ACTIVELY INTERFERE WITH ENFORCEMENT
OF THE ORDERS OF THE COURT THROUGH
YOUR OWN ACTIONS OR THROUGH THE USE

OF STATE LAW ENFORCEMENT OFFICIALS
OR IN ANY OTHER WAY?

THIRD, WILL STATE LAW ENFORCE-
MENT OFFICIALS COOPERATE IN MAIN-
TAINING LAW AND ORDER AND
PREVENTING VIOLENCE IN CONNECTION
WITH FEDERAL ENFORCEMENT OF THE
COURT ORDERS? IN THIS CONNECTION,
WILL YOU AT ONCE TAKE STEPS TO PRO-
HIBIT MOBS FROM COLLECTING IN
THE OXFORD AREA DURING THIS DIFFI-
CULT PERIOD, AND WILL YOU CALL ON THE
UNIVERSITY OFFICIALS TO ISSUE
REGULATIONS TO PREVENT STUDENTS
FROM PARTICIPATING IN DEMONSTRA-
TIONS OR MOB ACTIVITY? AS GOVERNOR
OF THE STATE OF MISSISSIPPI, WILL YOU
TAKE THE RESPONSIBILITY FOR MAIN-
TAINING LAW AND ORDER IN THAT STATE
WHEN THE COURT ORDERS ARE PUT INTO
EFFECT?

I WOULD LIKE TO HEAR FROM YOU THIS
EVENING BY WIRE.

I HOPE FOR YOUR COMPLETE COOPERA-
TION AND ASSISTANCE IN MEETING OUR
RESPONSIBILITIES.

JOHN F. KENNEDY
PRESIDENT OF THE UNITED STATES

In the midst of Kennedy's determination to remove all obstacles to Meredith's admittance, James Farmer wrote to the president.

———————————

NEW YORK NY 28 107

THE PRESIDENT
THE WHITE HOUSE

THE CONGRESS OF RACIAL EQUALITY SUP-
PORTS FULLY YOUR EFFORTS TO ENFORCE
FEDERAL LAW IN MISSISSIPPI AND TO ADMIT
JAMES MEREDITH TO THE UNIVERSITY OF
MISSISSIPPI IMMEDIATELY. WE COMMEND
THE COURTS AND THE JUSTICE DEPART-
MENT FOR THEIR FORTHRIGHT ACTIONS. IT
IS IMPERATIVE THAT THE INSURRECTION
OF GOVERNOR BARNETT AND HIS COHORTS
BE PUT DOWN QUICKLY FIRMLY AND DECI-
SIVELY.
    MOREOVER, JUSTICE NOW CALLS OUT FOR
THE MORAL FORCE OF YOUR OFFICE. WE
URGE YOU TO SPEAK PROMPTLY AND
FORTHRIGHTLY TO THE PEOPLE OF MISSIS-
SIPPI AND TO THE PEOPLE OF THE UNITED
STATES. WE URGE YOU PERSONALLY TO
ESCORT MEREDITH TO HIS CLASSES AND
THUS DEMONSTRATE TO THE WORLD THAT
THE AMERICAN WAY OF LIFE MEANS A LIFE
OF JUSTICE, EQUALITY, AND DEMOCRACY
FOR ALL. NEGRO AMERICANS LIKE ALL
DECENT AMERICANS WILL BACK YOU IN
SUCH A STAND.

JAMES FARMER NATIONAL DIRECTOR CON-
GRESS OF RACIAL EQUALITY

———————————

Kennedy did not personally escort James Meredith into the University of Mississippi. But he did make his enrollment possible by sending in United States marshals supported by the 70th Army Combat Battalion, U.S. Army military police, and troops from the Mississippi National Guard. At the same time he wrote to a Mississippi congressman declaring that the most effective tool for upholding the nation's laws was "your courage to accept those laws with which you disagree as well as those with which you agree."

THE WHITE HOUSE

WASHINGTON

October 26, 1962

Dear Congressman:

This will acknowledge your telegram to me of September 28 regarding the enforcement of the court orders requiring the admission of James Meredith to the University of Mississippi.

Under the Constitution it is my duty to enforce federal law, including the orders of the federal courts. When state and federal laws conflict, federal law must be paramount or this Nation could not continue to exist. I respect and appreciate your concern for the people of the State of Mississippi. In this connection, I refer you to my address of September 30, 1962, in which I said the following:

I recognize that the present period of transition and adjustment in our nation's southland is a hard one for many people. Neither Mississippi nor any other southern state deserves to be charged with all the accumulated wrongs of the last 100 years of race relations. To the extent that there has been failure, the responsibility for that failure must be shared by us all, by every state, by every citizen.

Mississippi and her university moreover are noted for her courage, for their contribution of talent and thought to the affairs of this nation. This is the state of Lucius Lamar and many others who have placed the national good ahead of sectional interest. This is the state which had four Medal of Honor winners in the Korean War alone. In fact, the Guard Unit federalized this morning, early, is part of the 155th Infantry, one of the ten oldest regiments in the Union and one of the most decorated for sacrifice and bravery in six wars.

In Mississippi in 1945 Jake Lindsey was honored by an unusual joint session of the Congress. I close therefore with this appeal to the students of the University, the people who are most concerned.

You have a great tradition to uphold, a tradition of honor and courage, won on the field of battle and on the gridiron as well as the university campus. You have a new opportunity to show that you are men of patriotism and integrity. For the most effective means of upholding the law is not the state policeman or the marshals or the National Guard. It is you. It lies in your courage to accept those laws with which you disagree as well as those with which you agree. The eyes of the nation and all the world are upon you and upon all of us, and the honor of your university and state are in the balance. I am certain the great majority of the students will uphold that honor.

There is in short no reason why the books on this case cannot now be quickly and quietly closed in the manner directed by the Court. Let us preserve both the law and the peace and then healing those wounds that are within we can turn to the greater crises that are without and stand united as one people in our pledge to man's freedom.

I appreciate hearing from you.

Sincerely,
John Kennedy

Honorable Thomas G. Abernethy
House of Representatives
Washington, D. C.

Among the civil rights leaders who heralded Kennedy's actions regarding James Meredith was A. Phillip Randolph, president of both the Brotherhood of Sleeping Car Porters and the Negro American Labor Council.

WUX NEW YORK 1 414P EDT

1961 Oct 2

THE PRESIDENT
THE WHITE HOUSE

THE OFFICERS AND MEMBERS OF THE
BROTHERHOOD OF SLEEPING CAR PORTERS
AND THE NEGRO AMERICAN LABOR COUN-
CIL EXTEND HEARTIEST CONGRATULA-
TIONS ON YOUR GREAT STATESMANSHIP IN
HANDLING THE CONTROVERSY INVOLVING
GOVERNOR BARNETT OF MISSISSIPPI AND
THE ADMISSION OF JAMES MEREDITH TO
THE UNIVERSITY OF THAT STATE

A PHILIP RANDOLPH INTL PRESIDENT
BROTHERHOOD OF SLEEPING CAR PORTERS

One month later, Kennedy, who, on November 20, 1962, signed an executive order banning racial discrimination in all federal assisted housing, received another congratulatory telegram, this one from King.

THE PRESIDENT
THE WHITE HOUSE

DEAR MR KENNEDY THE ISSUANCE TODAY
OF THE EXECUTIVE ORDER OUTLAWING
DISCRIMINATION IN ALL FEDERALLY AS-
SISTED HOUSING CARRIES THE WHOLE
NATION CLOSER TO THE REALIZATION OF
THE AMERICAN DREAM. IT COMES AS A
GREAT BEACON LIGHT OF HOPE TO ALL
FREEDOM LOVING AMERICANS EVERY-
WHERE. THIS EXECUTIVE ORDER IF VIGOR-
OUSLY ENFORCED WILL BE A MOMENTOUS

STEP TOWARD ENDING LEGAL DISCRIMINA-
TION IN THE SOUTH AND SETTLE HOUSING
DISCRIMINATION IN THE NORTH. YOUR
COURAGEOUS ACTION TODAY REVEALS NOT
ONLY YOUR COMMITMENT TO A CAMPAIGN
PROMISE BUT ALSO TO THE PRINCIPLES OF
JUSTICE AND FREEDOM SO BASIC TO OUR
DEMOCRATIC HERITAGE. FAITHFULLY
YOURS

MARTIN LUTHER KING JR.

It would be the last communication of that type for some time. By mid-1962, violence, including murder, against Freedom Riders, demonstrators, and activists had escalated to an alarming point. Nowhere was this violence more in evidence than in Birmingham, Alabama, where the city's public safety commissioner Theophilus "Bull" Connor had become a symbol of unbridled bigotry through his use of attack dogs, fire hoses, and even a tank against civil rights marchers. As the second year of his administration drew to a close, Kennedy received an urgent telegram from King, one that included a dire warning.

ATLANTA GA 15 240P EST

THE PRESIDENT
THE WHITE HOUSE

DEAR MR KENNEDY, A VIRTUAL REIGN OF
TERROR IS STILL ALIVE IN BIRMINGHAM
ALABAMA IT IS BY FAR THE WORST BIG CITY

IN RACE RELATIONS IN THE UNITED STATES
MUCH OF WHAT HAS GONE ON HAS HAD
THE TACIT CONSENT OF HIGH PUBLIC OFFI-
CIALS ONCE MORE WE HAVE BEEN SHOCKED
BY THE BOMBING OF BETHEL BAPTIST
CHURCH 25 SMALL CHILDREN MIRACU-
LOUSLY ESCAPED INJURY AND DEATH IF
SUCH ACTS OF VIOLENCE GO UNCHECKED

AND THE GESTAPO LIKE METHODS OF PO-
LICE OFFICIALS NOT HALTED WE MAY SEE IN
THIS CITY A TRAGIC AND DEVASTATING
RACIAL HOLOCAUST I APPEAL TO YOU TO
USE THE INFLUENCE OF YOUR GREAT OF-
FICE TO PERSUADE THE PEOPLE OF THIS
COMMUNITY TO FACE THE REALITY OF
DESEGREGATION THIS UNFORTUNATE
INCIDENT POINTS UP THE IMMEDIATE
NEED FOR A WHITE HOUSE CONFERENCE ON
DESEGREGATION VERY TRULY YOURS

MARTIN LUTHER KING JR. PRESIDENT
SOUTHERN CHRISTIAN LEADERSHIP
CONFERENCE

Despite the volatile situation in Birmingham, King and his friend and associate Reverend Ralph Abernathy, along with their followers, refused to halt their protest demonstrations and marches. Then, on April 13, 1963, Kennedy received the following telegram from Martin Luther King's executive assistant.

BIRMINGHAM ALA APR 13 717P CST

THE PRESIDENT
THE WHITE HOUSE

DEAR MR KENNEDY, DR MARTIN LUTHER
KING JR AND THE REVEREND RALPH D
ABERNATHY ARE PRESENTLY CONFINED
IN THE BIRMINGHAM CITY JAIL BOTH
WERE ARRESTED ALONG WTH 50 OTHER
CITIZENS IN VIOLATION OF THE CONSTI-
TUTIONAL GUARANTEES OF THE FIRST
AND FOURTEENTH AMENDMENTS. BOTH
ARE NOW IN SOLITARY CONFINEMENT
ALLEGEDLY FOR "THEIR OWN SAFETY" WE
SUBMIT THAT THESE TWO DISTIN-
GUISHED AMERICANS ARE POLITICAL
PRISONERS AND NOT CRIMINALS. WE ASK
THAT YOU USE THE INFLUENCE OF YOUR
HIGH OFFICE TO PERSUADE THE CITY
OFFICIALS OF BIRMINGHAM TO AFFORD
AT LEAST A MODICUM OF HUMAN TREAT-
MENT NEITHER OF THESE MEN HAVE
MATTRESSES OR BED LINEN VERY TRULY
YOURS
    SOUTHERN CHRISTIAN LEADERSHIP CON-
FERENCE WYATT TEE WALKER

EXECUTIVE ASSISTANT TO DR. KING

*It was far from the first time that King had been arrested. One of his
earliest incarcerations had taken place in Georgia during the 1960*

presidential campaign. Then, against the advice of several of his strate-
gists, Kennedy had called King's wife, offering to help her in gaining
King's release, a move that many political pundits believed was respon-
sible for his winning the black vote by a wide margin across the nation.
Now, Kennedy made another phone call to Coretta King, engendering
a grateful response from her husband.

BIRMINGHAM ALA APR 16 438P CST

THE PRESIDENT
THE WHITE HOUSE

I AM DEEPLY GRATEFUL TO YOU FOR TAKING
TIME OUT OF YOUR EASTER WEEKEND TO
TELEPHONE MY WIFE CONCERNING THE
BIRMINGHAM SITUATION. YOUR ENCOUR-
AGING WORDS AND THOUGHTFUL CON-
CERN GAVE HER RENEWED STRENGTH TO
FACE THE DIFFICULT MOMENTS THROUGH
WHICH WE ARE NOW PASSING SUCH MORAL
SUPPORT GREATLY ENHANCES OUR HUM-
BLE EFFORTS TO MAKE THE AMERICAN
DREAM A REALITY

MARTIN LUTHER KING JR.

King was eventually released from his imprisonment, but the situation
in Birmingham and throughout the South continued to deteriorate.
Still, Kennedy refrained from taking the type of bold action that civil
rights leaders were demanding. In arguably the harshest communica-
tion yet sent to the president, James Farmer predicted what would

*happen if Kennedy did not overcome "his fear" and continued to
merely "watch and wait."*

VU NEW YORK NY 8 1222P EDT

THE PRESIDENT
THE WHITE HOUSE

TACTICS OF BIRMINGHAM POLICE APPEAR
TO BE AIMED AT INTENTIONALLY PRO-
VOKING WIDE SCALE VIOLENCE THERE
CAN BE NO TRUCE WITH POLICE BRUTAL-
ITY AND POLICE LAWLESSNESS SUCH AS WE
WITNESS IN BIRMINGHAM EVEN IF GUNS
OF ALABAMA SUCCEED IN QUELLING NON-
VIOLENT STRUGGLE IN BIRMINGHAM IT
WILL RISE UP AGAIN IN PLACE AFTER
PLACE UNTIL SUCH TIME AS THE PRESI-
DENT OF THE UNITED STATES OVERCOMES
HIS FEAR OF SPEAKING OUT AND DECIDES
TO ACT FORCEFULLY TO SECURE FREE-
DOM OF NEGRO AMERICANS POLITICS
HAVE TOO LONG RULED THE ACTS OF
GOVERNMENT ON BEHALF OF CIVIL
RIGHTS NO COMPROMISE WITH JUSTICE IS
POSSIBLE THE DEMONSTRATIONS IN BIR-
MINGHAM MUST CONTINUE UNTIL THE
RIGHTS OF ALL AMERICANS ARE SECURED I
URGE YOU TO DO MORE THAN WATCH AND
WAIT WHILE AMERICANS STRUGGLE
AGAINST ARMED MIGHT OF TYRANNY IN
ALABAMA

JAMES FARMER NATIONAL DIRECTOR
CORE

Not all African Americans shared Farmer's understandable frustra-
tion. There were private black citizens who had long felt quite differ-
ently about Kennedy's efforts on behalf of civil rights.

November 19, 1962

The President
The White House
Washington 25, D. C.

Dear Sir:

I want you to know that since you have been President, I have been proud to salute the flag of the United
States of America. In the past when I came to the part
"liberty and justice for all" I could not make the words
come out.

I know that I am a good American who happens to
be a Negro and who knows that all advancements must
come from within.

May God give you wisdom and strength to do that
that is wise and when your sun sets and your life's work is
done, I pray that you find holy rest and peace at the last.

Sincerely,
M. Earl Grant, President
Family Savings and
Loan Association

Actually, Kennedy had, for some time, been preparing a message to Congress, pushing for civil rights legislation in several areas. He finally sent it in February 1963.

February 28, 1963

To the Congress of the United States:

"Our Constitution is color blind," wrote Mr. Justice Harlan before the turn of the century, "and neither knows nor tolerates classes among citizens." But the practices of the country do not always conform to the principles of the Constitution. And this Message is intended to examine how far we have come in achieving first-class citizenship for all citizens regardless of color, how far we have yet to go, and what further tasks remain to be carried out—by the Executive and Legislative Branches of the Federal Government, as well as by state and local governments and private citizens and organizations.

One hundred years ago the Emancipation Proclamation was signed by a President who believed in the equal worth and opportunity of every human being. That Proclamation was only a first step—a step which its author unhappily did not live to follow up, a step which some of its critics dismissed as an action which "frees the slave but ignores the Negro." Through these long one hundred years, while slavery has vanished, progress for the Negro has been too often blocked and delayed. Equality before the law has not always meant equal treatment and opportunity. And the harmful, wasteful and wrongful results of racial discrimination and segregation still appear in virtually every aspect of national life, in virtually every part of the Nation.

The Negro baby born in America today—regardless of the section or state in which he is born—has about one-half as much chance of completing high school as a white baby born in the same place on the same day—one-third as much chance of completing college—one-third as much chance of becoming a professional man—twice as much chance of becoming unemployed—about one-seventh as much chance of earning $10,000 per year—a life expectancy which is seven years less—and the prospects of earning only half as much.

No American who believes in the basic truth that "all men are created equal, that they are endowed by their Creator with certain unalienable Rights," can fully excuse, explain or defend the picture these statistics portray. Race discrimination hampers our economic growth by preventing the maximum development and utilization of our manpower. It hampers our world leadership by contradicting at home the message we preach abroad. It mars the atmosphere of a united and classless society in which this Nation rose to greatness. It increases the costs of public welfare, crime, delinquency and disorder. Above all, it is wrong.

Therefore, let it be clear, in our own hearts and minds, that it is not merely because of the Cold War, and not merely because of the economic waste of discrimination, that we are committed to achieving true equality of opportunity. The basic reason is because it is right.

The cruel disease of discrimination knows no sectional or state boundaries. The continuing attack on this problem must be equally broad. It must be both private and public—it must be conducted at national, state and local levels—and it must include both legislative and executive action.

In the last two years, more progress has been made in securing the civil rights of all Americans than in any comparable period in our history. Progress has been made—through executive action, litigation, persuasion and private initiative—in achieving and protecting equality of opportunity in education, voting, transportation, employment, housing, government, and the enjoyment of public accommodations.

But pride in our progress must not give way to relaxation of our effort. Nor does progress in the Executive Branch enable the Legislative Branch to escape its own obligations. On the contrary, it is in the light of this nationwide progress, and in the belief that Congress will wish once again to meet its responsibilities in this matter, that I stress in the following agenda of existing and prospective action important legislative as well as administrative measures.

1. THE RIGHT TO VOTE

The right to vote in a free American election is the most powerful and precious right in the world—and it must not be denied on the grounds of race or color. It is a potent key to achieving other rights of citizenship. For American history—both recent and past—clearly reveals that the power of the ballot has enabled those who achieve it to win other achievements as well, to gain a full voice in the affairs of their state and nation, and to see their interests represented in the governmental bodies which affect their future. In a free society, those with the power to govern are necessarily responsive to those with the right to vote. . . .

An indication of the magnitude of the overall problem, as well as the need for speedy action, is a recent five-state survey disclosing over 200 counties in which fewer than 15% of the Negroes of voting age are registered to vote. This cannot continue. I am, therefore, recommending legislation to deal with this problem of judicial delay and administrative abuse in four ways:

First, to provide for interim relief while voting suits are proceeding through the courts in areas of demonstrated need, temporary Federal voting referees should be appointed to determine the qualifications of applicants for registration and voting during the pendency of a lawsuit in any county in which fewer than 15% of the eligible number of persons of any race claimed to be discriminated against are registered to vote. . . .

Second, voting suits brought under the Federal Civil Rights statutes should be accorded expedited treatment in the Federal courts. . . .

Third, the law should specifically prohibit the application of different tests, standards, practices, or procedures for different applicants seeking to register and vote in federal election. . . .

Fourth, completion of the sixth grade should, with respect to Federal elections, constitute a presumption that the applicant is literate. Literacy tests pose especially difficult problems in determining voter qualification. The essentially subjective judgment involved in each individual case, and the difficulty of challenging that judgment, have made literacy tests one of the cruelest and most abused of all voter qualification tests. . . .

Finally, the 87th Congress—after 20 years of effort— passed and referred to the states for ratification a Constitutional amendment to prohibit the levying of poll taxes as a condition to voting. Already thirteen states have ratified the proposed Amendment and in three more one body of the Legislature has acted. I urge every state legislature to take prompt action on this matter and to outlaw the poll tax—which has too long been an outmoded and arbitrary bar to voting participation by minority groups and others—as the 24th Amendment to the Constitution. This measure received bi-partisan sponsorship and endorsement in the Congress—and I shall continue to work with governors and legislative leaders of both parties in securing adoption of the anti-poll tax amendment.

II. EDUCATION

Nearly nine years have elapsed since the Supreme Court ruled that State laws requiring or permitting segregated schools violate the Constitution. That decision represented both good law and good judgment—it was both legally and morally right. Since that time it has become increasingly clear that neither violence nor legalistic evasions will be tolerated as a means of thwarting court-ordered desegregation, that closed schools are not an answer, and that responsible communities are able to handle the desegregation process in a calm and sensible manner. This is as it should be—for, as I stated to the Nation at the time of the Mississippi violence last September:

"... Our Nation is founded on the principle that observance of the law is the eternal safeguard of liberty, and defiance of the law is the surest road to tyranny. The law which we obey includes the final rulings of the courts, as well as the enactments of our legislative bodies. Even among law-abiding men, few laws are universally loved—but they are uniformly respected and not resisted. . . .

In [all] within its jurisdiction, the Executive Branch will continue its efforts to fulfill the Constitutional objective of an equal, non-segregated, educational opportunity for all children. . . .

I recommend, therefore, a program of Federal technical and financial assistance to aid school districts in the process of desegregation in compliance with the Constitution.

Finally, it is obvious that the unconstitutional and outmoded concept of "separate but equal" does not belong in the Federal statute books. This is particularly true with respect to higher education, where peaceful desegregation has been underway in practically every state for some time. I repeat, therefore, this Administration's recommendation of last year that this phrase be eliminated from the Morrill Land Grant College Act.

III. EXTENSION AND EXPANSION OF THE COMMISSION ON CIVIL RIGHTS

The Commission on Civil Rights, established by the Civil Rights Act of 1957, has been in operation for more than five years and is scheduled to expire on November 30, 1963. During this time it has fulfilled its statutory mandate by investigating deprivations of the right to vote and denials of equal protection of the laws in education, employment, housing and the administration of justice. The Commission's reports and recommendations have provided the basis for remedial action both by Congress and the Executive Branch. . . .

IV. EMPLOYMENT

Racial discrimination in employment is especially inju-
rious both to its victims and to the national economy. It
results in a great waste of human resources and creates
serious community problems. It is, moreover, inconsis-
tent with the democratic principle that no man should
be denied employment commensurate with his abilities
because of his race or creed or ancestry.

The President's Committee on Equal Employment
Opportunity, reconstituted by Executive Order in early
1961, has, under the leadership of the Vice President,
taken significant steps to eliminate racial discrimination by those who do business with the Government. . . .

Career civil servants will continue to be employed on
the basis of merit, and not color, in every agency of the
Federal Government, including all regional and local
offices.

This Government has also adopted a new Executive
policy with respect to the organization of its employees.
As part of this policy, only those Federal employee labor
organizations that do not discriminate on grounds of
race or color will be recognized. . . .

V. PUBLIC ACCOMMODATIONS

No act is more contrary to the spirit of our democracy
and Constitution—or more rightfully resented by a
Negro citizen who seeks only equal treatment—than
the barring of that citizen from restaurants, hotels, the-
atres, recreational areas and other public accommodations and facilities.

Wherever possible, this Administration has dealt
sternly with such acts. In 1961, the Justice Department

and the Interstate Commerce Commission successfully took action to bring an end to discrimination in rail and bus facilities. In 1962, the fifteen airports still maintaining segregated facilities were persuaded to change their practices, thirteen voluntarily and two others after the Department of Justice brought legal action. As a result of these steps, systematic segregation in interstate transportation has virtually ceased to exist. No doubt isolated instances of discrimination in transportation terminals, restaurants, rest rooms and other facilities will continue to crop up, but <u>any such discrimination will be dealt with promptly</u>.

In addition, restaurants and public facilities in buildings leased by the Federal Government have been opened up to all Federal employees in areas where previously they had been segregated. . . .

In short, the Executive Branch of the Federal Government, under this Administration and in all of its activities, now stands squarely behind the principle of equal opportunity, without segregation or discrimination, in the employment of Federal funds, facilities and personnel. All officials at every level are charged with the responsibility of implementing this principle—and a formal inter-departmental action group, under White House chairmanship, oversees this effort and follows through on each directive. For the first time, the full force of Federal executive authority is being exerted in the battle against race discrimination.

CONCLUSION

". . . The program outlined in this message should not provide the occasion for sectional bitterness. No state or section of this Nation can pretend a self-righteous role, for every area has its own civil rights problems.

Nor should the basic elements of this program be imperiled by partisanship. The proposals put forth are consistent with the platforms of both parties and with the positions of their leaders. Inevitably there will be dis-agreement about means and strategy. But I would hope that on issues of constitutional rights and freedom, as in matters affecting our national security, there is a funda-mental unity among us that will survive partisan debate over particular issues.

The centennial of the issuance of the Emancipation Proclamation is an occasion for celebration, for a sober assessment of our failures, and for rededication to the goals of freedom. Surely there could be no more mean-ingful observance of the centennial than the enactment of effective civil rights legislation and the continuation of effective executive action.

John F. Kennedy

Kennedy's letter to Congress was a clear indication of the bold new stance he was adopting regarding civil rights. Then, in June 1963, a confrontation took place that profoundly affected both Kennedy and the course of the civil rights movement. In events reminiscent of the James Meredith affair, Alabama governor George Wallace, whose campaign pledge had been "segregation now, segregation tomorrow, segregation forever," made it clear that he would, if necessary, physi-cally prevent African American students from enrolling at the Univer-sity of Alabama. When two black students appeared on campus and attempted to enter the building where enrollment took place, Wallace placed himself in the doorway, blocking their way. Outraged at the governor's actions, Kennedy sent federal marshals to demand that the students be allowed to enter. Wallace, however, refused to budge, forcing Kennedy to federalize the Alabama National Guard. Finally, Wallace stepped aside.

For Kennedy, the confrontation was a turning point. That same evening, although seriously concerned he might well be committing political suicide, he announced in a television and radio address to the nation that he was sending a bill to Congress asking it to enact laws that would, at last, give African Americans the right to "receive equal service in places . . . such as hotels and restaurants and theaters and retail stores" and the right "to register to vote . . . without interference or fear of reprisal." Afterward, reflecting on his address, Kennedy confided to an aide, "Sometimes you look at what you've done and the only thing you ask yourself is, 'What took you so long to do it?'"

The television cameras had hardly been removed when Kennedy received another telegram from Dr. King.

THE PRESIDENT
THE WHITE HOUSE

DEAR MR PRESIDENT I HAVE JUST LISTENED
TO YOUR SPEECH TO THE NATION IT WAS
ONE OF THE MOST ELOQUENT PROFOUND
AND UNEQUIVOCAL PLEAS FOR JUSTICE
AND THE FREEDOM OF ALL MEN EVER MADE
BY ANY PRESIDENT YOU SPOKE PASSION-
ATELY TO THE MORAL ISSUES INVOLVED IN
THE INTEGRATION STRUGGLE I AM SURE
THAT YOUR ENCOURAGING WORDS WILL
BRING A NEW SENSE OF HOPE TO THE MIL-
LIONS OF DISINHERITED PEOPLE OF OUR
COUNTRY YOUR MESSAGE WILL BECOME A

HALLMARK IN ANNALS OF AMERICAN
HISTORY. . . .

MARTIN LUTHER KING JR.

For John Kennedy, it was a proud moment. But his proposed legisla-
tion did not bring an end to civil unrest. In many quarters, in fact, it
strengthened the resolve of those intent on denying African Americans
their long overdue equal rights and opportunities. The day after Ken-
nedy's address, Medgar Evers, field secretary for the NAACP, was
gunned down in his driveway as his wife and children looked on. Three
days later, Kennedy received a telegram from Jackie Robinson, who,
along with lamenting the loss of Evers, raised an alarming and tragi-
cally prophetic specter.

1963 JUN 15 AM 7 26

WA 043 NL PD
TDN BROOKYN NY 14

THE PRESIDENT
THE WHITE HOUSE

IT MIGHT SEEM FANTASTIC TO IMAGINE
THAT EVEN IN THE STATE OF MISSISSIPPI
ANYONE WOULD SEEK TO DO INJURY TO A
NON-VIOLENT LEADER LIKE DR MARTIN
KING AS HE GOES THERE THIS MORNING
ON A MISSION OF SORROW. YET IT WAS
FANTASTIC BUT TRUE THAT SOME DE-
PRAVED ASSASSIN GUNNED DOWN ANOTHER

MAN OF NON-VIOLENCE THE LATE MED-
GAR EVERS WHOSE FUNERAL DR KING
AND HIS ASSOCIATES WILL BE ATTENDING
TODAY IN JACKSON. SHOULD HARM COME
TO DR KING TO ADD TO THE MISERY
WHICH DECENT AMERICANS OF BOTH
RACES EXPERIENCED WITH THE MURDER
OF MR EVERS THE RESTRAINT OF MANY
PEOPLE ALL OVER THIS NATION MIGHT
BURST ITS BONDS AND BRING ABOUT A
BRUTAL BLOODY HOLOCAUST THE LIKE OF
WHICH THIS COUNTRY HAS NOT SEEN. I
THEREFORE IMPLORE YOU IN THE SPIRIT
OF YOUR RECENT MAGNIFICENT APPEAL
FOR JUSTICE TO UTILIZE EVERY FEDERAL
FACILITY TO PROTECT A MAN SORELY
NEEDED FOR THIS ERA. FOR TO MILLIONS
MARTIN KING SYMBOLIZES THE BEARING
FORWARD OF THE TORCH FOR FREEDOM
SO SAVAGELY WRESTED FROM THE DYING
GRIP OF MEDGAR EVERS AMERICA NEEDS
AND THE WORLD CANNOT AFFORD TO
LOSE HIM TO THE WHIMS OF MURDEROUS
MANIACS

JACKIE ROBINSON

Kennedy, who had embraced the battle for civil rights late in his career, would go to his premature grave with the battle far from resolved. In the final months of his life, he would continue to push his civil rights agenda, including making a point of acknowledging those Southern leaders with the courage to overturn long-held discriminatory practices.

July 3, 1963

Dear Governor:

   Upon my return, I learned of your issuing an executive order forbidding racial discrimination in all businesses licensed by the Commonwealth of Kentucky and its agencies. This is a most significant step and I believe it can have an impact beyond the boundaries of Kentucky in demonstrating to so many other states and communities the desirability of recognizing the unreasonableness, inequity and basic inhumanity of practices precluding Americans from buying goods or services in certain commercial establishments solely on the artificial distinction of color.

   Your action is bold, appropriate, and constructive and I congratulate you.

                                                    Sincerely,
                                                    John F. Kennedy

Honorable Bert T. Combs
Governor of Kentucky
Frankfort, Kentucky

Though many African Americans and liberals were frustrated by Kennedy's cautious approach to civil rights, others were grateful for his attention to the issue and for the gains he did achieve. Typical of these was a letter he received, only a month before he was murdered, from the international musical and political icon, the American-born French singer, dancer, and actress Josephine Baker.

Josephine Baker
Les Milandes
Castelnaud-Fayrac
Dordogne
Les Milandes, October 9, 1963

Mr. President:

I was particularly touched by the kind things about me that His Excellency Lee G. White wrote in your name in his letter of September 30, 1963.

I wish to express to you my gratitude and my sincere good wishes for Mrs. Kennedy and yourself, and to tell you how deeply I appreciate the noble and courageous effort you have made to reach a satisfactory and just solution of the serious segregation problem in the United States and race problems in general.

I shall always be ready to work for the victory of that cause, and I shall spare no efforts to serve it, as long as the fight is fair on both sides and conducted calmly and with dignity.

In fact, it would not be possible for me to take sides. I have always been in favor of a rapprochement in a spirit of brotherhood, and I shall protest with the same vigor against discrimination, from whichever side it may come, and against all violence without exception, since I am convinced that violence will be a bad course to take in the future.

I shall be very happy to return to the United States, the country of my birth, to which I am still deeply attached, in order to contribute my services at two charity concerts, one to be given in Carnegie Hall on October 12, and the other in Philadelphia on the 18th of the same month, for the benefit of the "March of Dimes."

I beg you to accept, Mr. President, the expression of my highest esteem.

Please convey to Mrs. Kennedy my children's kind regards and my own, and my very friendly sentiments.

(Signed) Josephine Baker

CHAPTER 4

★　★　★　★　★

World in Crisis

"WHEN I RAN for the Presidency of the United States..." John Kennedy stated, "I couldn't realize...how heavy and constant would be the burdens." And no wonder. No American president had ever faced a greater array of major challenges or more potentially catastrophic crises than did Kennedy.

In one of his first briefings after being elected, Kennedy was told of a bold plan developed during the Eisenhower administration. Designed to overthrow Cuban leader Fidel Castro and replace him with a noncommunist government friendly to the United States, the plan called for an invasion of Cuba by Cuban exiles secretly trained in invasion tactics by the Central Intelligence Agency.

After his military leaders assured him that the invasion would be both totally secret and successful, Kennedy approved the plan, and on April 17, 1961, the invasion was launched at a Cuban coastal area known as the Bay of Pigs. Too large to be kept secret and too small to be successful, it was a total disaster. Having learned of the impending attack, Castro had positioned twenty thousand troops on the beaches to repel the assault. In the disaster that followed, more than one hundred invaders were killed and almost twelve hundred were captured.

He had been president for only three months, but it would be the greatest defeat of John Kennedy's career. He took full responsibility for the fiasco, stating, "There's an old saying that victory has a hundred fathers and defeat is an orphan." To his surprise, the American public rallied around him. "It's amazing," he said afterward, "the more I screw up, the higher my ratings go."

The American public may have forgiven Kennedy, but Soviet premier Nikita Khrushchev had a much different reaction. Astounded that the young president would allow himself to become trapped in such a blunder, he sought to take advantage of what he perceived as Kennedy's weaknesses when, two months after the Cuban debacle, the two leaders met for the first time in Vienna.

Throughout the meetings, a bombastic and belligerent Khrushchev bullied Kennedy, treating the president, in Kennedy's words, "like a little boy." Returning home, Kennedy observed, "I think I know why he treated me like this. He thinks because of the Bay of Pigs that I'm inexperienced. Probably thinks I'm stupid. Maybe most important, he thinks I had no guts."

The issue that had most commanded Kennedy's and Khrushchev's attention in Vienna was Berlin, the city that, at the end of World War II, had been split into Soviet-occupied East Berlin and Western-occupied West Berlin. By the time that the two leaders met in Vienna, some four million East Germans, smarting under the oppressive communist regime, had left their homes and fled into West Berlin, a development that dramatically weakened the East German economy and, as one observer noted, "dramatized to all the world their choice of freedom over communism."

Assessing the situation, Kennedy remarked, "This is unbearable for Khrushchev. East Germany is hemorrhaging to death. The entire Eastern bloc is in danger. He has to do something to stop this. Perhaps a wall. And there's not a damn thing we can do about it."

Prophetic words. On August 13, 1961, workers began constructing the long, heavily guarded wall dividing the eastern and western parts of Berlin. From that moment on, Berlin was at the heart of the cold war. As the scholars at the John F. Kennedy Presidential Memorial Library and Museum have noted, the wall would be "a chilling symbol of the Iron Curtain that divided all of Europe between communism and democracy."

Prophetic also was Kennedy's declaration that the wall would go up without armed intervention. "All wars start from stupidity," he declared. "God knows I'm not an isolationist, but it seems particularly stupid to risk a million Americans over an argument about access rights on an Autobahn in the Soviet zone of Germany, or because the Germans want Germany reunified. If I'm going to threaten Russia with a nuclear war, it will be for much bigger and more important reasons than that. Before I back Khrushchev against a wall and put him to a final test, the freedom of all Western Europe will have to be at stake."

Alarmingly, little more than a month later, there was a "bigger and more important reason." And not only was the freedom of Western Europe hanging in the balance but also the survival of the world. That Khrushchev would authorize the placing of nuclear missiles in Cuba, capable of striking both the U.S. East Coast and targets as far west as Montana, revealed above all else that his opinion of the American president as being weak, inexperienced, and indecisive had not changed since Vienna. Kennedy proved him wrong. During a thirteen-day period in which the world held its breath, Kennedy showed himself to be bolder than Khrushchev had anticipated, informing the Soviet premier and people throughout the globe that "it shall be the policy of [the United States] to regard any nuclear missile launched from Cuba . . . as an attack on the United States, requiring a full retaliatory response on the Soviet Union." He also established his decisiveness, rejecting an

all-out bombing invasion of Cuba, which his military men had vehemently urged, in favor of a quarantine blocking the passage of
Soviet missile-carrying ships.

In the end, however, it was the frank and mostly secret exchange
of letters—providing an unprecedented, continuous line of communication between two men who held the fate of the world in
their hands—that prevented the unthinkable from taking place.
For Kennedy, it was his greatest triumph. In England, Prime Minister Harold Macmillan declared that the American president, by
his actions, had earned his place in history. As Theodore Sorensen
would observe, Cuba, which had been the locale of Kennedy's
greatest failure, had become the site of his greatest success.

Both Kennedy and Khrushchev were shaken by how danger-
ously close they had come to nuclear war. "The two most powerful
nations had been squared off against each other," Khrushchev
stated, "each with its finger on the button." "It is insane," Kennedy
said, "that two men sitting on opposite sides of the world should
be able to decide to bring an end to civilization."

Now, again through a series of private letters, the two men
opened their most serious dialogue on achieving nuclear disarmament. At the same time, Kennedy pursued what he termed his
"strategy of peace." Speaking at American University in Washington D.C., he declared, "If we cannot end our differences at least we
can make the world a safe place for diversity." Calling for an end to
the cold war, he said that "in the final analysis, our most basic
common link is that we share this small planet. We all breathe
the same air. We all cherish our children's future. And we are all
mortal."

On August 5, 1963, a treaty banning nuclear testing in the atmosphere, in outer space, and underwater was signed. It was called
the Limited Test Ban Treaty since agreement could not be reached
on monitoring underground nuclear testing. But as Kennedy told
the nation, a limited test ban was "safer by far for the United States
than an unlimited nuclear arms race."

He had indeed gained his place in history through his actions during the Cuban missile confrontation and in achieving a long-sought-after nuclear arms treaty. But he continued to be tested, particularly in a place far removed from the Caribbean, Berlin, and the Soviet Union. When Kennedy took office, few Americans had heard of South Vietnam or North Vietnam, let alone knew where they were. Yet, in his battle against the spread of communism, which came to dominate his presidency, these two adjoining Asian countries presented him with his greatest dilemma. As communist North Vietnam took aim at noncommunist South Vietnam, Kennedy was faced with the question: Should he send in combat troops to help prevent the north Vietnamese takeover, or should he keep the United States out of the conflict?

Kennedy's dilemma was exacerbated by the conflicting advice he received from both inside and outside the White House. Secretary of State Dean Rusk, Secretary of Defense Robert McNamara, and chief military adviser Maxwell Taylor were vocal in their belief that the United States needed to stay in Vietnam until the war was won. Under Secretary of State George Ball and elder statesman W. Averell Harriman vehemently disagreed. Senate Majority Leader Mike Mansfield, stating that "South Vietnam could be a quicksand for us," told Kennedy that the only possible results of such a decision would be either "an indecisive and costly war along the Korean line, a major war with China . . . [or] a total world conflict." Influential Democratic senator Stuart Symington of Missouri, on the other hand, cabled Kennedy from Saigon, saying, "It seems to me we ought to try to hold this place. Otherwise this part of the world is sure to go down the drain."

Kennedy himself seemed to equivocate. As late as September 2, 1963, in an interview with newsman Walter Cronkite, he proclaimed that the war needed to be left up to the South Vietnamese. "It is their war," he said. We can help them, we can send them equipment, we can send our men out there as advisers . . . but in the final analysis it is their people and their government who have to win or lose the struggle. All we can do is help." Yet, according to Theodore Sorensen, during the same period, Kennedy stated that abandoning South Vietnam "only makes it easy for the Communists. I think we should stay."

Shortly before he left for his fatal trip to Dallas, Kennedy ordered Michael Forrestal, one of the chief aides to national security adviser McGeorge Bundy, to prepare a study of every option he had in Vietnam, including "how to get out of there." Perhaps the best insight into what he really intended to do can be found in statements that, according to his close friend and biographer William Manchester, he made to Mike Mansfield. According to Manchester, Kennedy told the senate majority leader that he agreed with him that every American, including the sixteen thousand "advisers" Kennedy had sent to South Vietnam, should be brought home. "But," Manchester quoted Kennedy as saying, "I can't do it until 1965." According to Manchester, as soon as Mansfield left their meeting, Kennedy turned to his aide and confidante Kenneth O'Donnell and said, "In 1965 I'll become one of the most unpopular presidents in history. I'll be damned everywhere as a Communist appeaser. But I don't care. If I tried to pull out completely now from Vietnam, we would have another Joe McCarthy Red scare on our hands, but I can do it after I'm reelected, so we had better make damned sure I am reelected."

★   ★   ★   ★   ★

On April 18, 1961, as the Bay of Pigs invasion entered its second day, Kennedy received a letter from Nikita Khrushchev. Charging the United States with armed aggression, the Soviet leader warned Kennedy that if he did not stop the "little war," he would risk "an incomparable conflagration" with the Soviet Union.

Moscow, April 18, 1961

Mr. President,

I send you this message in an hour of alarm, fraught
with danger for the peace of the whole world. Armed aggression has begun against Cuba. It is a secret to no one
that the armed bands invading this country were trained,
equipped and armed in the United States of America.
The planes which are bombing Cuban cities belong to
the United States of America, the bombs they are dropping are being supplied by the American Government.

All of this evokes here in the Soviet Union an understandable feeling of indignation on the part of the
Soviet Government and the Soviet people.

Only recently, in exchanging opinions through our
respective representatives, we talked with you about
the mutual desire of both sides to put forward joint efforts directed toward improving relations between our
countries and eliminating the danger of war. Your statement a few days ago that the USA would not participate
in military activities against Cuba created the impression that the top leaders of the United States were taking into account the consequences for general peace
and for the USA itself which aggression against Cuba
could have. How can what is being done by the United
States in reality be understood, when an attack on Cuba
has now become a fact?

It is still not late to avoid the irreparable. The Government of the USA still has the possibility of not allowing
the flame of war ignited by interventions in Cuba to
grow into an incomparable conflagration. I approach
you, Mr. President, with an urgent call to put an end to
aggression against the Republic of Cuba. Military ar-

mament and the world political situation are such at this time that any so-called "little war" can touch off a chain reaction in all parts of the globe.

As far as the Soviet Union is concerned, there should be no mistake about our position: We will render the Cuban people and their government all necessary help to repel armed attack on Cuba. We are sincerely interested in a relaxation of international tension, but if others proceed toward sharpening, we will answer them in full measure. And in general it is hardly possible so to conduct matters that the situation is settled in one area and conflagration extinguished, while a new conflagration is ignited in another area.

I hope that the Government of the USA will consider our views as dictated by the sole concern not to allow steps which could lead the world to military catastrophe.

In his immediate reply, Kennedy informed Khrushchev that he was under a "serious misapprehension" as to what was taking place in Cuba. Intensifying the cold war rhetoric, Kennedy warned Khrushchev not to use the United States' determination to support Cubans "who wish to see a democratic system in an independent Cuba" as an excuse to "inflame other areas of the world."

Washington, April 18, 1961

Mr. Chairman:

You are under a serious misapprehension in regard to events in Cuba. For months there has been evident and growing resistance to the Castro dictatorship. More than 100,000 refugees have recently fled from Cuba into neighboring countries. Their urgent hope is naturally to assist their fellow Cubans in their struggle for freedom. Many of these refugees fought alongside Dr. Castro against the Batista dictatorship; among them are prominent leaders of his own original movement and government.

These are unmistakable signs that Cubans find intolerable the denial of democratic liberties and the subversion of the 26th of July Movement by an alien-dominated regime. It cannot be surprising that, as resistance within Cuba grows, refugees have been using whatever means are available to return and support their countrymen in the continuing struggle for freedom. Where people are denied the right of choice, recourse to such struggle is the only means of achieving their liberties.

I have previously stated, and I repeat now, that the United States intends no military intervention in Cuba. In the event of any military intervention by outside force we will immediately honor our obligations under the inter-American system to protect this hemisphere against external aggression. While refraining from military intervention in Cuba, the people of the United States do not conceal their admiration for Cuban patriots who wish to see a democratic system in an independent Cuba. The United States Government can take no action to stifle the spirit of liberty.

I have taken careful note of your statement that the events in Cuba might affect peace in all parts of the world. I trust that this does not mean that the Soviet Government, using the situation in Cuba as a pretext, is planning to inflame other areas of the world. I would like to think that your government has too great a sense of responsibility to embark upon any enterprise so dangerous to general peace.

I agree with you as to the desirability of steps to improve the international atmosphere. I continue to hope that you will cooperate in opportunities now available to this end. A prompt cease-fire and peaceful settlement of the dangerous situation in Laos, cooperation with the United Nations in the Congo and a speedy conclusion of an acceptable treaty for the banning of nuclear tests would be constructive steps in this direction. The regime in Cuba could make a similar contribution by permitting the Cuban people freely to determine their own future by democratic processes and freely to cooperate with their Latin American neighbors.

I believe, Mr. Chairman, that you should recognize that free peoples in all parts of the world do not accept the claim of historical inevitability for Communist revolution. What your government believes is its own business; what it does in the world is the world's business. The great revolution in the history of man, past, present and future, is the revolution of those determined to be free.

John F. Kennedy

While, both publicly and privately, Kennedy took sole responsibility for the Bay of Pigs disaster, he made it clear that he was determined to learn from what historians would eventually call the "perfect failure." Among the "lessons" he received was one from political scientist Edward Banfield, who reached back to the early-sixteenth-century writings of Machiavelli to remind Kennedy of the folly of trusting exiles to carry out one's goals.

HARVARD UNIVERSITY
FACULTY OF ARTS AND SCIENCES

April 25

Dear Former Colleague,

How Dangerous It Is To Trust To the Representation of Exiles

". . . And as to their vain hopes and promises, such is their extreme desire to return to their homes that they naturally believe many things that are not true, and add many others on purpose; so that, with what they really believe and what they say they believe, they will fill you with hopes to that degree that if you attempt to act upon them you will incur a fruitless expense, or engage in an undertaking that will involve you in ruin."

Machiavelli, Discourses, Ch 31

Cordially,
Ed Banfield

In the wake of the Bay of Pigs disaster, as Kennedy and Khrushchev prepared to hold their first face-to-face meetings in Vienna, they carried with them the hopes of an anxious world, hopes expressed by the dozens of cables, letters, and telegrams that Kennedy received at the U.S. embassy in the Austrian capital.

To the President of the United States of America
Mr. John Kennedy

We greet with great pleasure and satisfaction the meeting of the President of the United States Mr. Kennedy and the Prime Minister of Soviet Union Mr. Khrouchtchev [sic].

We hope that this your meeting will be an expression of the mutual desire for peace and that the results of your conference will contribute to positive results in important international problems of day, such as the conclusion of peace treaty with Germany, banning of nuclear weapons and their tests and fulfillment of general disarmament. We express our urgent desire that your meeting would strengthen friendly and confident relations between United States and Soviet Union and thus contribute to positive peaceful development of the whole world situation.

We will follow with keen interest your meeting wishing that it would have as good and as positive results as possible for the cause of peace.

In Helsinki the 26th May 1961

Meeting of Uudenmaan Rauhanneuvosto

In the name of the meeting

Voitto Mikkola
Secretary

Several of the messages from private citizens that Kennedy received in Vienna, like this one, warned of the dire consequences that would result if the leaders of the world's two greatest powers could not find a path to peace.

NEW HAVEN CONN 48 1 1055P

LT PRESIDENT KENNEDY
US EMBASSY VIENNA

DEAR PRESIDENT KENNEDY SURELY
COMPROMISES CAN BE FOUND TO END
ARMS RACE NEITHER COMMUNISM NOR
CAPITALISM BOTH IMPERFECT AS THEY
NOW EXIST HAS RIGHT TO THREATEN
MANKIND WITH EXTERMINATION
SENDING SAME MESSAGE TO PREMIER
KHRUSHCHEV

SEYMOUR SEGALOFF BLOSSOM SEGALOFF 23
DIXWELL AVE

*Some of the communiqués offered simple but direct words of encour-
agement.*

PRESIDENT KENNEDY CARE AMERICAN
EMBASSY VIENNA=

WE KNOW YOU WILL BE RIGHT =
RUBY AND BOB +

*Others, from private citizens, including the man famous for the devel-
opment of shock therapy, offered solutions.*

Lothar B. Kalinowsky
115 East 62nd Street
New York 26, N.Y.
Regent 7.0600

May 28, 1961

The President,
Mr. John F. Kennedy
American Embassy
Vienna, Austria

Dear Mr. President:

A possibility which a layman presents to you at this crucial moment as a simultaneous solution to several problems would be to place Berlin under United Nations control, and to make it the headquarters of the United Nations.

This would help to solve the Berlin question, to take Berlin out of the reunification of Germany, restore it as an important hub between West and East, and finally solve some of the serious problems resulting from the United Nations site in New York.

As to my background, I can only refer to data in "Who's Who".

Most respectfully yours,
Lothar B. Kalinowsky, M.D.

And at least one took a very different tone.

4125 Broadway
Indianapolis
Indiana

Dear President Kennedy,

There is a rumor that you intend to retreat on Berlin in return for a neutral Laos. Don't do it! Don't betray us—Americans, Germans, the world.

Yours truly,
Mrs. Richard Manetta

The most touching of all came from a Minnesota boy.

May 27, 1961

Dears Pres. Kennedy and Dear Mr. Kruschev,

I am 11 year old and I wonder what My future and the future of 11 year old Russian boys will be? If you President Kennedy and you Mr Kruschev will try to be real friend Maybe the American boys and the Russian boys will in the year of 1999. If both of you are real friends it will mean life to all boys and girls. Please try to be friends and help the whole world.

I save stamps so would you help me out by both signing these stamps [I sent you] and put the date on them and mail them to me. . . . I hope I can get you each to sign the stamps I sent to you and Mr. Kruschev.

K for Kennedy and K for Kruschev and K for Kindness so Why not be real friends,

Your friend,
George H. Garland

Route #1—Box 592
Excelsior, Minn.

On August 13, 1961, the day that the Soviets began stringing barbed wire as a prelude to constructing the Berlin Wall, West Berlin mayor Willy Brandt was on a train heading for the next stop in his campaign to win the German chancellorship. When the train reached its destination and Brandt learned of the closing of the border, he immediately flew to Berlin to assess the situation. Three days later, outraged at the United States, as well as England and France for, in his view, having done nothing to prevent the building of the wall, Brandt sent an angry cable to Kennedy.

17 AUGUST 1961

DEAR MR. PRESIDENT:

AFTER DEVELOPMENTS LAST THREE DAYS MY CITY, WISH CONVEY TO YOU IN PERSONAL, INFORMAL LETTER SOME OF MY THOUGHTS AND VIEWPOINTS.

MEASURES OF ULBRICHT REGIME, SUPPORTED BY SOVUNION AND OTHER EAST BLOC COUNTRIES, HAVE ALMOST FULLY DESTROYED REMNANTS FOUR-POWER STATUS. WHILE IN THE PAST ALLIED COMMANDANTS HAVE EVEN PROTESTED AGAINST PARADES BY SO-CALLED PEOPLES' ARMY, THIS TIME, AFTER MILITARY OCCUPATION OF EAST SECTOR BY PEOPLES' ARMY, THEY HAVE LIMITED THEMSELVES TO DELAYED AND NOT VERY VIGOROUS STEP.

ILLEGAL SOVEREIGNTY OF EAST BERLIN
GOVERNMENT WAS ACKNOWLEDGED BY
ACQUIESCING IN THE RESTRICTIONS OF
THE NUMBER OF CROSSING POINTS AND OF
ENTRY INTO THE EAST SECTOR. I REGARD
THIS ENCROACHMENT AS THE MOST SERI-
OUS IN THE POSTWAR HISTORY OF THIS
CITY SINCE THE BLOCKADE.

THIS DEVELOPMENT HAS NOT CHANGED
WILL TO RESIST OF WEST BERLIN POPULA-
TION, BUT HAS TENDED TO AROUSE DOUBTS
AS TO DETERMINATION OF THREE POWERS
AND THEIR ABILITY TO REACT. IN THIS CON-
NECTION THE DECISIVE FACTOR IS THAT
THE WEST HAS ALWAYS SPECIFICALLY IN-
VOKED THE EXISTING FOUR-POWER STATUS.

I AM WELL AWARE THAT EXISTING GUAR-
ANTEES FOR FREEDOM OF POPULATION,
PRESENCE OF TROOPS AND FREE ACCESS
APPLY ONLY WEST BERLIN. HOWEVER, THIS
IS MATTER OF A DEEP WOUND IN LIFE OF
GERMAN PEOPLE AND OF BEING FORCED
OUT OF SPHERES OF COMMON RESPONSIBIL-
ITY (BERLIN AND GERMANY AS A WHOLE)
AFFECTING WHOLE WESTERN PRESTIGE.

I SEE POLITICAL PSYCHOLOGICAL DAN-
GERS IN TWO RESPECTS:

(1) INACTIVITY AND MERE DEFENSIVE
POSTURE CAN BRING ABOUT CRISIS
OF CONFIDENCE IN WESTERN
POWERS;

(2) INACTIVITY AND MERE DEFENSIVE
POSTURE CAN LEAD TO EXAGGER-

John Kennedy was an early supporter of Martin Luther King Jr. and helped arrange his release from custody after a 1960 jailing in Atlanta. But King, like many African American leaders, felt Kennedy was too cautious and constantly pressed the president to take stronger action on civil rights. (Library of Congress)

Jackie Robinson, who broke the color line in the major leagues, was an outspoken advocate for equality after leaving baseball. He wrote bluntly to President Kennedy, warning that if he neglected civil rights greater turmoil would follow. (Associated Press)

As racial tensions continued to rise, Mississippi's segregationist governor Ross Barnett attempted to obstruct African American student James Meredith from enrolling at Ole Miss in September 1962. In a sternly worded telegram, Kennedy questioned Barnett about his interference with federal court orders. (Associated Press)

Kennedy meets in the Oval Office with several civil rights leaders assembled for the March on Washington. (He did not attend the march, perhaps a reason for the air of awkwardness in the photo.) Martin Luther King Jr. and John Lewis are at left, next to Kennedy is A. Philip Randolph, and at right is Whitney Young.

The crises in Birmingham, Mississippi, and elsewhere persuaded Kennedy to take bolder steps on behalf of racial equality, beginning with a major civil rights bill. Here, Kennedy addresses the nation on his proposed legislation. African American leaders hailed the president's action as a historic step forward.

One black public figure who praised Kennedy's progress on civil rights was singer Josephine Baker. Baker lived in France but had long been outspoken on American racial issues; here (at center) she appears at a public protest over the acquittal of Emmett Till's murderers. (Corbis)

Kennedy delivers his now-famous speech to thousands of Berliners in June 1963. "Freedom is indivisible," he told the crowd, "and when one man is enslaved, all are not free."

Kennedy meets with West Berlin Mayor Willy Brandt. The president's "Ich bin ein Berliner" speech did much to repair the once strained relations between the two leaders.

Kennedy and Nikita Khrushchev meet in Vienna in June 1961. During their meetings, the Russian leader dominated the novice president—emboldening him, many believe, to install offensive nuclear missiles in Cuba.

A meeting of the Executive Committee, or "ExComm," convened to deal with the Cuban missile crisis in October 1962. In an atmosphere of unrelenting tension, Kennedy and his advisers gingerly groped for a way to face down the Soviet Union without provoking nuclear war. At right, President Kennedy leans over the table with Secretary of State Dean Rusk; Robert Kennedy, the attorney general, paces at left.

Each of the ExComm members had his own opinion as to how to respond to the presence of nuclear missiles in Cuba. Kennedy (with back to camera) talks with Special Assistant McGeorge Bundy, Assistant Secretary of Defense Paul Nitze, Chairman of the Joint Chiefs of Staff General Maxwell Taylor, and Secretary of Defense Robert McNamara.

Kennedy and Arthur Schlesinger Jr. meet in the Oval Office. Schlesinger would prove to be one of the president's most informed and trusted advisers.

Kennedy calls on a reporter during one of his many regular press conferences. No president has ever welcomed these exchanges with the press more than Kennedy.

Throughout his presidency, Kennedy regarded British prime minister Harold Macmillan as his most valued ally. He regularly counted on him for advice and support.

Kennedy signs the Nuclear Test Ban Treaty in October 1963. Speaking of himself and his Soviet counterpart, Nikita Khrushchev, Kennedy said, "It is insane that two men, sitting on opposite sides of the world, should be able to decide to bring an end to civilization." The letters exchanged by Kennedy and Khrushchev were a vital part of the process by which their understanding was achieved.

Linus Pauling earned the Nobel Prize in Chemistry in 1954; eight years later, for his ardent antiwar advocacy, he received the Nobel Prize for Peace. He wrote passionately to President Kennedy urging nuclear disarmament—and later to thank him for achieving the test ban treaty.

A public speech by Kennedy on the conflict in Indochina, March 1961. The growing war in Vietnam and the ineffective, corrupt government of South Vietnam's Ngo Dinh Diem bedeviled the Kennedy administration.

Diem in a 1957 photo. In letters Kennedy expressed support for the Vietnamese leader but carefully made few military commitments. (U.S. Air Force)

Jacqueline Kennedy was an indispensable asset to JFK both as a candidate's wife and even more so as first lady. Here she charms French culture minister André Malraux.

John Kenneth Galbraith was both a key presidential adviser and a close friend of the Kennedy family. Here, as U.S. ambassador to India, he escorts Jacqueline Kennedy during her trip to that country.

JFK at the helm of the Coast Guard yacht *Manitou*, August 1962.

A characteristic Kennedy pose from a speech in Pennsylvania, October 1962. Kennedy believed in "vigor" and showed it as an orator.

JFK in the Oval Office with his children, Caroline and John (John-John), in October 1962. Kennedy described this shot, taken by White House photographer Cecil Stoughton, as his favorite picture.

Kennedy had always relished his Irish heritage. But even he was overwhelmed by the extraordinary welcome he received during a presidential visit to his ancestral home in June 1963.

Kennedy meets with Israeli premier David Ben-Gurion in 1961. The two would exchange highly charged letters over Israel's nuclear program, which the United States tried strenuously, and unsuccessfully, to hold back, fearing its effect on Middle East and cold war tensions. (Corbis)

Jacqueline Kennedy, flanked by the president's brothers Robert and Edward, walks in her husband's funeral procession, November 25, 1963. To the right of Edward Kennedy is their brother-in-law, Peace Corps director Sargent Shriver.

ATED SELF-CONFIDENCE ON PART OF
EAST BERLIN REGIME WHOSE NEWS-
PAPERS ALREADY TODAY BOAST OF
SUCCESS ITS DEMONSTRATION OF
MILITARY POWER.

SOVUNION HAS ACHIEVED HALF ITS FREE
CITY PROPOSALS THROUGH USE GERMAN
PEOPLES' ARMY. THE SECOND ACT IS A QUES-
TION OF TIME. AFTER SECOND ACT BERLIN
WOULD BE LIKE A GHETTO, WHICH HAS NOT
ONLY LOST ITS FUNCTION AS REFUGE OF
FREEDOM AND SYMBOL OF HOPE FOR RE-
UNIFICATON BUT WHICH WOULD ALSO BE
SEVERED FROM FREE PART GERMANY. IN-
STEAD OF FLIGHT TO BERLIN, WE MIGHT
THEN EXPERIENCE BEGINNING OF FLIGHT
FROM BERLIN.
IN THIS SITUATION I CONSIDER IT PROPER
THAT WESTERN POWERS, WHILE DEMAND-
ING RE-ESTABLISHMENT FOUR-POWER
RESPONSIBILITIES, PROCLAIM AT SAME
TIME A THREE-POWER STATUS FOR WEST
BERLIN. THREE POWERS SHOULD REITER-
ATE GUARANTEE THEIR PRESENCE IN WEST
BERLIN UNTIL GERMAN REUNIFICATION
AND, IF NECESSARY, HAVE THIS SUPPORTED
BY PLEBISCITE POPULATION WEST BERLIN
AND FEDREP. MUST ALSO BE SAID CLEARLY
THAT GERMAN QUESTION IS IN NO WAY
SETTLED FOR WESTERN POWERS BUT THAT
THEY MUST INSIST UPON PEACE SETTLE-
MENT CORRESPONDING TO RIGHT OF SELF-
DETERMINATION OF GERMAN PEOPLE AND

SECURITY INTERESTS OF ALL CONCERNED. WOULD ALSO CONSIDER ADVISABLE THAT WEST ON OWN INITIATIVE BRING BERLIN QUESTION BEFORE UN, AT LEAST ON BASIS THAT USSR HAS VIOLATED DECLARATION HUMAN RIGHTS IN MOST FLAGRANT MANNER. APPEARS BETTER TO ME PUT USSR IN POSITION OF GUILTY PARTY THAN TO HAVE TO DISCUSS SAME THEME AFTER MOTION BY OTHER STATES.

I EXPECT FROM SUCH STEPS NO SIGNIFICANT MATERIAL CHANGE PRESENT SITUATION AND RECOLLECT NOT WITHOUT BITTERNESS DECLARATIONS REJECTING NEGOTIATIONS WITH USSR ON BASIS ONE SHOULD NOT NEGOTIATE UNDER PRESSURE. WE NOW HAVE STATE OF ACCOMPLISHED EXTORTION, AND ALREADY I HEAR IT WILL NOT BE POSSIBLE TURN DOWN NEGOTIATIONS. IN SUCH SITUATION, WHEN POSSIBILITY OF INITIATIVE FOR ACTION IS ALREADY SO SMALL, IT IS ALL THE MORE IMPORTANT AT LEAST TO DEMONSTRATE POLITICAL INITIATIVE.

AFTER ACQUIESCENCE IN SOV STEP WHICH IS ILLEGAL, AND HAS BEEN TERMED ILLEGAL, AND IN VIEW MANY TRAGEDIES OCCURING TODAY EAST BERLIN AND SOVZONE, WE WILL NOT BE SPARED RISKS OF ULTIMATE DECISION. IT WOULD BE WELCOMED IF AMERICAN GARRISON WERE TO BE DEMONSTRATIVELY STRENGTHENED.

I CONSIDER SITUATION SERIOUS ENOUGH, MR. PRESIDENT, TO WRITE TO YOU IN ALL

FRANKNESS AS IS POSSIBLE ONLY BETWEEN
FRIENDS WHO TRUST EACH OTHER COM-
PLETELY.

(SIGNED) YOUR WILLY BRANDT

On August 17, 1961, in a letter authorized by Kennedy, the United States formally protested the Soviet Union's "flagrant and particularly serious actions in Berlin."

The Embassy of the United States presents its compliments to the Minister of Foreign Affairs and upon instructions of its Government has the honor to direct the most serious attention of the Government of the U.S.S.R. to the following.

On August 13, East German authorities put into effect several measures regulating movement and the boundary of the western sectors and the Soviet sector of the city of Berlin. These measures have the effect of limiting, to a degree approaching complete prohibition, passage from the Soviet sector to the western sector of the city. These measures were accompanied by the closing of the sector boundary by a sizable deployment of police forces and by military detachments brought into Berlin for this purpose.

All this is a flagrant, and particularly serious, violation of the quadripartite status of Berlin. Freedom of movement with respect to Berlin was reaffirmed by the quadripartite agreement of New York of May 4, 1949, and by the decision taken at Paris on June 20, 1949, by the Council of the Ministers of Foreign Affairs of the Four Powers. The United States Government has never accepted that limitations can be imposed on freedom of movement within Berlin. The boundary between the Soviet sector and the western sectors of Berlin is not a state frontier. The United States Government considers the measures which the East German authorities have taken are illegal. It reiterates that it does not accept the pretension that the Soviet sector of Berlin forms a part of the so-called "German Democratic Republic" and that Berlin is situated on its territory. Such a pretension is in itself a violation of the solemnly pledged word of the U.S.S.R. in the Agreement on the Zones of Occupation in Germany and the administration of Greater Berlin. Moreover, the United States Government cannot admit the right of the East German authorities to authorize their armed forces to enter the Soviet sector of Berlin.

By the very admission of the East German authorities, the measures which have just been taken are motivated by the fact that an ever increasing number of inhabitants of East Germany wish to leave this territory. The reasons for this exodus are known. They are simply the internal difficulties in East Germany.

To judge by the terms of a declaration of the Warsaw Pact powers published on August 13, the measures in question are supposed to have been recommended to the East German authorities by those powers. The United States Government notes that the powers which associated themselves with the U.S.S.R. by signing the Warsaw Pact are thus intervening in a domain in which they have no competence.

It is to be noted that this declaration states that the measures taken by the East German authorities are "in the interests of the German peoples themselves". It is difficult to see any basis for this statement, or to understand why it should be for the members of the Warsaw

Pact to decide what are the interests of the German people. It is evident that no Germans, particularly those
whose freedom of movement is being forcibly restrained,
think this is so. This would become abundantly clear if
all Germans were allowed a free choice, and the principle of self-determination were also applied in the Soviet
sector of Berlin and East Germany.

The United States Government solemnly protests
against the measures referred to above, for which it holds
the Soviet Government responsible. The United States
Government expects the Soviet Government to put an
end to these illegal measures. This unilateral infringe-
ment of the quadripartite status of Berlin can only increase existing tension and dangers.

*Outraged as he was by the Soviets' actions, Kennedy was also far from
pleased with the tone of the letter he had received from Willy Brandt.
But he realized that both the situation and the letter required a carefully conceived and worded reply. Clearly stating his belief that the issue of a divided Berlin, serious as it was, was not one that warranted
going to war over, Kennedy pledged a significant reinforcement of
American and Allied troops as an answer to the "long-range Soviet
threat to Berlin and to us all."*

August 18, 1961

Dear Mayor Brandt:

I have read with great care your personal informal letter of August 16th and I want to thank you for it. In these
testing days it is important for us to be in close touch. For
this reason I am sending my answer by the hand of Vice

President Johnson. He comes with General Clay, who is well known to Berliners; and they have my authority to discuss our problems in full frankness with you.

The measures taken by the Soviet Government and its puppets in East Berlin have caused revulsion here in America. This demonstration of what the Soviet Government means by freedom for a city, and peace for a people, proves the hollowness of Soviet pretensions; and Americans understand that this action necessarily constitutes a special blow to the people of West Berlin, connected as they remain in a myriad of ways to their fellow Berliners in the eastern sector. So I understand entirely the deep concerns and sense of trouble which prompted your letter.

Grave as this matter is, however, there are, as you say, no steps available to us which can force a significant material change in this present situation. Since it represents a resounding confession of failure and of political weakness, this brutal border closing evidently represents a basic Soviet decision which only war could reverse. Neither you nor we, nor any of our Allies, have ever supposed that we should go to war on this point.

Yet the Soviet action is too serious for inadequate responses. My own objection to most of the measures which have been proposed—even to most of the suggestions in your own letter—is that they are mere trifles compared to what has been done. Some of them, moreover, seem unlikely to be fruitful even in their own terms. This is our present judgment, for example, on the question of an immediate appeal to the United Nations, although we shall continue to keep this possibility under lively review.

On careful consideration I myself have decided that the best immediate response is a significant reinforcement of the Western garrisons. The importance of this reinforcement is symbolic—but not symbolic only. We know that the Soviet Union continues to emphasize its demand for the removal of Allied protection from West Berlin. We believe that even a modest reinforcement will underline our rejection of this concept.

At the same time, and of even greater basic importance, we shall continue and accelerate the broad buildup of the military strength of the West upon which we are decided, and which we view as the necessary answer to the long-range Soviet threat to Berlin and to us all.

Within Berlin, in the immediate affairs of the city, there may be other specific appropriate steps to take. These we shall review as rapidly and sympathetically as possible, and I hope you will be sure to express your own views on such measures clearly to Vice President Johnson and his party. Actions which effectively demonstrate our continued commitment to freedom in Berlin will have our support.

I have considered with special care your proposal of a three-power status for West Berlin. My judgment is that a formal proclamation of such a status would imply a weakening of the four-power relationship on which our opposition to the border-closing depends. Whatever may be the immediate prospects, I do not believe that we should now take so double-edged a step. I do agree that the guarantees which we have pledged to West Berlin should be continuously affirmed and reaffirmed, and this we are doing. Moreover, I support your proposal of an appropriate plebiscite demonstrating the continuing conviction of West Berlin that its destiny is freedom in connection with the West.

More broadly, let me urge it upon you that we must not be shaken by Soviet actions which in themselves are confessions of weakness. West Berlin today is more important than ever, and its mission to stand for freedom has never been so important as now. The link of West Berlin to the Free World is not a matter of rhetoric. Important as the ties to the East have been, painful as is their violation, the life of the city, as I understand it, runs primarily to the West—its economic life, its moral basis, and its military security. You may wish to consider and to suggest concrete ways in which these ties might be expanded in a fashion that would make the citizens of West Berlin more actively conscious of their role, not merely as an outpost of freedom, but as a vital part of the Free World and all its enterprises. In this double mission we are partners, and it is my own confidence that we can continue to rely upon each other as firmly in the future as we have in the past.

  With warm personal regards,

                                        Sincerely,

It was during the Berlin crisis that what must be regarded as one of the most significant developments of the entire cold war took place. In a letter to Kennedy, Nikita Khrushchev suggested that he and the American president use the exchange of personal, private correspondence as a means of expressing their admittedly often opposing views "without a backward glance at the press, at the journalists."

                                Moscow,
                                September 29, 1961

Dear Mr. President,

  At present I am on the shore of the Black Sea. When they write in the press that Khrushchev is resting on the Black Sea it may be said that this is correct and at the same time incorrect. This is indeed a wonderful place. As a former Naval officer you would surely appreciate the merits of these surroundings, the beauty of the sea and the grandeur of the Caucasian mountains. Under this bright southern sun it is even somehow hard to believe that there still exist problems in the world which, due to lack of solutions, cast a sinister shadow on peaceful life, on the future of millions of people.

But as you will fully understand, I cannot at this time permit myself any relaxation. I am working, and here I work more fruitfully because my attention is not diverted to routine matters of which I have plenty, probably like you yourself do. Here I can concentrate on the main things.

I have given much thought of late to the development of international events since our meeting in Vienna, and I have decided to approach you with this letter. The whole world hopefully expected that our meeting and a frank exchange of views would have a soothing effect, would turn relations between our countries into the correct channel and promote the adoption of decisions which could give the peoples confidence that at last peace on earth will be secured. To my regret—and, I believe, to yours—this did not happen. . . .

My thoughts have more than once returned to our meetings in Vienna. I remember you emphasized that you did not want to proceed towards war and favoured living in peace with our country while competing in the peaceful domain. And though subsequent events did not proceed in the way that could be desired, I thought it might be useful in a purely informal and personal way to approach you and share some of my ideas. If you do not agree with me you can consider that this letter did not

exist while naturally I, for my part, will not use this correspondence in my public statements. After all only in
confidential correspondence can you say what you think
without a backward glance at the press, at the journalists.

As you see, I started out by describing the delights of
the Black Sea coast, but then I nevertheless turned to
politics. But that cannot be helped. They say that you
sometimes cast politics out through the door but it
climbs back through the window, particularly when the
windows are open. . . .

I have already told you, Mr. President, that in striving
for the conclusion of a German peace treaty we do not
want somehow to prejudice the interests of the United
States and their bloc allies. Neither are we interested in
exacerbating the situation in connection with the conclusion of a German peace treaty. What need have we of
such exacerbation? It is in the Western countries that
they create all sorts of fears and allege that the socialist
States intend well-nigh to swallow up West Berlin. You
may believe my word, the word of the Soviet Government that neither we nor our allies need West Berlin.

I do not doubt that, given good will and desire, the
Governments of our countries could find a common
language in the question of a German peace treaty too.
Naturally in the solution of that question it is necessary
to proceed from the obvious fact, which even a blind
man cannot fail to see, that there exist two Sovereign
German states. . . .

There remains the question of West Berlin which must
also be solved when a German peace treaty is concluded.
From whatever side we approach the matter, we probably
will not be able to find a better solution than the transfor-
mation of West Berlin into a free city. And we shall proceed towards that goal. If, to our regret, the Western

Powers will not wish to participate in a German peace settlement and the Soviet Union, together with the other countries that will be prepared to do so, has to sign a treaty with the German Democratic Republic we shall nonetheless provide a free city status for West Berlin. . . .

You, yourself, understand that we are a rich country, our expanse is boundless, our economy is on the upgrade, our culture and science are in their efflorescence. Acquaint yourself with the Program of our Party which determines our economic development for twenty years to come. This is indeed a grand and thrilling Program. What need have we of war? What need have we of acquisitions? And yet it is said that we want to seize West Berlin! It is ridiculous even to think of that. What would that give us? What would that change in the ratio of forces in the world arena? It gives nothing to anyone. . . .

Accept my respects
N. Khrushchev

In his reply, Kennedy wholeheartedly agreed with the Soviet chairman's suggestion of the exchange of letters and said that such a correspondence, "directed only to each other," would "give us each a chance to address the other in frank, realistic, and fundamental terms."

Hyannis Port,
October 16, 1961

Dear Mr. Chairman:

I regret that the press of events has made it impossible for me to reply earlier to your very important letter of last month. I have brought your letter here with me to Cape Cod for a weekend in which I can devote all the time necessary to give it the answer it deserves.

My family has had a home here overlooking the Atlantic for many years. My father and my brothers own homes near my own, and my children always have a large group of cousins for company. So this is an ideal place for me to spend my weekends during the summer and fall, to relax, to think, to devote my time to major tasks instead of constant appointments, telephone calls and details. Thus, I know how you must feel about the spot on the Black Sea from which your letter was written, for I value my own opportunities to get a clearer and quieter perspective away from the din of Washington.

I am gratified by your letter and your decision to suggest this additional means of communication. Certainly you are correct in emphasizing that this correspondence must be kept wholly private, not to be hinted at in public statements, much less disclosed to the press. For my part the contents and even the existence of our letters will be known only to the Secretary of State and a few others of my closest associates in the government. I think it is very important that these letters provide us with an opportunity for a personal, informal but meaningful exchange of views. There are sufficient channels now existing between our two governments for the more formal and official communications and public statements of position. These letters should supplement those channels, and give us each a chance to address the other in frank, realistic and fundamental terms. Neither of us is going to convert the other to a new social, economic or political point of view. Neither of us will be induced by a letter to desert or subvert his own cause. So these letters can be free from the polemics of

the "cold war" debate. That debate, will, of course, proceed, but you and I can write messages which will be
directed only to each other.

The importance of this additional attempt to explore
each other's view is well-stated in your letter; and I believe it is identical to the motivation for our meeting in
Vienna. Whether we wish it or not, and for better or
worse, we are the leaders of the world's two greatest rival powers, each with the ability to inflict great destruction on the other and to do great damage to the rest of
the world in the process. We therefore have a special
responsibility—greater than that held by any of our
predecessors in the pre-nuclear age—to exercise our
power with fullest possible understanding of the other's
vital interests and commitments. As you say in your letter, the solutions to the world's most dangerous problems are not easily found—but you and I are unable to
shift to anyone else the burden of finding them. You
and I are not personally responsible for the events at the
conclusion in [of] World War II which led to the present situation in Berlin. But we will be held responsible if
we cannot deal peacefully with problems related to this
situation. . . .

My attitude concerning Berlin and Germany now, as it
was then, is one of reason, not belligerence. There is peace
in that area now—and this government shall not initiate
and shall oppose any action which upsets that peace.

You are right in stating that we should all realistically
face the facts in the Berlin and German situations—
and this naturally includes facts which are inconvenient
for both sides to face as well as those we like. And one of
those facts is the peace which exists in Germany now. It
is not the remains of World War II but the threat of
World War III that preoccupies us all. Of course, it is

not "normal" for a nation to be divided by two different armies of occupation this long after the war; but the fact is that the area has been peaceful—it is not in itself the source of the present tension—and it could not be rendered more peaceful by your signing a peace treaty with the East Germans alone.

. . . Your letter makes it clear that you are not interested in taking any step which would only be "exacerbating the situation." And I think this is a commendable basis on which both of us should proceed in the future. . . .

I hope you will believe me, Mr. Chairman, when I say that it is my deepest hope that, through this exchange of letters and otherwise, we may improve relations between our nations, and make concrete progress in deeds as well as words toward the realization of a just and enduring peace. That is our greatest joint responsibility— and our greatest opportunity.

Sincerely,

While Kennedy, in his determination to avoid going to war with the Soviets over Berlin, welcomed the opportunity presented by the exchange of private letters with Khrushchev, he had no idea how far the Russians would push their aggression in Germany beyond the building of the Berlin Wall. Realizing his obligations as commander in chief, he sent a top secret letter to General Lauris Norstad, commander of the North Atlantic Treaty Organization forces in Europe, setting forth a sequence of contingency plans should the Berlin situation escalate—including, if necessary, not only the use of nuclear weapons but also "General Nuclear war."

Washington,
October 20, 1961.

Dear General Norstad:

Since your visit here I have given further thought to the two principal subjects of our discussion in relation to the Berlin situation, namely, contingency planning and the preparatory build-up in NATO military strength. . . .

My present thinking on the preferred sequence of types of actions that we should take in the event of any abrogation of Western rights in Berlin is reflected in the sequence of four courses of action designated by Roman numerals in the enclosed outline. The import of this sequence should be clear to you, and I desire that it serve as the guidance for your discussions with our Allies and for your planning of detailed military operations. . . .

Two aspects of my present thinking about Berlin planning and preparation deserve especial emphasis.

First: What I want is a sequence of graduated responses to Soviet/GDR actions in denial of our rights of access. The purpose is to maintain our rights and preserve our alliance. The responses after Phase I should begin with the non-military and move to the military. We cannot plan in advance the exact time each response should be initiated, for one reason, because we cannot now predict the date of Soviet/GDR action, for another because we cannot foresee the duration or the consequences of each response. . . .

Second: At this juncture I place as much importance on developing our capacity and readiness to fight with significant non-nuclear forces as on measures designed primarily to make our nuclear deterrent more credible. In saying this I am not in any sense depreciating the need for realization by the U.S.S.R. of the tremendous power of our nuclear forces and our will to use them, if necessary, in support of our objectives. Indeed, I think the two aspects are interrelated. It seems evident to me that our nuclear deterrent will not be credible to the Soviets unless they are convinced of NATO's readiness to become engaged on a lesser level of violence and are thereby made to realize the great risks of escalation to nuclear war. I will be interested to hear of any suggestion from you as to how we might intensify that realization.

When contingency plans have been completed and received through established channels, the Joint Chiefs of Staff will review them with me and my other advisors.

Sincerely,
John F. Kennedy

Enclosure

Washington,
October 20, 1961.

U.S. POLICY ON MILITARY ACTIONS IN A BERLIN CONFLICT

In the event military force is applied in the Berlin situation, it is United States policy that the nature and sequence of such use should preferably be:

I *If* Soviet/GDR administrative or other action
interferes with Berlin access by ground or air
but is short of definitive blockage, *then* the
tripartite powers should execute Berlin contingency plans, to include tripartitely agreed
probes of Soviet intentions by a platoon or
smaller force on the ground and by fighter escort in the air; they should continue to use
fully any unblocked mode of access.

(*Comment*: Through this point, risks of major war, unless Soviets wish to start one, are
not materially raised by any tripartite action,
and therefore, decision on execution is tripartite rather than NATO responsibility.)

II *If*, despite the above tripartite actions, Soviet/
GDR action indicates a determination to
maintain significant blockage of our access to
Berlin, *then* the NATO Allies should undertake such non-combatant activity as economic embargo, maritime harassment, and
UN action. Simultaneously, they should mobi-
lize and reinforce rapidly to improve capability
for taking actions listed below. Meanwhile,
they should use fully any unblocked access to
Berlin . . .

III *If*, despite the above Allied actions, our
Berlin access is not restored, the Allies should
take appropriate further action to clarify
whether the Soviets/GDR intend to maintain
blockage of air or ground access, or both,
while making clear our intention to obtain re-
opened access. *Then* embark on one or more of
the following expanded military courses of
action:

A. European Theatre

1. Expanding non-nuclear air action, against a background of expanded ground defensive strength, to gain local air superiority. Extend size and scope as necessary . . .

2. Expanding non-nuclear ground operations into GDR territory in division and greater strength, with strong air support.

(*Comment*: This is a politically oriented military operation aiming to display to the Soviets the approaching danger of possibly irreversible escalation. Military overpowering of determined Soviet resistance is not feasible. The risks rise, as do the military pressures on the Soviets.)

B. World Wide

Maritime control, naval blockade, or other world-wide measures, both for reprisal and to add to general pressure on the Soviets . . .

IV *If,* despite Allied use of substantial non-nuclear forces, the Soviets continue to encroach upon our vital interests, *then* the Allies should use nuclear weapons, starting with one of the following courses of action but continuing through C below if necessary:

A. Selective nuclear attacks for the primary purpose of demonstrating the will to use nuclear weapons.

B. Limited tactical employment of nuclear weapons to achieve in addition significant tactical advantage such as preservation of the integrity of Allied forces committed, or to extend pressure toward the objective.

C. General Nuclear war.

   (*Comment*: The Allies only partially control the timing and scale of nuclear weapons use. Such use might be initiated by the Soviets, at any time after the opening of small-scale hostilities, Allied initiation of limited nuclear action may elicit a reply in kind; it may also prompt unrestrained pre-emptive attack.)

Throughout the crisis over Berlin, Kennedy would be buoyed by encouragement from highly influential individuals. One such show of support would come in the form of a warm handwritten letter from Great Britain's Queen Elizabeth II.

May 14th 1962

Dear Mr. President,

   I have seen my Prime Minister who has just returned from his visit to the United States and Canada, and he has told me how much he enjoyed being there, and particularly how much he valued this chance to talk personally with you at this present difficult stage in the affairs of the West.

   It is a great comfort to me to know that you and he are so close, and that you have confidence in each other's judgment and advice; I am sure that these meetings

May 14th 1962.

BUCKINGHAM PALACE

Dear Mr. President,

I have seen my Prime Minister who has just returned from his visit to the United States and Canada, and he has told me how much he enjoyed being there, and particularly how much he valued this chance to talk personally with you at this present difficult stage in the affairs of the West.

It is a great comfort to me to know that you and he are so close, and that you have confidence in each other's judgement and advice; I am sure that these meetings and this personal trust and understanding are of the greatest importance to both our peoples.

I was also glad to hear from Mr. Macmillan that my Ambassador and his wife are getting on so well and that you are finding them useful. David is, as you know, very highly thought of here,

During the Cold War, Kennedy developed a close relationship with British prime minister Harold Macmillan, as noted in this supportive letter from Queen Elizabeth II.

and this personal trust and understanding are of the greatest importance to both our peoples.

I was also glad to hear from Mr. Macmillan that my Ambassador and his wife are getting on so well and that you are finding them useful. He is, as you know, very highly thought of here, and so it is excellent news that he and Cissie are making their mark in Washington.

It was a great pleasure to meet Mrs. Kennedy again when she came here to lunch in March at the end of her strenuous tour. I hope her Pakistan horse will be a success—please tell her that mine became very excited by jumping with the children's ponies in the holidays, so I hope hers will be calmer!

During the CENTO meeting last month, I had the chance of a very enjoyable and interesting talk with Mr. Rusk when the Foreign Ministers dined with us.

My husband who is now in Canada is going to have the pleasure of visiting the World Fair in Seattle in June, and then a week later will be in New York for a dinner engagement. I envy him the chance of being in the United States again—we have had two such happy visits there.

> Your sincere Friend
> *Elizabeth*

Kennedy would also appreciate the support he received from his predecessor, Dwight D. Eisenhower, particularly concerning Kennedy's actions regarding Berlin.

> May 17, 1962

Dear General:

As you perhaps know, I have been a great admirer of yours since our first meeting in Frankfurt, in 1945,

when I accompanied Secretary Forrestal on a trip to
Europe. I agree with your view concerning the differences that could easily arise between us, and will certainly do everything in my power to prevent any
misunderstandings of thought, actions, or motive from
eroding our association. I fully understand that there
will be differences on some matters, especially on domestic issues, and at the same time, feel that in matters
of national concern, especially in foreign affairs, we
will see eye to eye.

Let me express my appreciation for your support in
the Berlin crisis, in the foreign trade discussion, and especially on foreign aid. Your continued interest in our
national security problems, and your ready acceptance
of intelligence and operational briefings concerning
Southeast Asia, leads me to feel that your important
support and judgment are readily at the nation's command, for which I am truly grateful.

Thank you for your recent letter, and its encouragement. I have received word on your suggestion concerning the title for General Heaton, and at the appropriate
time will make that change.

With best wishes and warm regards—and those of
longstanding.

> Sincerely,
> *General Dwight D.*
> *Eisenhower*
> Gettysburg, Pennsylvania

*As had been the case since he was elected president, one of Kennedy's
greatest supporters throughout the events in Berlin was former president Harry S. Truman.*

——————————————

July 24, 1962

Dear Mr. President:

It was a pleasure to me this morning to talk to you and tell you how I felt with regard to the difficulties you have been having. Very few people ever called me up on those matters when I was in trouble and I felt that maybe you would like to hear from me.

I hope you will remember that, under no circumstances, would I interrupt your busy day except to give you my ideas of what you have been doing. I think they are all right!

Sincerely yours,
Harry S. Truman

Although tensions between the world's two superpowers continued to increase, particularly in March 1962, when both nations resumed nuclear arms testing, the two cold war rivals did not go to war over Berlin. On June 26, 1963, Kennedy visited West Berlin. Peering out at a crowd of more than 1.5 million people, Kennedy discarded his prepared remarks and delivered a speech that presidential historian Michael Beschloss later described as "a kind of angry poetry." Looking out over the sea of humanity, Kennedy said, "There are many people in the world who really don't understand, or say they don't, what is the great issue between the free world and the Communist world. Let them come to Berlin. There are some who say that Communism is the way of the future. Let them come to Berlin. . . ."

Pausing to let the thunderous roar that greeted these words subside, Kennedy declared, "Freedom has many difficulties and democracy is not perfect, but we have never had to put up a wall to keep our people

*in, to prevent them from leaving us." His concluding statement brought
the greatest and most prolonged cheers of all: "All free men, wherever
they may live, are citizens of Berlin, and, therefore, as a free man, I
take pride in the words 'Ich bin ein Berliner.'"*

*He had given many speeches, but none would be more triumphant.
And he knew it. Turning to an aide as Air Force One left Germany, Kennedy said, "We'll never have another day like this one as long as we live."
On July 3, 1963, Kennedy received a letter from Willy Brandt, very different in tone than the one Brandt had written when the Berlin Wall was
first constructed.*

3 July 1963

The President
of the United States of America
Mr. John F. Kennedy
Washington D.C. / USA

Dear Mr. President,

I want to express to you once again my heartfelt gratitude for your visit to Berlin.

You will have seen yourself how much this occasion
meant to my fellow-citizens and to myself and how intense are the feelings of gratitude and of confidence in
you that found expression during that memorable day.

Your visit to Germany had strengthened the Western community, and it helped many people understand
correctly your strategy of peace. I hope that through
contributions of our own we will be able both to help
you and to move forward, step by step, toward solving
our own problems.

I should also like to thank you warmly for the hand-

some gifts that you brought for my sons and myself;
they will always remind me of a great day in the history
of my city and of your role in giving direction to the
struggle for a better world.

> With kindest regards,
> Sincerely yours,
> *Willy Brandt*

*On October 21, 1962, Kennedy, in a "top secret" letter, informed British
prime minister Harold Macmillan of clandestine developments that
were taking place in Cuba, creating a "crisis of the most serious sort."*

10/21/62

Dear Prime Minister:

I am sending you this most private message to give
you advance notice of a most serious situation and of
my plan to meet it. I am arranging to have David Bruce
report to you more fully tomorrow morning, but I want
you to have this message tonight so that you may have as
much time as possible to consider the dangers we will
now have to face together.

Photographic intelligence has established beyond
question, in the last week, that the Soviet Union has
engaged in a major build-up of medium-range missiles
in Cuba. Six sites have so far been identified, and two of
them may be in operational readiness. In sum, it is clear
that a massive secret operation has been proceeding in
spite of repeated assurances we have received from the
Soviet Union on this point.

After careful reflection, this Government has decided to prevent any further buildup by sea and to demand the removal of this nuclear threat to our hemisphere. When he sees you tomorrow, Ambassador Bruce will have at hand the substance of a speech which I will give on Monday evening, Washington time.

This extraordinarily dangerous and aggressive Soviet step obviously creates a crisis of the most serious sort, in which we shall have to act most closely together. I have found it absolutely essential, in the interest of security and speed, to make my first decision on my own responsibility, but from now on I expect that we can and should be in the closest touch, and I know that together with our other friends we will resolutely meet this challenge. I recognize fully that Khrushchev's main intention may be to increase his chances at Berlin, and we shall be ready to take a full role there as well as in the Caribbean. What is essential at this moment of the highest test is that Khrushchev should discover that if he is counting on weakness or irresolution, he has miscalculated.

I venture to repeat my hope that the nature of this threat and of my first decision to meet it be held most privately until announcements are made here.

Sincerely,
John F. Kennedy

The next day Kennedy wrote the first of what would be more than twenty letters and telegrams exchanged between the American president and the Soviet chairman during what would become known as the Cuban missile crisis.

THE WHITE HOUSE

WASHINGTON,

OCTOBER 22, 1962.

Sir:

A copy of the statement I am making tonight concerning developments in Cuba and the reaction of my Government thereto has been handed to your Ambassador in Washington. In view of the gravity of the developments to which I refer, I want you to know immediately and accurately the position of my Government in this matter.

In our discussions and exchanges on Berlin and other international questions, the one thing that has most concerned me has been the possibility that your Government would not correctly understand the will and determination of the United States in any given situation, since I have not assumed that you or any other sane man would, in this nuclear age, deliberately plunge the world into war which it is crystal clear no country could win and which could only result in catastrophic consequences to the whole world, including the aggressor.

At our meeting in Vienna and subsequently, I expressed our readiness and desire to find, through peaceful negotiation, a solution to any and all problems that divide us. At the same time, I made clear that in view of the objectives of the ideology to which you adhere, the United States could not tolerate any action on your part which in a major way disturbed the existing over-all balance of power in the world. I stated that an attempt to force abandonment of our responsibilities and commitments in

Berlin would constitute such an action and that the United States would resist with all the power at its command.

It was in order to avoid any incorrect assessment on the part of your Government with respect to Cuba that I publicly stated that if certain developments in Cuba took place, the United States would do whatever must be done to protect its own security and that of its allies.

Moreover, the Congress adopted a resolution expressing its support of this declared policy. Despite this, the rapid development of long-range missile bases and other offensive weapons systems in Cuba has proceeded. I must tell you that the United States is determined that this threat to the security of this hemisphere be removed. At the same time, I wish to point out that the action we are taking is the minimum necessary to remove the threat to the security of the nations of this hemisphere. The fact of this minimum response should not be taken as a basis, however, for any misjudgment on your part.

I hope that your Government will refrain from any action which would widen or deepen this already grave crisis and that we can agree to resume the path of peaceful negotiations.

Sincerely,
JFK

From the moment that the missiles were discovered in Cuba, the Joint Chiefs of Staff urged Kennedy to launch an airstrike against the missile sites. Weighing all his options, Kennedy asked Executive Committee member C. Douglas Dillon to prepare a report listing the advantages that might be gained from such a course of action.

Mr. President:

—Scenario for Airstrike against offensive missile bases and bombers in Cuba

ADVANTAGES

1. Carries out President's pledge to eliminate offensive threat to U.S. and Hemisphere from Cuba and avoids any erosion of U.S. momentum and position. The pledge carried out shows that U.S. has will to fight and to protect vital interests (of great importance vis-à-vis Berlin).

2. Since directed at offensive weapons, keeps issue focused on Soviet nuclear presence in Cuba in defiance of OAS and majority of Security Council.

3. Sharp, possible one time action, may carry smaller risks of further escalation than a series of confrontations over a period of time. Soviet decision to risk major war unlikely to be decisively affected by this action in an area non-vital to the Soviets.

4. Prompt action will avoid danger of a growth of hands-off Cuba movement throughout Latin America which might make it increasingly difficult to strike at offensive weapons. Present willingness of Latin Americans to support strong action probably cannot be maintained indefinitely.

5. Signals clearly that U.S. not prepared to bargain bases in Cuba for positions in Berlin, NATO and elsewhere.

6. It could demonstrate to Cubans, Castro and others, the weakness of Soviet position in Cuba. In the absence of a strong Soviet reaction in defense of Cuba, we would start the process of disenchantment and disaffection requisite to undermining Castro and Cuban reliance on the Soviet Union. We would also weaken any tendencies to rely on Soviets elsewhere in the world.

7. Removes a military threat to U.S. from Cuban territory.

8. Denies Khrushchev a possible cheap victory through successful maintenance of offensive weapons in Cuba.

On May 23, the day on which Kennedy authorized the naval quarantine of Cuba, Khrushchev replied to the president's letter, stating for the first of many times that the missile sites had been erected solely for defensive purposes and that the world would see "catastrophic consequences" if the United States did not remove the quarantine.

Moscow, October 23, 1962

Mr. President.

I have just received your letter, and have also acquainted myself with the text of your speech of October 22 regarding Cuba.

I must say frankly that measures indicated in your statement constitute a serious threat to peace and to the security of nations. The United States has openly taken the path of grossly violating the United Nations

Москва, 23 октября 1962 года

Господин Президент,

Только что получил Ваше письмо, а также ознакомился с текстом Вашего выступления 22 октября в связи с Кубой.

Должен откровенно сказать, что намеченные в Вашем заявлении меры представляют собой серьезную угрозу миру и безопасности народов. Соединенные Штаты открыто становятся на путь грубого нарушения Устава Организации Объединенных Наций, на путь нарушения международных норм свободы судоходства в открытых морях, на путь агрессивных действий как против Кубы, так и против Советского Союза.

Заявление Правительства Соединенных Штатов Америки нельзя оценить иначе как неприкрытое вмешательство во внутренние дела Кубинской Республики, Советского Союза и других государств. Устав Организации Объединенных Наций и международные нормы не дают права ни одному государству устанавливать в международных водах проверку судов, направляющихся к берегам Кубинской Республики.

Мы, разумеется, не можем признать за Соединенными Штатами и право установления контроля за оружием, необходимым Республике Куба для укрепления своей обороноспособности.

Его Превосходительству
Джону КЕННЕДИ,
Президенту Соединенных Штатов
Америки

Soviet premier Nikita Khrushchev's letter (in the original Russian) to President Kennedy in response to Kennedy's announcement of a naval blockade of Cuba

Charter, the path of violating international norms of freedom of navigation on the high seas, the path of aggressive actions both against Cuba and against the Soviet Union.

DEPARTMENT OF STATE
DIVISION OF LANGUAGE SERVICES

(TRANSLATION)

DECLASSIFIED
E.O. 11652, Sec. 3(E) and 5(D) or (E)
State Dept Bulletin #1795
By MK...... NARS, Date 11/27/73

LS NO. 45989
T-85/T-94
Russian

[Embossed Seal of the USSR]

Moscow, October 23, 1962

Mr. President:

I have just received your letter, and have also acquainted myself
with the text of your speech of October 22 regarding Cuba.

I must say frankly that the measures indicated in your statement
constitute a serious threat to peace and to the security of nations. The
United States has openly taken the path of grossly violating the United
Nations Charter, the path of violating international norms of freedom of
navigation on the high seas, the path of aggressive actions both against
Cuba and against the Soviet Union.

The statement by the Government of the United States of America can
only be regarded as undisguised interference in the internal affairs of
the Republic of Cuba, the Soviet Union and other states. The United
Nations Charter and international norms give no right to any state to
institute in international waters the inspection of vessels bound for
the shores of the Republic of Cuba.

And naturally, neither can we recognize the right of the United
States to establish control over armaments which are necessary for the
Republic of Cuba to strengthen its defense capability.

We reaffirm that the armaments which are in Cuba, regardless of the
classification to which they may belong, are intended solely for defensive
purposes in order to secure the Republic of Cuba against the attack of an
aggressor.

His Excellency
    John Kennedy,
        President of the United States of America

GPO-918904

The State Department's translation of Khrushchev's October 23 letter

The statement by the Government of the United States of America can only be regarded as undisguised interference in the internal affairs of the Republic of Cuba, the Soviet Union, and other states. The United Nations Charter and international norms give no right to any state to institute in international waters the inspection of vessels bound for the shores of the Republic of Cuba.

And naturally, neither can we recognize the right of the United States to establish control over armaments which are necessary for the Republic of Cuba to strengthen its defense capability.

We affirm that the armaments which are in Cuba, regardless of the classification to which they may belong, are intended solely for defensive purposes, in order to secure the Republic of Cuba against the attack of an aggressor.

I hope that the United States Government will display wisdom and renounce the actions pursued by you, which may lead to catastrophic consequences for world peace.

The viewpoint of the Soviet Government with regard to your statement of October 22 is set forth in a Statement of the Soviet Government, which is being transmitted to you through your Ambassador at Moscow.

N. Khrushchev

In his immediate reply, Kennedy, pointedly using the term "offensive" in reference to the missiles, asked Khrushchev to observe the terms of the quarantine.

WASHINGTON, OCTOBER 23, 1962, 6:51 P.M.

DEAR MR. CHAIRMAN:

I HAVE RECEIVED YOUR LETTER OF OCTO-
BER TWENTY-THIRD. I THINK YOU WILL
RECOGNIZE THAT THE STEP WHICH
STARTED THE CURRENT CHAIN OF
EVENTS WAS THE ACTION OF YOUR GOV-
ERNMENT IN SECRETLY FURNISHING
OFFENSIVE WEAPONS TO CUBA. WE WILL
BE DISCUSSING THIS MATTER IN THE
SECURITY COUNCIL. IN THE MEANTIME,
I AM CONCERNED THAT WE BOTH SHOW
PRUDENCE AND DO NOTHING TO ALLOW
EVENTS TO MAKE THE SITUATION
MORE DIFFICULT TO CONTROL THAN IT
ALREADY IS.
    I HOPE THAT YOU WILL ISSUE IMMEDI-
ATELY THE NECESSARY INSTRUCTIONS TO
YOUR SHIPS TO OBSERVE THE TERMS OF THE
QUARANTINE, THE BASIS OF WHICH WAS
ESTABLISHED BY THE VOTE OF THE ORGANI-
ZATION OF AMERICAN STATES THIS AFTER-
NOON, AND WHICH WILL GO INTO EFFECT
AT 1400 HOURS GREENWICH TIME OCTOBER
TWENTY-FOUR.

SINCERELY,
JFK

13

THE WHITE HOUSE
WASHINGTON

Kennedy's handwritten draft of a reply to Khrushchev

On October 24, the crisis reached its boiling point when Khrushchev responded by telling Kennedy that he could not agree to obey the terms of the quarantine, which he described as "piratical acts by American ships on the high seas." The Soviet leader warned Kennedy that not only would the Soviet Union oppose the quarantine by force but that it also had "everything necessary to do so."

Moscow, October 24, 1962.

Dear Mr. President:

I have received your letter of October 23, have studied it, and am answering you.

Just imagine, Mr. President, that we had presented you with the conditions of an ultimatum which you have presented us by your action. How would you have reacted to this? I think that you would have been indignant at such a step on our part. And this would have been understandable to us.

In presenting us with these conditions, you, Mr. President, have flung a challenge at us. Who asked you to do this? By what right did you do this? Our ties with the Republic of Cuba, like our relations with other states, regardless of what kind of states they may be, concern only the two countries between which these relations exist. And if we now speak of the quarantine to which your letter refers, a quarantine may be established, according to accepted international practice, only by agreement of states between themselves, and not by some third party. Quarantines exist, for example, on agricultural goods and products. But in this case the question is in no way one of quarantine, but rather of far more serious things, and you yourself understand this.

You, Mr. President, are not declaring a quarantine, but rather are setting forth an ultimatum and threatening that if we do not give in to your demands you will use force. Consider what you are saying! And you want to persuade me to agree to this! What would it mean to agree to these demands? It would mean guiding oneself in one's relations with other countries not by reason, but by submitting to arbitrariness. You are no longer appealing to reason, but wish to intimidate us.

No, Mr. President, I cannot agree to this, and I think that in your own heart you recognize that I am correct. I am convinced that in my place you would act the same way....

You wish to compel us to renounce the rights that every sovereign state enjoys, you are trying to legislate in questions of international law, and you are violating the universally accepted norms of that law. And you are doing all this not only out of hatred for the Cuban people and its government, but also because of considerations of the election campaign in the United States. What morality, what law can justify such an approach by the American government to international affairs? No such morality or law can be found, because the actions of the United States with regard to Cuba constitute outright banditry or, if you like, the folly of degenerate imperialism. Unfortunately, such folly can bring grave suffering to the peoples of all countries, and to no lesser degree to the American people themselves, since the United States has completely lost its former isolation with the advent of modern types of armament.

Therefore, Mr. President, if you coolly weigh the situation which has developed, not giving way to passions, you will understand that the Soviet Union cannot fail to reject the arbitrary demands of the United States. When you confront us with such conditions, try to put yourself in our place and consider how the United States would react to these conditions. I do not doubt that if someone attempted to dictate similar conditions to you—the United States—you would reject such attempt. And we also say—no.

The Soviet Government considers that the violation of the freedom to use international waters and international air space is an act of aggression which pushes mankind toward the abyss of world nuclear-missile war. Therefore, the Soviet Government cannot instruct the captains of the Soviet vessels bound for Cuba to observe the orders of American naval forces blockading that Island. Our instructions to Soviet mariners are to observe strictly the universally accepted norms of navigation in international waters and not to retreat one step from them. And if the American side violates these rules, it must realize what responsibility will rest upon it in that case. Naturally we will not simply be bystanders with regard to piratical acts by American ships on the high seas. We will then be forced on our part to take the measures we consider necessary and adequate in order to protect our rights. We have everything necessary to do so.

Respectfully,
N. Khrushchev

Kennedy replied on October 25, repeating, "It was not I who issued the first challenge in this race." Meanwhile, as the missile crisis escalated, people throughout the world waited anxiously for the next development. On the same day that Kennedy received Khrushchev's threaten-

ing letter, he also received one of a series of angry telegrams from renowned British philosopher, mathematician, historian, and social critic Lord Bertrand Russell.

YOUR ACTION DESPERATE. THREAT TO HUMAN SURVIVAL. NO CONCEIVABLE JUS- TIFICATION. CIVILIZED MAN CONDEMNS IT. WE WILL NOT HAVE MASS MURDER. ULTIMATUMS MEAN WAR. . . . END THIS MADNESS.

Kennedy's reply to Lord Russell was marked by a pointed admonishment.

October 26, 1962

Lord Bertrand Russell
Penrnyndeudracth
Merioneth County
Wales, England

I am in receipt of your telegrams.

We are currently discussing the matter in the United Nations. While your messages are critical of the United States, they make no mention of your concern for the introduction of secret Soviet missile weapons into Cuba. I think your attention might well be directed to the burglars rather than to those who have caught the burglars.

John F. Kennedy

On October 26, while Kennedy, at a meeting of his staff and advisers, was stating that he now believed that the quarantine alone would not force the Soviets to remove their Cuban missiles, ABC News reporter John Scali was contacted by Aleksandr Fomin (a cover for his real name, Aleksandr Feklisov) of the Soviet embassy with a Russian proposal for a formal end to the crisis. Later that day, Kennedy received a long, rambling letter from Khrushchev. Once again characterizing the missiles in Cuba as defensive weapons and accusing Kennedy of taking piratical measures in establishing the quarantine, Khrushchev nonetheless then repeated the offer earlier conveyed to Scali: In exchange for a lifting of the quarantine and a pledge from the United States that it would not invade Cuba, the Soviet Union would dismantle the missile sites and remove the missiles. In his reply, Kennedy agreed to the proposal.

WASHINGTON, OCTOBER 27, 1962, 8:05 PM.

DEAR MR. CHAIRMAN:

I HAVE READ YOUR LETTER OF OCTOBER 26TH WITH GREAT CARE AND WELCOMED THE STATEMENT OF YOUR DESIRE TO SEEK A PROMPT SOLUTION TO THE PROBLEM. THE FIRST THING THAT NEEDS TO BE DONE, HOWEVER, IS FOR WORK TO CEASE ON OFFENSIVE MISSILE BASES IN CUBA AND FOR ALL WEAPONS SYSTEMS IN CUBA CAPABLE OF OFFENSIVE USE TO BE RENDERED INOPERABLE, UNDER EFFECTIVE UNITED NATIONS ARRANGEMENTS.

ASSUMING THIS IS DONE PROMPTLY, I HAVE GIVEN MY REPRESENTATIVES IN NEW YORK INSTRUCTIONS THAT WILL PERMIT THEM TO WORK OUT THIS WEEKEND—IN

COOPERATION WITH THE ACTING SECRE-
TARY GENERAL AND YOUR REPRESENTA-
TIVE—AN ARRANGEMENT FOR A
PERMANENT SOLUTION TO THE CUBAN
PROBLEM ALONG THE LINES SUGGESTED IN
YOUR LETTER OF OCTOBER 26TH. AS I READ
YOUR LETTER, THE KEY ELEMENTS OF YOUR
PROPOSALS—WHICH SEEM GENERALLY
ACCEPTABLE AS I UNDERSTAND THEM—
ARE AS FOLLOWS:

1) YOU WOULD AGREE TO REMOVE THESE
   WEAPONS SYSTEMS FROM CUBA UNDER
   APPROPRIATE UNITED NATIONS OBSER-
   VATION AND SUPERVISION; AND UNDER-
   TAKE, WITH SUITABLE SAFEGUARDS, TO
   HALT THE FURTHER INTRODUCTION OF
   SUCH WEAPONS SYSTEMS INTO CUBA.

2) WE, ON OUR PART, WOULD AGREE—UPON
   THE ESTABLISHMENT OF ADEQUATE
   ARRANGEMENTS THROUGH THE UNITED
   NATIONS TO ENSURE THE CARRYING
   OUT AND CONTINUATION OF THESE
   COMMITMENTS—(A) TO REMOVE
   PROMPTLY THE QUARANTINE MEASURES
   NOW IN EFFECT AND (B) TO GIVE ASSUR-
   ANCES AGAINST AN INVASION OF CUBA. I
   AM CONFIDENT THAT OTHER NATIONS
   OF THE WESTERN HEMISPHERE WOULD
   BE PREPARED TO DO LIKEWISE.

IF YOU WILL GIVE YOUR REPRESENTATIVE
SIMILAR INSTRUCTIONS, THERE IS NO

REASON WHY WE SHOULD NOT BE ABLE TO
COMPLETE THESE ARRANGEMENTS AND
ANNOUNCE THEM TO THE WORLD WITHIN
A COUPLE OF DAYS. THE EFFECT OF SUCH A
SETTLEMENT ON EASING WORLD TENSIONS
WOULD ENABLE US TO WORK TOWARD A
MORE GENERAL ARRANGEMENT REGARD-
ING "OTHER ARMAMENTS", AS PROPOSED IN
YOUR SECOND LETTER WHICH YOU MADE
PUBLIC. I WOULD LIKE TO SAY AGAIN THAT
THE UNITED STATES IS VERY MUCH INTER-
ESTED IN REDUCING TENSIONS AND HALT-
ING THE ARMS RACE; AND IF YOUR LETTER
SIGNIFIES THAT YOU ARE PREPARED TO
DISCUSS A DÉTENTE AFFECTING NATO AND
THE WARSAW PACT, WE ARE QUITE PRE-
PARED TO CONSIDER WITH OUR ALLIES ANY
USEFUL PROPOSALS.

BUT THE FIRST INGREDIENT, LET ME
EMPHASIZE, IS THE CESSATION OF WORK ON
MISSILE SITES IN CUBA AND MEASURES TO
RENDER SUCH WEAPONS INOPERABLE,
UNDER EFFECTIVE INTERNATIONAL GUAR-
ANTEES. THE CONTINUATION OF THIS
THREAT, OR A PROLONGING OF THIS DIS-
CUSSION CONCERNING CUBA BY LINKING
THESE PROBLEMS TO THE BROADER QUES-
TIONS OF EUROPEAN AND WORLD SECU-
RITY, WOULD SURELY LEAD TO AN
INTENSIFICATION OF THE CUBAN CRISIS
AND A GRAVE RISK TO THE PEACE OF THE
WORLD. FOR THIS REASON I HOPE WE CAN
QUICKLY AGREE ALONG THE LINES IN THIS

LETTER AND IN YOUR LETTER OF OCTOBER 26TH.

John F. Kennedy

Khrushchev, however, was not quite done. He had one final demand: a pledge from Kennedy that the United States would remove its Jupiter missiles from Turkey. Recognizing the demand as a face-saving request, Kennedy agreed. The next day, following Radio Moscow's announcement of the proposed solution to the crisis, Kennedy wrote yet again to Khrushchev, ending his long telegram with the hope that as the two sides "step back from danger," they could work toward preventing such a crisis from happening again.

WASHINGTON, OCTOBER 28, 1962, 5:03 P.M.

DEAR MR. CHAIRMAN:

I AM REPLYING AT ONCE TO YOUR BROADCAST MESSAGE OF OCTOBER TWENTY-EIGHT EVEN THOUGH THE OFFICIAL TEXT HAS NOT YET REACHED ME BECAUSE OF THE GREAT IMPORTANCE I ATTACH TO MOVING FORWARD PROMPTLY TO THE SETTLEMENT OF THE CUBAN CRISIS. I THINK THAT YOU AND I, WITH OUR HEAVY RESPONSIBILITIES FOR THE MAINTENANCE OF PEACE, WERE AWARE THAT DEVELOPMENTS WERE APPROACHING A POINT WHERE EVENTS COULD HAVE BECOME UNMANAGEABLE. SO I WELCOME THIS MESSAGE AND CONSIDER

IT AN IMPORTANT CONTRIBUTION TO
PEACE.

THE DISTINGUISHED EFFORTS OF ACTING
SECRETARY GENERAL U THANT HAVE
GREATLY FACILITATED BOTH OUR TASKS. I
CONSIDER MY LETTER TO YOU OF OCTOBER
TWENTY-SEVENTH AND YOUR REPLY OF
TODAY AS FIRM UNDERTAKINGS ON THE
PART OF BOTH OUR GOVERNMENTS WHICH
SHOULD BE PROMPTLY CARRIED OUT. I HOPE
THAT THE NECESSARY MEASURES CAN AT
ONCE BE TAKEN THROUGH THE UNITED
NATIONS AS YOUR MESSAGE SAYS, SO THAT
THE UNITED STATES IN TURN CAN REMOVE
THE QUARANTINE MEASURES NOW IN EF-
FECT. I HAVE ALREADY MADE ARRANGE-
MENTS TO REPORT ALL THESE MATTERS TO
THE ORGANIZATION OF AMERICAN STATES,
WHOSE MEMBERS SHARE A DEEP INTEREST
IN A GENUINE PEACE IN THE CARIBBEAN
AREA....

MR. CHAIRMAN, BOTH OF OUR COUN-
TRIES HAVE GREAT UNFINISHED TASKS AND
I KNOW THAT YOUR PEOPLE AS WELL AS
THOSE OF THE UNITED STATES CAN ASK
FOR NOTHING BETTER THAN TO PURSUE
THEM FREE FROM THE FEAR OF WAR. MOD-
ERN SCIENCE AND TECHNOLOGY HAVE
GIVEN US THE POSSIBILITY OF MAKING
LABOR FRUITFUL BEYOND ANYTHING THAT
COULD HAVE BEEN DREAMED OF A FEW
DECADES AGO.

I AGREE WITH YOU THAT WE MUST DE-
VOTE URGENT ATTENTION TO THE PROB-

LEM OF DISARMAMENT, AS IT RELATES
TO THE WHOLE WORLD AND ALSO TO
CRITICAL AREAS. PERHAPS NOW, AS WE
STEP BACK FROM DANGER, WE CAN TO-
GETHER MAKE REAL PROGRESS IN THIS
VITAL FIELD. I THINK WE SHOULD GIVE
PRIORITY TO QUESTIONS RELATING TO
THE PROLIFERATION OF NUCLEAR WEAP-
ONS, ON EARTH AND IN OUTER SPACE,
AND TO THE GREAT EFFORT FOR A NU-
CLEAR TEST BAN. BUT WE SHOULD ALSO
WORK HARD TO SEE IF WIDER MEA-
SURES OF DISARMAMENT CAN BE AGREED
AND PUT INTO OPERATION AT AN EARLY
DATE. THE UNITED STATES GOVERN-
MENT WILL BE PREPARED TO DISCUSS
THESE QUESTIONS URGENTLY, AND IN
A CONSTRUCTIVE SPIRIT, AT GENEVA OR
ELSEWHERE.

JOHN F. KENNEDY

The crisis was over. And Kennedy, as reflected in a telegram he received from Prime Minister Harold Macmillan, had regained the prestige he had lost over the Bay of Pigs.

PMUK 004/62
1833 ZULU OCTOBER 28

IT WAS INDEED A TRIAL OF WILLS AND
YOURS HAS PREVAILED. WHATEVER DAN-
GERS AND DIFFICULTIES WE MAY HAVE TO

FACE IN THE FUTURE I AM PROUD TO FEEL
THAT I HAVE SO RESOURCEFUL AND SO
FIRM A COMRADE.

*In his letter to Khrushchev confirming the settlement of the Cuban
missile crisis, Kennedy's statement "Perhaps now, as we step back
from danger, we can together make real progress in this vital field"
referred to nuclear disarmament, an issue he had felt passionately
about since his days as a senator. As a candidate for his party's presidential nomination, he had strongly supported the Eisenhower administration's participation in a conference in Geneva on the
discontinuance of nuclear arms testing. Concerned that the upcoming
election might temper Eisenhower's efforts, Kennedy had written to the
president.*

March 30, 1960

The President
The White House
Washington, D.C.

Dear Mr. President:

I have been greatly disturbed by the possibility
that our current nuclear test ban negotiations might be
jeopardized by the approach of the Presidential election.

You have consistently indicated your own belief that
the present Geneva negotiations may be bringing us
close to a final agreement to end testing. I share this
belief with you. At the same time, you may be under-
standably reluctant to decide on a small-test moratorium
which might bind your successor in office.

As a candidate for the Presidential nomination—although only one candidate among many—let me assure you that, if elected President, I will undertake to carry out in good faith any moratorium extending beyond your term of office which you now decide to be in the best interests of the nation. I realize that such an assurance from a single candidate has only a limited value. But I hope that it will help you to proceed—unhindered by thoughts of the coming election—with your efforts to bring about agreement on this vital matter, and thus bring us one step closer to world peace.

Sincerely yours,
John F. Kennedy

Beginning in the 1950s, one of the most active and fervent advocates of nuclear disarmament was the distinguished American scientist Linus Pauling, who, in his lifetime, was awarded both the Nobel Prize in Chemistry and the Nobel Peace Prize for his campaign against aboveground nuclear testing. In July 1961, Pauling, alarmed at the escalating United States–Soviet Union confrontation over the issue of a divided Berlin, sent President Kennedy an impassioned letter criticizing his administration for placing the ongoing Geneva test ban negotiations in jeopardy.

July 21, 1961

Dear Mr. President:

With all the intensity I can muster, I urge that, in your negotiations with the Soviet Union, you not take actions that increase the chance of nuclear war, such as the threat to use military force if the negotiations do not proceed in the way that you desire.

No dispute can justify nuclear war. The time has come when problems such as that involving Berlin and the German peace treaty must be settled by recourse to principles of justice, rather than by threat of military action or by military action itself.

After sixteen years, it is of course high time that the German peace treaty be made. But the world cannot take the chance of a unified and armed Germany. A Germany armed with nuclear weapons would represent an increased threat to world peace. I hope that you are giving serious consideration to the possibility of initiating negotiations to extend the principle of demilitarization to a region in central Europe, including West Germany, East Germany, Poland, Czechoslovakia, and possibly other countries. The problem of achieving such an arrangement is a difficult one, but the contribution that it would make to world security is so great that the problem should be attacked and solved.

I urge also that you make an honest effort to achieve the completion of the test-ban treaty, by proposing, in good faith, some reasonable compromises on the questions that remain unsettled. The United States has not yet proposed reasonable compromises in good faith. Until this is done, it will not be possible to place the blame on the U.S.S.R., in case that the Geneva bomb-test negotiations are broken off.

Sincerely yours,
Linus Pauling

Linus Pauling's partner in his campaign to end nuclear testing was his wife, Ava Helen Pauling, who devoted her life to such causes as women's rights, racial equality, and the peace movement. Particularly alarmed at the nuclear proliferation menace of the arms race, Mrs. Pauling reached out to a fellow mother, Jacqueline Kennedy.

15 July 1961

Dear Mrs. Kennedy:

Your children, like all other children in the world, are laying down in their bones, along with the calcium, Strontium 90. This substance is present in the world because of the explosion of nuclear bombs. If more bombs are tested, the amount of Strontium 90 will increase, and your children, accordingly, will have a greater chance of being injured by this radioactive material in their bones.

I urge you to use your influence to safeguard your children as well as all of the children of the world by keeping the United States Government from resuming nuclear testing under any circumstances.

The Geneva negotiations must continue until agreement is reached.

Sincerely yours,
Ava Helen Pauling

The man who would soon warn that "mankind must put an end to war or war will put an end to mankind" was already more than convinced of the life-threatening danger hanging over the head of every man, woman, and child living in a nuclear age. However, in August 1961, the Soviet

Union resumed its testing. The following month, Life *magazine devoted an entire issue to the building of bomb shelters in case of nuclear attack. Included was an open letter to the American people from their president.*

THE WHITE HOUSE

September 7, 1961

My Fellow Americans:

Nuclear weapons and the possibility of nuclear war are facts of life we cannot ignore today. I do not believe that war can solve any of the problems facing the world today. But the decision is not ours alone.

The government is moving to improve the protection afforded you in your communities through civil defense. We have begun, and will be continuing throughout the next year and a half, a survey of all public buildings with fallout shelter potential, and the marking of those with adequate shelter for 50 persons or more. We are providing fallout shelter in new and in some existing federal buildings. We are stocking these shelters with one week's food and medical supplies and two weeks' water supply for the shelter occupants. In addition, I have recommended to the Congress the establishment of food reserves in centers around the country where they might be needed following an attack. Finally, we are developing improved warning systems which will make it possible to sound attack warning on buzzers right in your homes and places of business.

More comprehensive measures than these lie ahead, but they cannot be brought to completion in the immediate future. In the meantime there is much that you can do to protect yourself – and in doing so strengthen your nation.

I urge you to read and consider seriously the contents in this issue of LIFE. The security of our country and the peace of the world are the objectives of our policy. But in these dangerous days when both these objectives are threatened we must prepare for all eventualities. The ability to survive coupled with the will to do so therefore are essential to our country.

John F. Kennedy

As part of his campaign to prepare Americans in the event of a nuclear attack, Kennedy ordered the Defense Department to create materials to support his effort. When one of the first of these materials was ready for dissemination, the president asked John Kenneth Galbraith to review it. Galbraith's assessment was far from positive.

November 9, 1961

Dear Mr. President:

At your request, I have gone over the Department of Defense draft pamphlet called "Fallout Protection— What to Know About Nuclear Attack—What to Do About It." I must tell you that I have read this document with grave misgiving, though not without realization of the serious problems moral and political which the whole issue involves.

It is evident first of all that we will be seriously criticized if we seem not to be taking sensible precautions. And we would be morally delinquent if people died in a catastrophe where they might be saved by our foresight. However, there is a right and a wrong way to discharge our responsibilities and this pamphlet represents, I fear, the wrong way. I have five specific objections, as follows:

1. The pamphlet does not make clear that it is American policy to avoid a holocaust. Civilian defense represents contingency planning, with the word contingency strongly underlined. As a government we hope and indeed intend to save our people from this disaster. This is not made clear in the present pamphlet.

2. The present pamphlet is a design for saving Republicans and sacrificing Democrats. These are the people who have individual houses with basements in which basement or lean-to fallout shelters can be built. There is no design for civilians who live in wooden three deckers, tenements, low cost apartments, or other congested areas. I am not at all attracted by a pamphlet which seeks to save the better elements of the population, but in the main writes off those who voted for you. I think it particularly injudicious, in fact it is absolutely incredible, to have a picture of a family with a cabin cruiser saving itself by going out to sea. Very few members of the UAW can go with them.

3. The rest of the social philosophy underlying this pamphlet is equally offensive.

    While maintenance of an Army and Navy and their protection in case of an attack are well recognized functions of the State, the protection of the civilian is herewith assigned to private enterprises. This is on the theory that the civilian is too expensive a luxury to protect. The pamphlet even makes a virtue of this by saying: 'The anticipation of a new market for home shelters is helpful and in keeping with the free enterprise way of meeting changing conditions in our lives.' All this, of course, is related to the social discrimination in survival. We don't want to pay the price of deep urban shelters so we are writing off the slum dwellers.

4. I also worry a little bit about the effect on the Soviets of a great helter skelter shelter program such as this pamphlet could set off and with all the commercial publicity attached. Isn't it a rather ostentatious form of war preparation? I think we are also likely to set off a certain amount of racketeering on people's fears.

5. Finally, and perhaps a minor point, it seems to me that the pamphlet is extremely sanguine, both about life in the shelter and the world into which people emerge. The latter will be a barren and hideous place with no food, no transportation and full of stinking corpses. Perhaps this can't be said but I don't think the people who wrote this pamphlet quite realize it. . . .

Sincerely,
John Kenneth Galbraith

The resumption of Soviet nuclear testing engendered widespread alarm among disarmament activists, who were not only outraged by the Russian action but also fearful that Kennedy would be compelled to respond

in kind. Most vocal of all was Linus Pauling, who, in another letter to
the president, made no effort to hold back his feelings.

1 March 1962

Night Letter Durham NC

President John F. Kennedy, White House:

Are you going to give an order that will cause you to
go down in history as one of the most immoral men of all
time and one of the greatest enemies of the human race?

In a letter to the *New York Times* I state that nuclear
tests duplicating the Soviet 1961 tests would seriously
damage over 20 million unborn children, including those
caused to have gross physical or mental defect and also the
stillbirths and embryonic, neonatal and childhood deaths
from the radioactive fission products and carbon 14.

Are you going to be guilty of this monstrous immo-
rality, matching that of the Soviet leaders, for the political purpose of increasing the still imposing lead of the
United States over the Soviet Union in nuclear weapons technology?

Linus Pauling

Despite more temperate pleas from nuclear test opponents from
around the world, including famed theologian, philosopher, and medi-
cal missionary Dr. Albert Schweitzer, Kennedy felt he had no choice
but to order the resumption of American testing. In June 1962, he wrote
to Schweitzer explaining the reasons for his decision.

June 6, 1962

Dear Dr. Schweitzer:

I read your letter on the nuclear testing problem with interest and sympathy. I can assure you that no decision I have taken in my Administration has given me more concern and sorrow than the decision to resume nuclear testing. It was a tragic choice; and I made it only because the alternative seemed to me to offer even greater dangers to or hopes for world peace, to unborn generations to come, and to the future of humanity.

If I had any assurance that the Soviet Union would not test again, I would never have directed that our tests be resumed. But it is impossible to believe that our refusal to test would have deterred the Soviet Union from initiation of a new test series whenever it suited their plans. The Soviet leaders have shown their contempt for world opinion in the past, and deference to this opinion is not likely to constrain them in the future. If the Soviet Union had been able to launch a new series without intervening tests on our part, it is conceivable that a grave shift in the world balance of power might have resulted, with fateful consequences for all our hopes for peace and freedom.

From the start of my Administration, I have tried to negotiate an agreement with the Soviet Union outlawing all nuclear tests. As you know, the Soviet Union has shown little interest in having such an agreement. Until the Soviet Union accepts a meaningful test ban agreement, I can see no choice, as the man responsible for the future of my country and my people, but to take

necessary steps to protect the security position of the
United States.

You raise the question of the need for international
inspection. At present, national systems are able to de-
tect seismic shocks but not reliably identify them—i.e.,
they are not reliably able to distinguish an explosion
from an earthquake. Until detection methods improve,
there can be no alternative to some limited form of on-
site inspection. Obviously such inspection would apply
to the United States and Great Britain as well as to the
Soviet Union.

I need hardly say that, as the father of two children, I
share your concern over the pernicious effect of radio-
activity. I can only say that I had to weigh this against
the alternative—that is, unlimited testing by the Soviet
Union alone, leading to a steady increase in Soviet nuclear strength until the Communist world could be
ready for a final offensive against the democracies. I believe that the Soviet leadership includes men genuinely
devoted to the cause of peace. Our strength reinforces
them in their arguments with their extremist colleagues. It would seriously underline their position if
their country were permitted to acquire decisive nuclear
superiority.

Nothing lies closer to my heart than the hope of
bringing about general and complete disarmament under conditions of reliable international control. You are
one of the transcendent moral influences of our century. I earnestly hope that you will consider throwing
the great weight of that influence behind the movement
for general and complete disarmament. I am happy to
attach an outline of the basic provisions for such a
treaty. I also enclose a study by our Arms Control and

Disarmament Agency on "The Detection and Identification of Underground Nuclear Explosions" and a copy of my speech of March 2 setting forth the considerations which led me to conclude in favor of the resumption of testing.

Sincerely,
John F. Kennedy

In attempting to deal with the agonizing decision of whether or not to resume nuclear testing, Kennedy continually sought and received advice from his closest ally, British prime minister Harold Macmillan. By 1962, as the following two letters reveal, the two had developed what many saw as something akin to a father/son relationship.

May 25, 1961.

Dear Mr. President

I write to wish you many happy returns of May 29. I had always imagined that your birthday was on March 17; but the boys in my back room tell me that that is not so and that it is on May 29.

This letter comes with every good wish for the future to you and yours.

I value our friendship. I rejoice that relations between the United States and my country are so close and happy.

Harold Macmillan

Dear Harold:

Jacqueline and I found our short stay in London an entirely pleasant and memorable experience. We were tremendously impressed by the enthusiastic and friendly reception with which we were met at every turn. In particular we wish to thank you and Lady Dorothy for the most enjoyable luncheon at Admiralty House.

I also want to thank you for your cheerful note about my birthday, which I should have acknowledged before, if I had not been on the wing since before it arrived.

Finally I want to say one word about our talks in London and about our relations in general. It was a very helpful meeting, for me, and I value our open and friendly conversations more and more. London felt near home to us all. And so I am sorry to see that one or two crabbed minds have suggested that somehow in trying to get on better with de Gaulle America is getting on less well with England. It's not so, as we both know, and I'll find a chance to clear the point up soon.

Sincerely,

The Right Honorable
Harold Macmillan, MP
The Prime Minister
Admiralty House
London

Evidence of the closeness of the Kennedy/Macmillan relationship could be further seen in letters relating first to the serious illness of Joseph P.

Kennedy Sr. and then to the death of Kennedy's infant son, Patrick
Bouvier Kennedy.

Message from Prime
Minister Macmillan
to the President – 12/20/61

   I have heard with the deepest regret of the serious
illness of your father. I am afraid this must be a very
great anxiety and sorrow to you. I do hope that you will
have better news in the course of the day.

   With regard to our meeting I am of course entirely at
your service. We would be glad to welcome you here as
arranged if you desire. Or I will go with Lord Hume either to Palm Beach or to Washington as you may wish.
There is no need to settle before 8:00 p.m. your time tonight. Deepest sympathy.

August 30, 1963

Dear Prime Minister:

   Our deepest thanks to you and Lady Dorothy for your
generous message of sympathy. You were very kind to
think of us at this difficult time, and your message was a
comfort to us. Mrs. Kennedy and I are very grateful to you.

Sincerely,
John Kennedy

The Right Honorable
Harold Macmillan, M.P.

Prime Minister
London, England

I appreciate more than I can say your kind and thoughtful letter to me.

Kennedy had not undertaken the resumption of nuclear testing without informing Macmillan of his decision, all in the hope that in taking this critical step "we may not be too far apart."

February 27, 1962

Dear Mr. Prime Minister:

· Since I last talked with David Ormsby Gore, I have had a most careful review of the testing problem with my senior advisers, and I should now inform you that they have unanimously recommended to me that the United States should resume tests in the atmosphere, starting about April 15. I myself believe that their advice is correct, and that once this decision is definitely taken, it should be promptly announced to the American people, and not allowed to dribble out in gossip and rumor. Our present plan is that I should announce such a decision in a television address to the American people on Thursday evening, the first of March. But before this decision becomes final, I wish to take this further opportunity of consultation with you, and I am sending you this letter in the hope that we may talk it over tomorrow, if you wish.

The military reasons which are leading me to this decision are, I think, familiar to you and to your advisers.

The essence of it is that I do not believe we can accept a further moratorium on atmospheric testing while the Soviet Union remains free to move onward from what it learned last fall and test again and again. My central concern is not with the size of any particular weapon—the Western stockpile is large enough, in all conscience, from that point of view. The problem is rather one of assuring the effectiveness of our strategic deterrent against possible surprises in missile or anti-missile technology in future years. Until we can get a reasonably safeguarded agreement, of the sort which you and we have worked for in recent years, I feel that I have no alternative.

There remain a number of tactical questions on which I hope we may not be too far apart. You will see that I have somewhat changed my thinking since I talked to David Ormsby Gore a week ago. It now seems plain to me that I should not allow the Disarmament Committee to begin its work under the illusion that the United States is not yet settled in its own mind about the need for testing. I believe that a sudden announcement of a quick decision to resume, sometime in early April, would be seen as more of a blow to the work of the Disarmament Committee than a careful and moderate explanation of our position ahead of time. The honest way is to put the matter plainly now.

I would, however, intend to make it clear in any speech that the United States is still ready to sign and put into effect a properly safeguarded treaty which would protect the world from nuclear testing. I would like to be able to say that Great Britain joined in this position. I would also plan to say that if any such agreement could be signed in the next six weeks, there would be no American atmospheric testing.

The test series which we now propose is essentially the same as that which has been discussed at length between your experts and ours. I am giving David Ormsby Gore a short memorandum which contains a precise description of the current proposals. The one notable addition is a pair of what are called "systems tests." These are designed to show whether all of the components of our basic POLARIS and ATLAS missiles work together as well as the individual parts have done in separate testing. If we had not reached a decision to test on other grounds, these two, in my judgment, could be omitted. But once the general decision is made, I believe it would be wise to accept the strong and unanimous military advice that such tests would be necessary to give our commanders proper confidence in our basic strategic deterrent systems.

I shall be at my desk all day tomorrow, Wednesday, and would hope to be able to talk with you about this whole subject at any time that you wish.

With warm personal regards,

Sincerely,

The Right Honorable
Harold Macmillan, M. P.
The Prime Minister
London, England

Macmillan's response to Kennedy's letter contained the vital advice and suggestions that the American president had come to rely on from the prime minister.

February 28, 1962

Dear Mr. President,

Many thanks for your messages about nuclear testing. It is of course very short notice and as you frankly say represents a change of plan. I hope you will understand that I must put this before the Cabinet, which I will do tomorrow morning, Thursday, March 1.

With regard to the justification for the tests, I feel that the need to make them falls within the statement I made in the House of Commons on October 31, conforms with the discussions we had in Bemuda and the communiqué we then issued; and as the programme has been discussed between our experts I will stand by you on this in full. . . .

There will of course be a violent reaction in this country and I think in many parts of the world against this sudden decision and we shall have to face it. Worthy people all over the world are hoping against hope that the conference opening on March 14 will lead to some result and allow us to end what we called this sterile contest. At the same time I see the dangers of waiting. It is rather evenly balanced.

I must plead that you will meet us on two points. First on the date of your announcement. If you make it tomorrow night, March 1, it will be published here on Friday morning, March 2. The House of Commons meets on Fridays, but will not regard it as a suitable day for so dramatic a discussion, and would even suspect it had been arranged so as to avoid a debate until Monday. This is only my private difficulty. But I do feel also that we should give advance warning to the other three members of the Western Five, Canada, France and Italy—the first country being particularly sensitive about decisions of this kind being taken without prior knowledge. . . .

Now as to the contents of the statement. If you wished to put us absolutely straight with world opinion you could say that tests would be resumed on June 1, by which time the Committee of Eighteen ought to report to the United Nations, unless the Russians had signed a test agreement by then. But if this is really too far off for you could we not at least postpone the date from April 15 to say, May 3? That would allow us to argue that we had given two months' grace from the date of the announcement, and we would point out that the Russians could get in touch with us immediately for preliminary talks for a treaty. . . .

I should be grateful if you could let me have a message in time for the Cabinet which meets at 11.00 a.m. tomorrow morning (6.00 a.m. your time).

One last point which I am sure you have considered. The Russians may do one of two things. First they may boycott the conference on the grounds that your statement is a provocative action. Secondly, and more tiresome, they may take some action over Berlin which will precipitate a crisis. And we must remember that it is not altogether impossible that Khrushchev really wants to get in touch with us for some constructive purpose.

With warm regard,
Yours sincerely,
Harold Macmillan

In one of his final communications with Macmillan before a treaty was finally achieved, Kennedy asked the man, to whom he had now addressed his letters with the words "Dear Friend," for a vital piece of advice—how to keep the French and German governments from throwing a roadblock into making the long-sought-after treaty a reality.

7/4/63

Dear Friend:

Now that I am back in Washington, I want to thank you again for your kindness to me and to all my party at Birch Grove House. We packed a lot of work into a short time, and I think our meeting proved again how useful these sessions are.

It was particularly kind of Lady Dorothy not only to permit our invasion but to do so much to make everyone comfortable. Both dinner on Saturday and lunch on Sunday were meals of the sort that would make my wife ask if the cook would like to live in the United States.

The big problem before us now is the mission of our two colleagues to Moscow, and I know our people are in closest touch as the work goes forward. I agree with what you said in the House yesterday, and I particularly agree that the most important thing at the moment is to try to keep our French and German friends from throwing any cold water in public. I have sent a message to the Chancellor trying to make this point quietly, and we have made the same suggestion to the French Ambassador here. What troubles me is that General de Gaulle may see nothing to his advantage in any agreement of the sort which may now be possible, and we are thinking hard here about possible ways of leading him to a less negative attitude. If you have any thoughts on this aspect of the problem, I should be very glad to hear them. . . .

> With renewed thanks, and
> warm personal wishes,
> Sincerely,
> *John F. Kennedy*

Despite their resumption of testing, both Kennedy and Khrushchev continued to pursue the goal of disarmament. In their continuing exchange of letters there was much disagreement and quibbling over the mechanisms necessary for monitoring underground testing. But on July 25, 1963, representatives of the United States, the Soviet Union, and the United Kingdom reached an agreement on a treaty banning nuclear testing in the air, in space, and underwater. A day earlier, Kennedy had written to President Harry Truman asking him for his reaction to the wording of the treaty.

July 24, 1963

Dear President Truman:

I was glad to have a chance to talk to you today.

I am enclosing a copy of the tentative agreement, although it will not be final until it is initialed. It gives us, it seems to me, a reasonable solution and it may lead to the lessening of the threat of war—although we must watch with care future developments.

I will talk to you again this week and I will be glad to

have someone come out there and discuss the matter with you if you have any questions concerning it.

With warm regards.

John Kennedy

In his reply Truman, while expressing approval of the treaty, also expressed certain "mental reservations."

July 26, 1963

Dear Mr. President:

I appreciated your thoughtfulness in sending me an advance copy of the "Treaty Banning Nuclear Weapon Tests."

I have read the text with care and have no hesitancy about going along with the general sense of it.

I know, however, that you would not want me to withhold any mental reservations that I might have, and I, therefore, wish to touch on one or two of these:

a. The last three lines in paragraph two of the "Preamble" which would "eliminate the incentive to the production and testing of all kinds of weapons" is rather sweeping.

b. In Article 1, the provision: "—or any other nuclear explosion" would seem to curb developments for peaceful purposes. Of course, this is an area best understood by the men of science.

The same thought occurs to me in connection with paragraph a. of Article 1—as well as that of paragraph 2.

The intent of Article IV, I think, I understand—but it does raise some concern about "the other fellow."

These are thoughts I wanted to share with you, and are expressed for no other purpose.

Sincerely,
Harry Truman

The Honorable John F. Kennedy
The White House
Washington, D. C.

The Test Ban Treaty was a historic achievement. Among the congratulations Kennedy received was a letter from Linus Pauling, much different in tone from the previous one the Nobel laureate had sent the president.

1 August 1963

President John F. Kennedy
The White House
Washington, D.C.

Dear Mr. President:

I write to express my gratitude to you for your successful effort in arranging that an international agreement be formulated to stop the testing of nuclear weapons (except possibly underground).

I wish you success in achieving the ratification of this treaty by the Senate. I believe that the action of the

United States, Great Britain, and the Soviet Union in
having made this agreement will go down in history as
one of the greatest events in the history of the world.

With the repeated expression of my support for your
efforts,

I am

Sincerely yours,
Linus Pauling

*In his letter, Pauling expressed the hope that Kennedy would succeed
in getting the U.S. Senate to ratify the Test Ban Treaty, something that
was not a complete certainty. In order to attain this goal, as important
as achieving the treaty itself, Kennedy sent the following letter to two of
the most important members of the Senate, Mike Mansfield and Everett Dirksen. The treaty was ratified on September 23.*

September 10, 1963

Dear Senator Mansfield and Senator Dirksen:

I am deeply appreciative of the suggestion which you
made to me on Monday morning that it would be helpful to have a further clarifying statement about the policy of this Administration toward certain aspects of our
nuclear weapons defenses, under the proposed test ban
treaty now before the Senate. I share your view that it is
desirable to dispel any fears or concerns in the minds of
Senators or of the people of our country on these matters. And while I believe that fully adequate statements
have been made on these matters before the various
committees of the Senate by the Secretary of State, the

Secretary of Defense, the Director of Central Intelligence, the Chairman of the Atomic Energy Commission, and the Joint Chiefs of Staff, nevertheless I am
happy to accept your judgment that it would be helpful
if I restated what has already been said so that there
may be no misapprehension.

In confidence that the Congress will share and support the policies of the Administration in this field,
I am happy to give these unqualified and unequivocal
assurances to the members of the Senate, to the entire
Congress, and to the country:

1. Underground nuclear testing, which is permit-
    ted under the treaty, will be vigorously and
    diligently carried forward, and the equipment,
    facilities, personnel and funds necessary for that
    purpose will be provided. As the Senate knows,
    such testing is now going on. While we must all
    hope that at some future time a more compre-
    hensive treaty may become possible by changes
    in the policies of other nations, until that time
    our underground testing program will continue.

2. The United States will maintain a posture of
    readiness to resume testing in the environments
    prohibited by the present treaty and it will take
    all the necessary steps to safeguard our national
    security in the event that there should be abro-
    gation or violation of any treaty provision. In
    particular, the United States retains the right
    to resume atmospheric testing forthwith if the
    Soviet Union should conduct tests in violation
    of the treaty.

3. Our facilities for the detection of possible vio-
    lations of this treaty will be expanded and im-

proved as required to increase our assurance against clandestine violation by others.

4. In response to the suggestion made by President Eisenhower to the Foreign Relations Committee on August 23, 1963, and in conformity with the opinion of the Legal Adviser of the Department of State, set forth in the report of the Committee on Foreign Relations, I am glad to emphasize again that the treaty in no way limits the authority of the Commander-in-Chief to use nuclear weapons for the defense of the United States and its allies, if a situation should develop requiring such a grave decision. Any decision to use such weapons would be made by the United States in accordance with its Constitutional processes and would in no way be affected by the terms of the nuclear test ban treaty.

5. While the abnormal and dangerous presence of Soviet military personnel in the neighboring island of Cuba is not a matter which can be dealt with through the instrumentality of this treaty, I am able to assure the Senate that if that unhappy island should be used either directly or indirectly to circumvent or nullify this treaty, the United States will take all necessary action in response.

6. The treaty in no way changes the status of the authorities in East Germany. As the Secretary of State has made clear, "We do not recognize, and we do not intend do recognize, the Soviet occupation zone of East Germany as a state or as an entity possessing national sovereignty, or to recognize the local authorities as a government. These authorities cannot alter these facts by the act of subscribing to the test ban treaty."

7. This government will maintain strong weapons laboratories in a vigorous program of weapons development, in order to ensure that the United States will continue to have in the future a strength fully adequate for an effective national defense. In particular, as the Secretary of Defense has made clear, we will maintain strategic forces fully ensuring that this nation will continue to be in a position to destroy any aggressor, even after absorbing a first strike by a surprise attack.

8. The United States will diligently pursue its programs for the further development of nuclear explosives for peaceful purposes by underground tests within the terms of the treaty, and as and when such developments make possible constructive uses of atmospheric nuclear explosions for peaceful purposes, the United States will seek international agreement under the treaty to permit such explosions.

I trust that these assurances may be helpful in dispelling any concern or misgivings which any member of the Senate or any citizen may have as to our determination to maintain the interests and security of the United States. It is not only safe but necessary, in the interest of this country and the interest of mankind, that this treaty should now be approved, and the hope for peace which it offers firmly sustained, by the Senate of the United States.

Once more, let me express my appreciation to you both for your visit and for your suggestions.

Sincerely,
/S/

The Honorable Mike Mansfield
The Honorable Everett McKinley Dirksen
United States Senate
Washington, D. C.

In the summer of 1961, author and journalist Theodore H. White, who in 1960 published The Making of the President, *set off on a trip to Southeast Asia. White had lived and worked in China throughout the 1930s and early 1940s and was deeply disturbed by what he encountered in Vietnam. When he returned to the United States, White, who had become a friend of Kennedy's while writing his book, sent the president a fourteen-page letter in which he candidly described the situation, as he saw it, in Vietnam. Following is an excerpt from that letter.*

The situation gets worse almost week by week. I say this despite the optimistic bullshit now hitting the papers. The guerrilas [guerrillas] now control almost all the southern delta—so much so that I could find no American who would drive me outside Saigon in his car even by day without military convoy.

There is a political breakdown here of formidable proportions. . . . If we mean to win, perhaps we must do more. But what? If there is another coup against [South Vietnam's President] Diem by his army, should we support it? If there is no natural coup and we are convinced that Diem is useless, should we incubate one? If we feel bound by honor not to pull or support a coup, shall we lay it on the line to Diem and intervene directly . . . or should we get the Hell out and make another line or policy elsewhere?

What perplexes the hell out of me is that the Commies on their side, seem to be able to find people willing to die for their cause. I find it discouraging to spend a night in a Saigon night club full of young fellows of 20 and 25 dancing and jitterbugging . . . while twenty miles away their Communist contemporaries are terrorizing the countryside.

By October 1961, the threat to South Vietnam posed by Hanoi was abundantly clear. Kennedy took the occasion of the sixth anniversary of the establishment of the Republic of Vietnam to write to its American-backed president, Ngo Dinh Diem, pledging that the United States "was determined to help Viet-Nam preserve its independence." In the letter, however, Kennedy offered no further concrete aid to Diem, stating that he was awaiting a report from the key military adviser he had sent to assess the situation before deciding upon possible additional actions.

October 24, 1961

Dear Mr. President:

On the sixth anniversary of the Republic of Viet-Nam, the United States of America is proud to pay tribute to the courage of the Vietnamese people. We have seen and marked well the anguish—and the glory—of a nation that refuses to submit to Communist terror. From the people that twice defeated the hordes of Kublai Khan, we could expect no less. America, and indeed all free men, must be grateful for the example you have set.

Mr. President, in 1955 we observed the dangers and difficulties that surrounded the birth of your Republic. In the years that followed, we saw the dedication and vigor of your people rapidly overcoming those dangers and difficulties. We rejoiced with you in the new rice springing again from fields long abandoned, in the new hospitals and roads and schools that were built, and in the new hopes of a people who had found peace after a long and bitter war. The record you established in providing new hope, shelter and security to nearly a million fleeing from Communism in the North stands out as one of the most laudable and best administered efforts in modern times.

Your brave people scarcely tasted peace before they were forced again into war. The Communist response to your growing strength and prosperity of your people was to send terror into your villages, to burn your new schools and to make ambushes of your new roads. On this October 26, we in America can still rejoice in the courage of the Vietnamese people, but we must also sorrow for the suffering, destruction and death which Communism has brought to Viet-Nam, so tragically represented in the recent assassination of Colonel Hoang Thuy Nam, one of your outstanding patriots.

Mr. President, America is well aware of the increased intensity which in recent months has marked the war against your people, and of the expanding scale and frequency of the Communist attacks. I have read your speech to the Vietnamese National Assembly in which you outline so clearly the threat of Communism to Viet-Nam. And I have taken note of the stream of threats and vituperation, directed at your government and mine, that flows day and night from Hanoi. Let me assure you again that the United States is determined to help Viet-Nam preserve its independence, protect its people against Communist assassins, and build a better life through economic growth.

I am awaiting with great interest the report of General Maxwell Taylor based on his recent talks and

observations in Viet-Nam, supplementing reports I have
received from our Embassy there over many months. I
will then be in a better position to consider with you additional measures that we might take to assist the republic of Viet-Nam in its struggle against the Communist
aggressors.

Mr. President, we look forward in these perilous days
to a future October 26, when Viet-Nam will again know
freedom and peace. We know that day is coming, and
we pray that it may be soon. I speak for the American
people when I say that we are confident of the success of
the Vietnamese nation, that we have faith in its strength
and valor, and that we know that the future of the Vietnamese people is not Communist slavery but the freedom and prosperity which they have defended and
pursued throughout their history.

Sincerely,
John F. Kennedy

*Kennedy's agonizing over what course to take in Vietnam was exacer-
bated by the ineffectiveness and the blatant corruption of the Diem
government and the specter of Soviet military intervention on behalf of
the North Vietnamese. In early November 1961, Kennedy received a
letter from Nikita Khrushchev. In the following excerpt from that letter, the Soviet chairman conveyed some of the same sentiments being
expressed by Americans in both the public and private sectors.*

November 10, 1961

. . . I as well as many other people feel rightfully
puzzled—how one can support a man like Ngo Dinh

Diem with his bloody regime who completely lost the respect of the people? Yet, the United States Government supports him, giving him economic and military assistance. And what does it mean to give military assistance to such a regime? It means to assist this regime of terrorism which managed to antagonize not only the population in the South of the country but also its neighbors because of its aggressive policy. Mr. Johnson, Vice-President of the United States, paid a visit to Ngo Dinh Diem; quite recently General Taylor visited South Vietnam. Some news agencies report of the intention of the US Government to send American troops to South Vietnam. I do not think that all this could contribute to the improvement of the situation in this part of Southeast Asia. Sending troops to suppress national-liberation movement[s] in other countries is by no means a way that corresponds to the interests of peace and, besides, what are the guarantees that the American troops would not get tied up in South Vietnam. I think that such a perspective is most real. But it is fraught with new complications, and to the difficulties that exist now in the international situation that you and I are trying to overcome. . . .

Sincerely,
N. Khrushchev

In December 1961, Kennedy responded to a letter from President Diem, pleading that Vietnam "must have further assistance from the United States if we are to win the war now being waged," by informing Diem that "we shall promptly increase our assistance to your defense effort." But this assistance meant more advisers and more money, not combat troops. In March 1962, with the debate escalating over what the extent of American involvement in Vietnam should be, Kennedy received a secret letter from

John Kenneth Galbraith. Now U.S. ambassador to India, Galbraith was, more than ever, one of Kennedy's most trusted advisers. Stating that he was aware of Kennedy's "distaste for diagnosis without remedy," Galbraith presented what he believed American policy in regard to Vietnam should be, accompanied by warnings that would later prove tragically prophetic.

New Delhi, March 2, 1962

. . . I continue to be sadly out of step with the Establishment. I can't think Diem has made any significant effort to improve his government either politically or administratively or will. We are increasingly replacing the French as the colonial military force and we will increasingly arouse the resentments associated therewith. Moreover, while I don't think the Russians are clever enough to fix it that way, we are surely playing their game. They couldn't be more pleased than to have us spend our billions in these distant jungles where it does us no good and them no harm.

Incidentally, who is the man in your administration who decides what countries are strategic? I would like to have his name and address and ask him what is so important about this real estate in the space age. What strength do we gain from an alliance with an incompetent government and a people who are so largely indifferent to their own salvation. Some of his decisions puzzle me. . . .

However this may be, and knowing your distaste for diagnosis without remedy, let me lay down four rules that should govern our policy in this part of the world. They are:

1. Keep up the threshold against the commitment of American combat forces. This is of the ut-

most importance—a few will mean more and more and more. And then, the South Vietnamese boys will go back to the farms. We will do the fighting.

2. Keep civilian control in Saigon. Once the military take over we will have no possibility of working out a disentanglement. . . .

3. We must keep the door wide open for any kind of a political settlement. In particular we must keep communications open by way of the Indians and even the Russians to Hanoi. If they give any indication of willingness to settle, we should jump at the chance. . . . Politics is not the art of the possible. It consists in choosing between the disastrous and the unpalatable. I wonder if those who talk of a ten-year war really know what they are saying in terms of American attitudes. We are not as forgiving as the French.

4. Finally, I hold to the view, whatever our public expressions, that any alternative to Diem is bound to be an improvement. I think I mentioned once before that no one ever sees an alternative to the man in power. But when the man in power is on the way down, anything is better.

Yours faithfully,
John Kenneth Galbraith

Kennedy could not help being moved by a letter he received from the sister of an American serviceman who had been killed—a letter that expressed the grief that was to enter so many American homes in the following decade. It also asked questions that would echo throughout the nation.

February 18, 1963

Dear Mr. President:

My brother, Specialist James Delmar McAndrew, was one of the seven crew members killed on January 11 in a Viet Nam helicopter crash.

The Army reports at first said that communist gunfire was suspected. Later, it said that the helicopter tragedy was due to malfunction of aircraft controls. I've wondered if the "malfunction of aircraft controls" wasn't due to "communist gunfire." However, that's neither important now, nor do I even care to know.

My two older brothers entered the Navy and the Marine Corps in 1941 immediately after the war started—they served all during the war and in some very important battles—then Jim went into the Marines as soon as he was old enough and was overseas for a long time. During those war years and even all during the Korean conflict we worried about all of them—but that was all very different. They were wars that our <u>country</u> were fighting, and everyone here <u>knew</u> that our sons and brothers were giving their lives for their country.

I can't help but feel that giving one's life for one's country is one thing, but being sent to a country where half <u>our</u> country never even <u>heard</u> of and being shot at without even a chance to shoot back is another thing altogether!

Please, I'm only a housewife who doesn't even claim to know all about the international situation—but we have felt so bitter over this—can the small number of our boys over in Viet Nam possibly be doing enough good to justify the awful number of casualties? It seems to me that if we are going to have our boys stay over there, that we should send enough to have a *chance*—or else to stay home. Those fellows are just sitting ducks in those darn helicopters. If a war is worth fighting—isn't it worth fighting to *win*?

Please answer this and help me and my family to reconcile ourselves to our loss and to feel that even though Jim died in Viet Nam—and it isn't our war—it wasn't in vain.

I am a good Democrat—and I'm not criticizing. I think you are doing a wonderful job—and God Bless You—

> Very sincerely,
> *Bobbie Lou Pendergrass*

Kennedy may well have seen an opportunity in Bobbie Lou Pendergrass's letter. Three days after receiving it, Kennedy replied to her. Along with expressing his sympathy for her loss, he set down what arguably may have been his clearest explanation as to why, although he stated " full scale war in Viet Nam is at the moment unthinkable," the United States was involved in that country.

March 6, 1963

Dear Mrs. Bobbie Lou Pendergrass:

I would like to express to you my deep and sincere sympathy in the loss of your brother. I can, of course, well understand your bereavement and the feelings which prompted you to write.

The questions which you posed in your letter can, I believe, best be answered by realizing why your brother—and other American men—went to Viet Nam in the first place. When this is understood, I am sure that the other related questions will be answered.

Americans are in Viet Nam because we have determined that this country must not fall under Communist domination. Ever since Viet Nam was divided, the Viet Namese have fought valiantly to maintain their independence in the face of the continuing threat from the North. Shortly after the division eight years ago it became apparent that they could not be successful in their defense without extensive assistance from other nations of the Free World community.

In the late summer of 1955, with the approval of President Eisenhower, an Advisory Group was established in Viet Nam to provide them with adequate weapons and equipment and training in basic military skills which are essential to survival in the battlefield. Even with this help, the situation grew steadily worse under the pressure of the Viet Cong. By 1961, it became apparent that the troubles in Laos and the troubles in Viet Nam could easily expand. It is also apparent that the Communist attempt to take over Viet Nam, is only part of a larger plan for bringing the entire area of Southeast Asia under their domination. Though it is only a small part of the area geographically, Viet Nam is now the most crucial.

If Viet Nam should fall, it will indicate to the people of Southeast Asia that complete Communist domination of their part of the world is almost inevitable. Your brother was in Viet Nam because the threat to the Viet Namese people is, in the long run, a threat to the Free World community, and ultimately a threat to us also. For when freedom is destroyed in one country, it is threatened throughout the world.

I have written to you at length because I know that it

is important to you to understand why we are in Viet Nam. James McAndrew must have foreseen that his service could take him into a war like this; a war in which he took part not as a combatant but as an advisor. I am sure that he understood the necessity of such a situation, and I know that as a soldier, he knew full scale war in Viet Nam is at the moment unthinkable.

I believe if you see this as he must have seen it, you will believe as he must have believed, that he did not die in vain. Forty-five American soldiers, including your brother, have given their lives in Viet Nam. In their sacrifice, they have earned the eternal gratitude of this Nation and other free men throughout the world.

Again, I would like to express to you and the members of your family my deepest personal sympathy.

Sincerely,
John F. Kennedy

John Kennedy's dilemma concerning what course of action he should take in Vietnam haunted him until the day of his assassination. Would he have pursued the disastrous course taken by his successors Lyndon Johnson and Richard Nixon? Or, after his reelection, would he have withdrawn all American forces from that troubled region? One thing is certain: "What would Kennedy have done if he had lived?" remains arguably the greatest of all "What if" questions in the history of foreign policy.

CHAPTER 5

★ ★ ★ ★ ★

A Triumph of Will

By NOVEMBER 1963, John Kennedy and his top political advisers were deep in preparations for the 1964 presidential campaign, an election that he looked forward to with confidence. This time there would be no narrow mandate. Given the foundations he had laid, the next four years would allow him to make great strides at home and abroad.

Kennedy had even allowed himself to seriously consider what he would do after his second term was over. He would still be only fifty years old, much too young to retire. He would certainly write his memoirs. He had also given serious thought to starting and editing a new Washington newspaper, staffed with the best newsmen whom he would be certain to attract. And he had already begun discussions with Harvard officials about the establishment of the John F. Kennedy Presidential Library, which he believed should be located there.

It was with the upcoming election in mind that Kennedy chose to go to Dallas in the third week of November 1963. It was a decision made despite the warnings of many of his party's leaders who feared what might happen to the liberal Democratic president in a city that was home to many right-wing extremists. Only a month earlier, Adlai Stevenson had been mobbed and spat upon after delivering a United Nations Day speech to a Dallas crowd. In early November, Byron Skelton, a member of the Democratic National Committee from Texas, had warned that the city simply wasn't safe for Kennedy and should be avoided. But the man who had narrowly escaped death both during the war and in more than one hospital regarded the threat of assassination as "one of the more unpleasant aspects of the job." When Senator William Fulbright of Arkansas told him directly, "Dallas is a very dangerous place. . . . I wouldn't go there," and "Don't you go," Kennedy responded by stating that if any president ever reached the point where he was afraid to visit any American city, he should immediately resign.

As he rode through Dallas streets in an open convertible and was cheered wildly by thousands of onlookers—an enthusiastic reception reminiscent of the one he had received in Fort Worth the day before—it was obvious that the vast majority of Dallas residents were far from extremists. But at 12:30 P.M. central standard time on November 22, 1963, John Kennedy was struck by two sniper's bullets and was pronounced dead at 1 P.M. At forty-six, he had become the youngest United States president to die.

As was the case with the December 7, 1941, Japanese attack on Pearl Harbor and the September 11, 2001, terrorist attacks, most people clearly remember where they were when they heard the news of Kennedy's assassination. His murder elicited an outpouring of emotion rivaled only by that after the assassination of Abraham Lincoln. Adlai Stevenson perhaps put it best when he said, "All of us will bear the grief of his death until the last day of ours."

Less than an hour after Kennedy was officially pronounced dead, Lee Harvey Oswald, a former U.S. Marine who had defected to the Soviet Union, was arrested for the crime. Two days later, while being transferred from Dallas police headquarters to the county jail, Oswald himself was shot and killed by Dallas night-club owner Jack Ruby. Arrested and convicted of murder, Ruby successfully appealed the verdict but then became ill and died before a new trial date could be set.

Oswald's murder and Ruby's death added to the complexity of the questions that had been on almost all Americans' minds since the shots had been fired in Dallas. Did Lee Harvey Oswald act alone? If not, who was responsible for John Kennedy's murder? Although the President's Commission on the Assassination of President Kennedy, known unofficially as the Warren Commission, appointed by President Lyndon Johnson to investigate the crime, concluded that Oswald was the lone assassin, public opinion polls continued to indicate that an overwhelming number of Americans believed that Kennedy's assassination was the result of a criminal conspiracy. A subsequent investigation by the Select Committee on Assassinations of the U.S. House of Representatives came to the same conclusion as the polls. What both the polls and the House committee report also revealed was that among those who believed in a conspiracy theory, there was no agreement on who might have been involved or what their motives might have been. All of which spawned speculations that continue to be raised in books, articles, television documentaries, and private investigations.

Was, for example, Vice President Lyndon Johnson, out of a burning desire to become president, part of a conspiracy to kill Kennedy? Was the KGB, seeking revenge for the way the Soviet Union had been forced to back down during the Cuban missile crisis, responsible for the assassination? Did Fidel Castro, in response to both the Bay of Pigs invasion and American attempts to remove him, arrange the murder of the president? Was the Mafia, outraged at Attorney General Robert Kennedy's unrelenting war against organized crime or by his brother's affair with Judith Exner, the mistress of boss Sam Giancana, responsible for Kennedy's death? Was the assassination the result of a conspiracy hatched by members of the nation's military-industrial complex who could not tolerate Kennedy's pursuit of a negotiated peace with the Soviet Union and an end to the cold war?

And there is another question that needs to be asked, one equally intriguing: Even if Kennedy had not been assassinated, would he, despite continual medical advancements, have lived long enough to complete a second term?

It is a legitimate question. To most of the world, Kennedy was the epitome of what he loved to term "vigor" (pronounced "vigah"), a model of glowing health and energy. It was a well-orchestrated lie. The history of illness that had plagued him throughout his childhood remained with him all his life. Kennedy, as a U.S. senator, as a presidential candidate, and as the president, was ill and in pain much of the time. Although the public was never aware of it, the man who projected such health and good humor relied heavily on drugs and pills, needed three hot baths a day, and spent many days in bed.

Much of the public knew that Kennedy had severe back problems. But what wasn't known was that by the time he was thirty, he had developed a condition so serious that as a congressman on a visit to London in 1947 he became ill enough to receive the last rites of the Catholic Church. The doctor who attended him diagnosed his condition as a failure of his adrenal glands, known as Addison's disease. At the time, the doctor told one of Kennedy's friends, "He hasn't got a year to live."

While the doctor's diagnosis of the disease proved correct, his timetable for Kennedy's demise fortunately proved to be wrong. But for the rest of his life, Kennedy was forced to rely on a variety of strong medications for pain management. By the time he entered the White House, he was regularly taking heavy doses of cortisone both orally and through injection. He also had another form of cortisone implanted in his thighs and replaced several times a year. There is strong evidence that the Kennedy family kept a supply of cortisone in safe deposit boxes around the country and overseas so that he would have access to it wherever he traveled.

As one of his aides recalled, Kennedy "used more pills, potions poultices, and other paraphernalia than would be found in a small dispensary."

Oddly enough, the man who, as an adult, received the last rites of the Catholic Church four times—and who, according to historian Richard Reeves, was "something of a medical marvel, kept alive by a complicated daily combination of pills and injections"— never let his physical ailments negatively affect the way he conducted his presidency. "He lived with pain," William Manchester wrote, "though only those who knew him well could tell when he was suffering. . . . This image was a triumph of will."

In death, John Kennedy became not only a martyr but also a cultural icon. Less than a week after the events in Dallas, thanks to an interview Jacqueline Kennedy gave to author and journalist Theodore H. White for a *Life* magazine article, the connection between the romantic Camelot myth and the Kennedy era was born. It remains etched in the public mind, never so eloquently expressed as by White in his book *In Search of History*. "The Kennedy administration," he wrote "became Camelot—a magic moment in American history . . . when great deeds were done, when artists, writers and poets met at the White House, and the barbarians beyond the walls held back."

The truth of the matter is that John Kennedy needed no myth to earn his place in history. Perhaps more than any other American president, he inspired a nation, symbolizing the hopes and aspirations of people everywhere. And he endowed us with a remarkable enormous legacy that, like the myths that surround him, endures.

Some fifty years after he envisioned it, the Peace Corps can boast of having had more than 210,000 volunteers working in 139 countries, and it is still growing. Although he did not live to see an American step on the moon, it was his vision and his determination that led us to the stars. By attaining the historic Nuclear Test Ban Treaty, he took the first steps toward steering the world away from self-destruction. Ultimately, he initiated the most meaningful civil rights legislation in the nation's history. And he helped elevate the arts to a position they had never held in America.

For a president who served little more than three years, for a man with considerable physical and moral chinks in his armor, it is an enormous achievement. As William Manchester proclaimed, "[Kennedy's] death was tragic, but his life had been a triumph, and that is how he should be remembered and celebrated, now."

★   ★   ★   ★   ★

In March 1992, Representative Paul Findley of Illinois, wrote in the Washington Report on Middle Eastern Affairs, *"It is interesting. . . . to notice that in all the words written and uttered about the Kennedy assassination, Israel's intelligence agency, the Mossad, has never been mentioned." Two years later in his book* Final Judgment, *author Michael Collins Piper actually accused Israel of the crime. Of all the conspiracy theories, it remains one of the most intriguing.*

What is indisputable is that although it was kept out of the eye of both the press and the public, a bitter dispute had developed between Israeli prime minister David Ben-Gurion, who believed that his nation's survival depended on its attaining nuclear arms capability, and Kennedy, who was vehemently opposed to it. In May 1963, Kennedy wrote to Ben-Gurion explaining why he was convinced that Israel's pursuit of nuclear weapons capability was a serious threat to world peace.

May 18, 1963

Dear Mr. Prime Minister:

I welcome your letter of May 12 and am giving it careful study.

Meanwhile, I have received from Ambassador Barbour a report of his conversation with you on May 14 regarding the arrangements for visiting the Dimona reactor. I should like to add some personal comments on that subject.

I am sure you will agree that there is no more urgent business for the whole world than the control of nuclear weapons. We both recognized this when we talked together two years ago, and I emphasized it again when I met with Mrs. Meir just after Christmas. The dangers in the proliferation of national nuclear weapons systems are so obvious that I am sure I need not repeat them here.

It is because of our preoccupation with this problem that my Government has sought to arrange with you for periodic visits to Dimona. When we spoke together in May 1961 you said that we might make whatever use we wished of the information resulting from the first visit of American scientists to Dimona and that you would agree to further visits by neutrals as well. I had assumed from Mrs. Meir's comments that there would be no problem between us on this.

We are concerned with the disturbing effects on world stability which would accompany the development of a nuclear weapons capability by Israel. I cannot imagine that the Arabs would refrain from turning to the Soviet Union for assistance if Israel were to develop a nuclear weapons capability—with all the consequences this would hold. But the problem is much larger than its impact on the Middle East. Development of a nuclear weapons capability by Israel would almost certainly lead other larger countries, that have so far refrained from such development, to feel that they must follow suit.

As I made clear in my press conference on May 8, we have a deep commitment to the security of Israel. In addition, this country supports Israel in a wide variety of other ways which are well known to both of us. . . .

I can well appreciate your concern for developments in the UAR [United Arab Republic]. But I see no present or imminent nuclear threat to Israel from there. I am assured that our intelligence on this question is good and that the Egyptians do not presently have any installation comparable to Dimona, nor any facilities potentially capable of nuclear weapons production. But, of course, if you have information that would support a contrary conclusion, I should like to receive it from you through Ambassador Barbour. We have the capacity to check it.

I trust this message will convey the sense of urgency and the perspective in which I view your Government's early assent to the proposal first put to you by Ambassador Barbour on April 2.

Sincerely,
John F. Kennedy

In his reply to Kennedy, Ben-Gurion defended his country's development of a nuclear reactor for both peaceful and military purposes and suggested a time when Dimona would be ready for inspection.

Jerusalem, May 27, 1963

Dear Mr. President,

I have given careful consideration to your letter of May 19 and to Ambassador Barbour's explanation of your policy in the conversations which I have had with him.

Let me assure you, at the outset, Mr. President, that our policy on nuclear research and development has not changed since I had the opportunity of discussing it with you in May 1961. I fully understand the dangers involved in the proliferation of nuclear weapons, and I sympathize with your efforts to avoid such a development. I fear that in the absence of an agreement between the Great Powers on general disarmament, there is little doubt that these weapons will, sooner or later, find their way into the arsenals of China and then of various European states and India. In this letter, however, I propose to deal not with the general international aspect on which you express your views so clearly in your letter—but with Israel's own position and attitude on this question.

In our conversation in 1961, I explained to you that we were establishing a nuclear training and research reactor in Dimona with French assistance. This assistance has been given on condition that the reactor will be devoted exclusively to peaceful purposes. I regard this condition as absolutely binding, both on general grounds of good faith and because France has extended military assistance of unique value to Israel in her struggle for self-defence, from the Arab invasion of 1948 down to the present day.

In the same sense I informed you in 1961 that we are developing this reactor because we believe, on the strength of expert scientific advice, that within a decade or so the use of nuclear power will be economically viable and of great significance for our country's development. I went on to add that we should have to follow developments in the Middle East. This is still our position today.

Between us and France there exists a bilateral

arrangement concerning the Dimona reactor similar to that which we have with the United States in the reactor at Nachal Sureiq. While we do not envisage a system of formal United States control at the Dimona reactor which the United States has not helped to establish or construct, as in the case of the reactor at Nachal Sureiq, we do agree to further annual visits to Dimona by your representatives, such as have already taken place.

The "start-up" time of the Dimona reactor will not come until the end of this year or early in 1964. At that time, the French companies will hand the reactor over to us. I believe that this will be the most suitable time for your representatives to visit the reactor. At that stage they will be able to see it in an initial stage of operation, whereas now nothing is going on there except building construction.

I hope, Mr. President, that this proposal meets the concern expressed in your letter of May 19.

In 1961, you suggested the possibility that a visit be carried out by a scientist from a "neutral" country. This idea is acceptable to us, but a visit by an American expert would be equally acceptable from our point of view.

I appreciate what you say in your letters, Mr. President, about the commitment of the United States to Israel's security. While I understand your concern with the prospect of a proliferation of nuclear weapons, we in Israel cannot be blind to the more actual danger now confronting us. I refer to the danger arising from destructive "conventional" weapons in the hands of neighboring governments which openly proclaim their intention to attempt the annihilation of Israel. This is our people's major anxiety. It is a well-founded anxiety, and I have nothing at this stage to add to my letter of

May 12 which is now, as I understand, receiving your active consideration.

Yours sincerely,
D. Ben-Gurion

Kennedy was far from satisfied with Ben-Gurion's reply, particularly his attempt to stall any inspection in Dimona. In secret, private conversations with the prime minister and in the following letter, Kennedy pressured Ben-Gurion for earlier and more frequent inspections of the nuclear site.

June 15, 1963

Dear Mr. Prime Minister:

I thank you for your letter of May 27 concerning American visits to Israel's nuclear facility at Dimona. I know your words reflect your most intense personal consideration of a problem that is not easy for you or for your Government, as it is not for mine.

I welcome your strong reaffirmation that the Dimona will be devoted exclusively to peaceful purposes. I also welcome your reaffirmation of Israel's willingness to permit periodic visits to Dimona.

Because of the crucial importance of this problem, however, I am sure you will agree that such visits should be of a nature and on a schedule which will more nearly be in accord with international standards, thereby resolving all doubts as to the peaceful intent of the Dimona project.

Therefore, I asked our scientist to review the alternative schedules of visits we and you have proposed. If Israel's purposes are to be clear to the world beyond reasonable doubt, I believe that the schedule which would best serve our common purposes would be a visit early this summer, another visit in June 1964, and thereafter at intervals of six months. I am sure that such a schedule should not cause you any more difficulty than that which you have proposed. It would be essential, and I take it that your letter is in accord with this, that our scientist have access to all areas of the Dimona site and to any related part of the complex, such as fuel fabrication facilities or plutonium separation plant, and that sufficient time be allotted for a thorough examination.

Knowing that you fully appreciate the truly vital significance of this matter to the future well-being of Israel, to the United States, and internationally, I am sure our carefully considered request will again have your most sympathetic attention.

Sincerely,
John F. Kennedy

On June 16, 1963, Ben-Gurion, who had been Israel's leader since its inception in 1948, resigned from office. Many believed his resignation was due in great measure to his dispute with Kennedy over Dimona. In a letter to Ben-Gurion's successor, Levi Eshkol, Kennedy left no doubt as to what the U.S. response would be if "we were unable to obtain reliable information" about the intent of the Dimona project, a threat that, according to one conspiracy theory, led to Israel's role in Kennedy's assassination.

July 4, 1963

Dear Mr. Prime Minister:

It gives me great personal pleasure to extend congratulations as you assume your responsibilities as Prime
Minister of Israel. You have our friendship and best
wishes in your new tasks. It is on one of these that I am
writing you at this time.

You are aware, I am sure, of the exchanges which I
had with Prime Minister Ben-Gurion concerning
American visits to Israel's nuclear facility at Dimona.
Most recently, the Prime Minister wrote to me on May
27. His words reflected a most intense personal consideration of a problem that I know is not easy for your
Government, as it is not for mine. We welcomed the
former Prime Minister's strong reaffirmation that Dimona will be devoted exclusively to peaceful purposes
and the reaffirmation also of Israel's willingness to permit periodic visits to Dimona.

I regret having to add to your burdens so soon after
your assumption of office, but I feel the crucial importance of this problem necessitates my taking up with
you at this early date certain further considerations,
arising out of Mr. Ben-Gurion's May 27 letter, as to the
nature and scheduling of such visits.

I am sure you will agree that these visits should be as
nearly as possible in accord with international standards, thereby resolving all doubts as to the peaceful intent of the Dimona project. As I wrote Mr. Ben-Gurion
this Government's commitment to and support of Israel
could be seriously jeopardized if it should be thought

that we were unable to obtain reliable information on a subject as vital to peace as the question of Israel's effort in the nuclear field.

Therefore, I asked our scientists to review the alternative schedules of visits we and you had proposed. If Israel's purposes are to be clear beyond reasonable doubt, I believe that the schedule which would best serve our common purposes would be a visit early this summer, another visit in June 1964, and thereafter at intervals of six months. I am sure that such a schedule should not cause you any more difficulty than that which Mr. Ben-Gurion proposed in his May 27 letter. It would be essential, and I understand that Mr. Ben-Gurion's letter was in accord with this, that our scientists have access to all areas of the Dimona site and to any related part of the complex, such as fuel fabrication facilities or plutonium separation plant, and that sufficient time be allotted for a thorough examination.

Knowing that you fully appreciate the truly vital significance of this matter to the future well-being of Israel, to the United States, and internationally, I am sure our carefully considered request will have your most sympathetic attention.

Sincerely,
John F. Kennedy

In March 1963, Kennedy was invited to attend Operation Sail, an event in which tall sailing ships came to the United States in a spectacular display of bygone days. In accepting the invitation, Kennedy described how important sailing had always been to him and what it had taught him.

April 3, 1963

From my first race on Nantucket Sound many years ago to my most recent outing as a weekend sailor, sailing has given me some of the most pleasant and exciting moments of my life. It also has taught me something of the courage, resourcefulness and strength required of men who sail the seas in ships. Thus, I am looking forward eagerly to Operation Sail. The sight of so many ships gathered from the distant corners of the world should remind us that strong, disciplined and venturesome men still can find their way safely across uncertain and stormy seas.

John F. Kennedy

No world leader knew the meaning of "stormy" better than Nikita Khrushchev, who had sailed with Kennedy to the brink of nuclear war. On October 10, 1963, Kennedy received the most optimistic communication from Khrushchev that the chairman had ever sent him. For the president, whose thoughts were turning increasingly toward reelection, the long telegram, expressing Khrushchev's belief that the Nuclear Test Ban Treaty "should become the beginning of a sharp turn toward broad relaxation of international tension" could not have been more welcome. Tragically, it would also be the last letter Kennedy ever received from the Soviet chairman.

MOSCOW, OCTOBER 10, 1963, 6 P.M.

DEAR MR. PRESIDENT:

TODAY IN THE THREE CAPITALS—MOSCOW, WASHINGTON AND LONDON, CARRYING

OUT THE FINAL ACT IN CONNECTION WITH
THE CONCLUSION OF THE TREATY BAN-
NING NUCLEAR WEAPON TESTS IN THE
ATMOSPHERE, IN OUTER SPACE AND
UNDERWATER—THE RATIFICATION INSTRU-
MENTS OF THE ORIGINAL PARTIES TO THIS
TREATY, THE SOVIET UNION, THE UNITED
STATES OF AMERICA AND GREAT BRITAIN
HAVE BEEN DEPOSITED.

THUS THE NUCLEAR WEAPON TEST
BAN TREATY HAS COME INTO FORCE. THIS
UNDOUBTEDLY IS A SIGNIFICANT DEVEL-
OPMENT IN INTERNATIONAL AFFAIRS
WHICH BRINGS JOY TO ALL PEOPLES. TO-
GETHER WITH THE SOVIET UNION, THE
UNITED STATES OF AMERICA AND GREAT
BRITAIN THE NUCLEAR WEAPON TEST
BAN TREATY HAS BEEN SIGNED BY MORE
THAN ONE HUNDRED STATES. IT CAN BE
SAID WITH ASSURANCE THAT THIS
TREATY HAS FOUND WARM RESPONSE
AND APPROVAL AMONG ALL PEOPLES OF
GOOD WILL.

IT HAS BEEN REPEATEDLY NOTED BY
REPRESENTATIVES OF OUR COUNTRIES
THAT THE TEST BAN TREATY IS IN ITSELF A
DOCUMENT OF GREAT INTERNATIONAL
SIGNIFICANCE AND THE HOPE HAS BEEN
EXPRESSED THAT THE CONCLUSION OF
THIS TREATY WILL HAVE A POSITIVE IN-
FLUENCE ON THE INTERNATIONAL CLI-
MATE, ON RELATIONS BETWEEN STATES.
ACTUALLY, THE CONCLUSION OF THE
NUCLEAR WEAPON TEST BAN TREATY HAS

INJECTED A FRESH SPIRIT INTO THE INTER-
NATIONAL ATMOSPHERE SHOWING THAT
NO MATTER HOW COMPLICATED CONTEM-
PORARY PROBLEMS, NO MATTER HOW
GREAT THE DIFFERENCES BETWEEN SO-
CIAL SYSTEMS OF OUR STATES, WE CAN
FIND MUTUALLY ACCEPTABLE SOLUTIONS
IN THE INTERESTS OF ALL MANKIND, IN
THE INTERESTS OF MAINTAINING PEACE IF
WE MANIFEST THE NECESSARY PUSH . . .
TOWARD THIS END.

BUT, IT IS UNDERSTOOD, AGREEMENT
ON BANNING EXPERIMENTAL NUCLEAR
EXPLOSIONS WITH ALL ITS IMPORTANCE
FOR PEOPLES, IN ITSELF DOES NOT SOLVE
THE PRINCIPAL INTERNATIONAL PROBLEM
OF OUR EPOCH—DOES NOT ELIMINATE
THE DANGER OF WAR. NOW IT IS
NECESSARY—AND OUR GOVERNMENTS
HAVE SPOKEN OUT IN FAVOR OF THIS—TO
DEVELOP FURTHER THE SUCCESS THAT WE
HAVE ACHIEVED, TO SEEK SOLUTIONS OF
OTHER RIPE INTERNATIONAL QUES-
TIONS. . . .

PEOPLES EXPECT THAT OUR GOVERN-
MENTS WILL NOW MANIFEST STILL MORE
PERSISTENCE AND CONSISTENCY IN THEIR
FURTHER ACTIVITIES IN THE INTERESTS OF
CONSOLIDATING PEACE. SO FAR AS THE
SOVIET GOVERNMENT IS CONCERNED,
INALTERABLY FOLLOWING THE COURSE OF
PEACEFUL COEXISTENCE OF STATES, IT IS
PREPARED TO EXERT NEW EFFORTS, TO DO
EVERYTHING DEPENDENT ON IT IN ORDER

THAT THE CHANGE FOR THE BETTER IN THE
INTERNATIONAL SITUATION WHICH HAS
BEEN NOTED AS A RESULT OF THE CONCLU-
SION OF THE NUCLEAR WEAPON TEST BAN
TREATY SHOULD BECOME THE BEGINNING
OF A SHARP TURN TOWARD BROAD RELAX-
ATION OF INTERNATIONAL TENSION.

PERMIT ME, MR. PRESIDENT, TO EXPRESS
THE HOPE THAT THE GOVERNMENT OF THE
UNITED STATES OF AMERICA FOR ITS PART
WILL MAKE AN APPROPRIATE CONTRIBU-
TION TO THE SOLUTION OF INTERNA-
TIONAL PROBLEMS WHICH IS DEMANDED BY
THE INTERESTS OF WEAKENING INTERNA-
TIONAL TENSIONS, THE INTERESTS OF
INSURING UNIVERSAL PEACE.

RESPECTFULLY YOURS,
N. KHRUSHCHEV

In the weeks following John Kennedy's assassination, Jacqueline Ken-
nedy received some one thousand letters of condolence. Hundreds of
letters from around the world also poured into the State Department.
Many were addressed to Deputy Assistant Secretary Katie Louch-
heim, who, at the time, held the highest-ranking position in the depart-
ment ever attained by a woman. Among the letters was the following
from the Russian journal Soviet Woman.

November 28, 1963

Katie Louchheim,
Deputy Assistant Secretary

for Public Affairs,
State Department,
Washington, D.C.,
U.S.A.

Dear Mrs. Louchheim,

We offer you our sincere condolences on the tragic death of the President of the United States America John Fitzgerald Kennedy, that outstanding statesman.

We Soviet people respected the late President as a man who contributed much towards the solution of disputed issues through negotiation on the international arena and who strove to promote mutual understanding and cooperation between our nations. . . .

Yours sincerely,
Maria Ovsyannikova
Editor-in-Chief
Journal "Soviet Woman"
Moskva, Kuznetski Most 22.

Another of the letters was sent by Mrs. William Leonhart, wife of the U.S. ambassador to Tanganyika.

Dear Katie:

I am afraid that I have not been able to concentrate on anything since the twenty-second. It still seems unreal. The effect on the Tanganyikans was like one great surge of grief, the President, as you have probably read, wept openly. He called a special session of his cabinet that night and declared Saturday a national day of mourning. Yesterday in his address to the Nation on the second Anniversary of Independence he again paid tribute to our President and the loss to the world. People continue to come in either here or at the Chancery, most just sit, don't say much, just seem to want us to say it isn't true.

Sincerely,
Pidge

Typical of the letters from ordinary citizens throughout the globe was the following from La Paz, Bolivia.

30 November 1963

Dear Friend:

With very great grief from the depths of my heart, I am sending you this letter to express my sincere condolences on the tragic death of the late President of the United States, John F. Kennedy.

This death—just when mankind was looking to him for its defense and for the defense of its sacred and inalienable rights, in a truly democratic regime—is a great tragedy for the whole world. My whole country has recognized it as such.

For his most worthy wife, Mrs. Jacqueline Kennedy and his adorable children, I pray to God and the Holy

Virgin that they be granted Christian consolation and blessings.

Sincerely,
A. Espinosa Schmidt

One of the first letters of condolence was sent to the new American president, Lyndon Johnson, by Nikita Khrushchev.

Moscow,
November 24, 1963

Dear Mr. President:

I am writing this message to you at a moment that holds a special place in the history of your country. The villainous assassination of Head of the American State John F. Kennedy is a grievous, indeed a very grievous loss for your country. I want to say frankly that the gravity of this loss is felt by the whole world, including ourselves, the Soviet people.

There is no need for me to tell you that the late President John F. Kennedy and I, as the Head of the Government of the socialist Soviet Union, were people of different poles. But I believe that probably you yourself have formed a definite view that it was an awareness of the great responsibility for the destinies of the world that guided the actions of the two Governments—both of the Soviet Union and of the United States—in recent years. These actions were founded on a desire to prevent a disaster and to resolve disputed issues through agreement with due regard for the most important, the most fundamental interests of ensuring peace.

An awareness of this responsibility, which I found John F. Kennedy to possess during our very first conversations in Vienna in 1961, laid down the unseen bridge of mutual understanding which, I venture to say, was not broken to the very last day in the life of President John F. Kennedy. For my own part, I can say quite definitely that the feeling of respect for the late President never left me precisely because, like ourselves, he based his policy on a desire not to permit a military collision of the major powers which carry on their shoulders the burden of the responsibility for the maintenance of peace.

And now, taking the opportunity offered by the visit to the United States of my First Deputy A.I. Mikoyan to attend the funeral of John F. Kennedy, I address these lines to you, as the new President of the United States of America in whom is vested a high responsibility to your people. I do not know how you will react to these words of mine, but let me say outright that in you we saw a comrade-in-arms of the late President, a man who always stood at the President's side and supported his line in foreign policy. This, I believe, gives us grounds to express the hope that the basis, which dictated to the leaders of both countries the need not to permit the outbreak of a new war and to keep the peace, will continue to be the determining factor in the development of relations between our two States.

Needless to say, on our part, and on my own part, as Head of the Government of the Soviet Union, there has been and remains readiness to find, through an exchange of views, mutually acceptable solutions for those problems which still divide us. This applies both to the problems of European security, which have been handed down to the present generation chiefly as a legacy of World War II, and to other international problems.

Judging by experience, exchanges of views and our contacts can assume various forms, including such an avenue as the exchange of personal messages, if this does not run counter to your wishes.

Recently we marked the Thirtieth Anniversary of the establishment of diplomatic relations between the U.S.S.R. and the U.S. This was a historic act in which an outstanding role was played by President Franklin D. Roosevelt. We have always believed that, being a representative of one and the same political party, the late President John F. Kennedy to a certain extent continued in foreign policy Roosevelt's traditions which were based on recognition of the fact that the coinciding interests of the U.S.S.R. and the U.S. prevail over all that divides them.

And it is to you Mr. President, as to a representative of the same trend of the United States policy which brought into the political forefront statesmen, such as Franklin D. Roosevelt and John F. Kennedy, that I want to say that if these great traditions could go on being maintained and strengthened, both Americans and Soviet people could, we are convinced, look optimistically into the future. We are convinced that this development of events would meet the sympathy of every state, and indeed of every individual who espouses and cherishes peace.

I would welcome any desire on your part to express your ideas in connection with the thoughts—though they may, perhaps, be of a somewhat general nature—

which I deemed it possible to share with you in this message.

Respectfully,
N. *Khrushchev*

Writing on "one of the last nights I will spend in the White House," Jacqueline Kennedy sent Nikita Khrushchev a very special message.

Washington,
December 1, 1963

Dear Mr. Chairman President,

I would like to thank you for sending Mr. Mikoyan as your representative to my husband's funeral. He looked so upset when he came through the line, and I was very moved.

I tried to give him a message for you that day—but as it was such a terrible day for me, I do not know if my words came out as I meant them to.

So now, in one of the last nights I will spend in the White House, in one of the last letters I will write on this paper at the White House, I would like to write you my message.

I send it only because I know how much my husband cared about peace, and how the relation between you and him was central to this care in his mind. He used to quote your words in some of his speeches—"In the next war the survivors will envy the dead."

You and he were adversaries, but you were allied in a

determination that the world should not be blown up. You respected each other and could deal with each other. I know that President Johnson will make every effort to establish the same relationship with you.

The danger which troubled my husband was that war might be started not so much by the big men as by the little ones.

While big men know the needs for self-control and restraint—little men are sometimes moved more by fear and pride. If only in the future the big men can continue to make the little ones sit down and talk, before they start to fight.

I know that President Johnson will continue the policy in which my husband so deeply believed—a policy of control and restraint—and he will need your help.

I send this letter because I know so deeply of the importance of the relationship which existed between you and my husband, and also because of your kindness, and that of Mrs. Khrushchev in Vienna.

I read that she had tears in her eyes when she left the American Embassy in Moscow, after signing the book of mourning. Please thank her for that.

Sincerely,
Jacqueline Kennedy

Acknowledgments

★ ★ ★ ★ ★

The editor of this book has made every attempt to contact the writers or estates of all the letters in this book for permission to print them. The publisher would appreciate hearing from any letter writer or estate whom the author has been unable to contact so that appropriate permission can be secured.

It is important to state that a book of this magnitude could not have been completed without the invaluable aid of many individuals. I am indebted to Sam Rubin, Steve Plotkin, and Laurie Austin of the John F. Kennedy Presidential Library and Museum for all their help. Thanks are due also to the John F. Kennedy Library Foundation's Karen Mullen for her aid and support. A special debt of gratitude is owed to Marilyn (Lynn) Farnell for her dedicated and superlative research and to Marie McHugh, Frances Mayo, Laura Phillips, and Karen and Carol Sandler for their many contributions. Special thanks are extended to Bloomsbury's Rob Galloway who, time and again, came to the rescue. Finally, it has been my great good fortune to have compiled this book under the guidance of publisher/editor Peter Ginna. There are simply not words adequate enough to describe all that he has contributed to this volume and I am eternally grateful.

As for the documents included in this volume, the vast majority are housed in the John F. Kennedy Presidential Library and Museum and are in the public domain. Other letters in this book, also in the public domain, are contained in the Library of Congress, the National Archives, the Franklin D. Roosevelt Presidential Library and Museum, and the United States Department of Health and Human Services.

Grateful acknowledgment is made to the following individuals and estates for their gracious permission to include other letters not in the public domain, and for their assistance in finding information about documents and copyright holders: The Briscoe Center for American History for the James Farmer letters; Bob Clark, supervisory archivist, Franklin D. Roosevelt Library, for the Eleanor Roosevelt letters; Dawn Evans, legal department, the Evangelistic Association, for the Billy Graham letter; Rich Ewig, American Heritage Center, University of Wyoming, for information regarding the Inga Arvad letter; James Galbraith for the Galbraith letters; Peter Gilbert and the Estate of Robert Lee Frost for the Robert Frost letters; Sig Gissler, administrator, Pulitzer Prizes, Columbia University, for the Pulitzer Prize letter; Brooke Hersey, literary executor for John Hersey, for his letter; Laura Hoguet, the Ed Banfield estate, for the Banfield letter; Mrs. Hulan Jack for the Hulan Jack letter; the John F. Kennedy Library Foundation for the Joseph Kennedy Jr. and the Rose Kennedy letters; Bruce Kirby, manuscript reference librarian, Library of Congress, for the A. Philip Randolph letters; Patrick Kerwin, manuscript reference librarian, Manuscript Division, Library of Congress, for the W. Averell Harriman letter; Daniel Linke, Seeley G. Mudd Manuscript Library, Princeton University, for the Adlai Stevenson and Bernard Baruch letters; William Marx for the Harpo Marx letter; John Natter, Office of the Secretary, United States Department of State for the John Kerry letter; Chris Petersen, Special Collections, Oregon State University, for the Linus Pauling and Mrs. Linus Pauling letters; Mrs. Rachel Robinson for the Jackie Robinson letters; Cynthia Schlesinger, for the Arthur Schlesinger Sr. and the Arthur Schlesinger Jr. letters; Thomas Schwartz, director, Herbert Hoover Presidential Library and Museum, for the Herbert Hoover letter; Ethan Wayne, president, John Wayne Enterprises, for the John Wayne letter. Letters by Martin Luther King Jr. are reprinted by arrangement with the heirs to the Estate of Martin Luther King Jr., c/o Writers House, New York, N.Y., as agent for the proprietor. Letters by Winston Churchill, copyright Winston S. Churchill, are reproduced with permission of Curtis Brown, London, on behalf of the Estate of Sir Winston Churchill.

Index

A Note on the Author

Martin W. Sandler is the author of *Lincoln Through the Lens* and *The Dust Bowl Through the Lens*. He has won five Emmy Awards for his writing for television and is the author of more than sixty books, two of which have been nominated for a Pulitzer Prize. Among Sandler's other books are the six volumes in his award-winning *Library of Congress American History Series for Young People*. Sandler has taught American History and American Studies at the University of Massachusetts at Amherst and at Smith College, and lives in Massachusetts.